Medicine and the Ethics of Care
Diana Fritz Cates and Paul Lauritzen, Editors

The Moral Theology of Pope John Paul II
Charles E. Curran

The Origins of Moral Theology in the United States: Three Different Approaches
Charles E. Curran

Shaping the Moral Life: An Approach to Moral Theology
Klaus Demmer, M.S.C.
Translated by Roberto Dell'Oro
James F. Keenan, S.J., Editor

Who Count as Persons? Human Identity and the Ethics of Killing
John F. Kavanaugh, S.J.

THE MORAL THEOLOGY

of

POPE JOHN PAUL II

CHARLES E. CURRAN

Georgetown University Press | Washington, D.C.

Georgetown University Press, Washington, D.C.
© 2005 by Georgetown University Press. All rights reserved.
Printed in the United States of America

10   9   8   7   6   5   4   3   2   1   2005

This book is printed on acid-free paper meeting the requirements of the American National Standard for Permanence in Paper for Printed Library Materials.

Library of Congress Cataloging-in-Publication Data

Curran, Charles E.
  The moral theology of Pope John Paul II / Charles E. Curran.
     p.   cm. — (Moral traditions series)
  Includes bibliographical references and index.
  ISBN 1-58901-042-6 (cloth : alk. paper)
     1. John Paul II, Pope, 1920—Ethics.   2. Christian ethics—Catholic authors.
  3. Catholic Church—Doctrines—History—20th century.   I. Title.   II. Series.
BJ1249.C8195   2005
  241'.042'092—dc22   2004022930

To my many friends in the theological community
especially
Beth Johnson and Dick McBrien

CONTENTS

ACKNOWLEDGMENTS

I AM GRATEFUL to my institution, Southern Methodist University (SMU), for providing me with the opportunity and support for my research. My students, faculty colleagues, the librarians at Bridwell Library, and the administration of the university have made SMU a very congenial and stimulating academic home for me. I am privileged to hold the Elizabeth Scurlock University Professorship of Human Values established by Jack and Laura Lee Blanton in memory of Laura Lee Blanton's mother. Laura Lee Blanton died in 1999. Thanks to the major and significant benefactions of the Blantons, Laura Lee Blanton continues to influence the life of SMU. Richard Brown, the director of Georgetown University Press, and James F. Keenan, the editor of its Moral Traditions series, together with the staff of the press, have been most supportive and helpful. This volume would never have seen the light of day without the competent word processing skills of my associate, Carol Swartz, who on a day-to-day basis is a considerate and congenial office mate, and I wish to acknowledge Rosemarie Gorman, who prepared the index.

Earlier versions of substantial parts of two chapters appeared in other publications. I gratefully acknowledge permission to republish parts of chapters 2 and 5 that first appeared in *Horizons: The Journal of the College Theology Society* in 2004 and in the founding symposium of the *University of St. Thomas Law Journal* in 2004, "God, the Person, History, and Law: Themes from the Work of Judge John T. Noonan Jr."

INTRODUCTION

THIS BOOK aims to give an appraisal of Pope John Paul II's moral theology. All recognize the significant role that John Paul II has played in the life of the Catholic Church during his very long papacy. As the bishop of Rome, he has often taught authoritatively on moral matters. As a result, a critical analysis of his teachings in the area of moral theology is most appropriate.

One immediate problem arises. Moral theology is not exactly the same as moral teachings. Moral theology is a second-order discourse that tries to explain systematically, thematically, and critically how Christians should act in this world. By definition, moral theology is in the area of theory, is an academic discipline, and deals with methodology as well as with substantive issues. Authoritative moral teaching primarily addresses the church audience with what is required for Christian living. The pope is not primarily writing moral theology as theory or an academic discipline.

Although it is true that moral theology is not the same as moral teaching, they are closely related. Moral teaching implicitly involves a moral theology. Behind moral teaching, there is a moral theology. This is especially true for Karol Wojtyla, who became Pope John Paul II. He was trained as a philosophical ethicist and taught and wrote extensively in the area of philosophical ethics. Philosophical ethics, like moral theology, is a second-order discipline dealing with the theory of the moral life. In addition, even as a philosophical ethicist, the future pope had a great interest in and concern for moral theology. In his authoritative moral teaching, Pope John Paul II is quite conscious of the more theoretical moral theology that lies behind his moral teachings. In addition, the pope has dedicated one encyclical, *Veritatis splendor*, to moral theology and moral theory. If there were just a small sample of moral teachings, it would be rather difficult to draw out the moral theory behind such teachings. But because the pope has written extensively in moral areas, one can more easily discern the moral theory behind his teachings.

A second problem arises from the very extensive authoritative writings of John Paul II. What documents should one study? The pope on any given day gives a number of different talks and addresses. For example, the Vatican website (http://www.vatican.va) contains more than fifty addresses given by the pope during his first visit to the United States in early October 1979. Obviously, he does not write all the speeches himself.

All agree that the more authoritative papal documents, by their very nature, are the most significant. Without doubt, the pope is quite heavily involved in writing these more authoritative documents. Documents addressed to the universal church are more important than documents addressed to individuals or particular churches.[1] The most authoritative papal documents are encyclicals that are addressed to the universal church, even though encyclicals of themselves do not contain infallible papal teaching. John Paul II has written fourteen encyclicals during his pontificate, some of which do not deal directly with moral teachings. But the majority of the encyclicals do, at least on occasion, propose moral teachings. In addition, three encyclicals develop Catholic social teaching, and *Veritatis splendor* deals directly with moral theory. Thus, the encyclicals form the primary sources for this study of John Paul II's moral teachings.

In this introduction, it is helpful to list the encyclicals that will be used and to describe them briefly:[2]

✝ *Redemptor hominis* (*RH*), 1979, considers the mystery of redemption in Christ Jesus but also its relation to the dignity and life of human beings.

✝ *Dives in misericordia* (*DM*), 1980, is the second panel of John Paul II's Trinitarian triptych dealing with the mercy of God the Father. The pope here draws out some implications for human existence because theology and anthropology are complementary.

✝ *Laborem exercens* (*LE*), 1981, commemorates the ninetieth anniversary of Leo XIII's *Rerum novarum*, understood by John Paul II as the beginning of modern Catholic social teaching. The encyclical develops the understanding and role of work, with special emphasis on the person who does the work.

✝ *Dominum et vivificantem* (*DV*), 1986, completes the Trinitarian triptych by discussing the role of the Holy Spirit. The encyclical intends to show the Spirit's life-giving power to bring about renewal in human beings, in society, and in the church.

✝ *Redemptoris mater* (*RMA*), 1987, develops the unique dignity, vocation, and mission of Mary in salvation history. The encyclical occasionally points out the ramifications of this for human existence.

✝ *Sollicitudo rei socialis* (*SRS*), 1987, commemorates the twentieth anniversary of Pope Paul VI's *Populorum progressio*. John Paul II here proposes the meaning of authentic human development, deploring the economic underdevelopment in the developing world and the economic superdevelopment in the industrial world.

✝ *Redemptoris missio* (*RM*), 1990, develops the evangelizing mission of the church. In the process, the encyclical occasionally talks about the relation of this mission to human life and action.

✝ *Centesimus annus* (*CA*), 1991, marks the centenary of Leo XIII's *Rerum novarum*. The encyclical concentrates on the social teaching of the church in light of Leo's encyclical and in light of the 1989 collapse of communism in Europe.

✝ *Veritatis splendor* (*VS*), 1993, develops in depth issues regarding the very foundations of moral theology in light of a crisis of truth that not only exists in the world at large but also has had an influence within the church itself.

✝ *Evangelium vitae* (*EV*), 1995, follows in the aftermath of *Veritatis splendor* and concentrates on the dignity and value of human life, with special attention to the practical issues of killing, abortion, euthanasia, and capital punishment.

✝ *Ut unum sint* (*UUS*), 1995, concentrates on ecumenism and ecumenical relationships from the viewpoint of the Catholic Church but occasionally mentions implications for moral life.

✝ *Fides et ratio* (*FR*), 1998, discusses from a pastoral perspective the important question of the relationship between faith and reason, and between theological and philosophical inquiry. The document explores the proper role of reason in theology and also in moral theology.

✝ *Ecclesia de eucharistia* (*EE*), 2003, concentrates on the Eucharist and its role in the life of the church.

There are also other types of papal documents that are addressed to the whole church, such as apostolic exhortations and apostolic letters, and that are not as authoritative as encyclicals.[3] When appropriate, this study considers these documents; for example, the apostolic exhortation *Familiaris consortio* (1981) dealing with family, and the apostolic letter *Mulieris dignitatem* (1988) treating the dignity and role of women. This volume also occasionally uses less authoritative documents dealing with a specific topic, such as the "World Day of Peace Message" given at the beginning of each year.

The discussion in this book on marriage and sexuality pays special attention to a particular genre of teaching—the speeches given at the weekly audiences at the beginning of John Paul II's service as bishop of Rome. As such, talks to general audiences have little or no authoritative character. They are often just greetings to the various people in attendance and exhortations to live a better life. One can assume popes themselves often do not bother writing such talks. But such is not the case with the first audience talks given by the new Pope John Paul II. From September 1979 to November 1984, the pope dedicated his audience talks (with some interruptions) to developing his teaching on marriage and sexuality. He had already written this material before he became pope and was going to use it for another purpose. Quite frankly, the talks do not seem appropriate for the occasion. They are somewhat theoretical and too detailed for a general audience. In addition, because each individual talk is a part of a larger whole, it is difficult to understand the full meaning of any short talk without seeing the whole picture. I am sure that most of those in attendance at the audiences did not follow what the pope was saying. But these talks, even though they have little or no importance from the viewpoint of authoritative teaching, are a gold mine for one who wants to know and study John Paul II's approach to human sexuality and marriage. These talks have been collected in one volume with the English title *The Theology of the Body: Human Love in the Divine Plan.*[4] Chapter 5 will rely heavily on these talks.

This book addresses the moral teaching and moral theology of John Paul II as pope. I do not consider directly his philosophical or ethical writings that were published before he became pope.[5] Obviously, these writings help to explain the approach he takes as pope, but this book deals explicitly only with the papal writings themselves.

Because the book considers moral theology as such, its focus is the papal writing on the subject of morality. I do not discuss the life and actions of the pope. Many biographies of John Paul II have been written from different perspectives about his life and accomplishments, but this book does not directly consider biographical materials.[6] Likewise, discussions of the life and state of the Catholic Church today lie beyond the scope of this volume.

Many commentators have already discussed aspects of John Paul II's moral theology. Two edited volumes in English examine his moral teaching.[7] But there has never been a monograph in English focusing on his moral theology as such. I occasionally refer to some of these commentaries on the papal teaching, but my primary concern is the papal teaching itself and not the different reactions to that teaching by others.

I make no attempt to propose my own systematic moral theology or to develop in a positive manner specific methodological or substantive issues such as natural law, the use of scripture in moral theology, conscience, moral norms, marriage and sexual ethics, or social ethics in this volume, but instead analyze and criticize the moral theology of John Paul II. The basis for this appraisal is my understanding of the Catholic moral tradition today. But, as the last chapter insists, this is a living tradition.

Catholic moral theology addresses both method and substantive areas. This book appraises the moral theology of John Paul II in six main chapters. The first chapter discusses the theological presuppositions of John Paul II's moral teaching and moral theology. Subsequent chapters address his theological methodology, his ethical methodology, and his fundamental moral theology, together with his understanding of human life. The final two chapters consider the specific issues of marriage and sexuality and Catholic social teaching.

Because this book primarily addresses Catholic moral theology, it makes no attempt to bring directly into the discussion other traditions of Christian moral theology or philosophical writings. Thus, for example, I do not directly refer to Protestant ethics as such or to postmodernism. My analysis and criticism of John Paul II's moral theology comes from my own approach to moral theology. In the past, I have on occasion disagreed with some aspects of his moral theology and continue to do so. I have tried to be fair in this analysis, but obviously my own position colors my approach. The critical reader must decide for herself or himself what is the more fitting approach to, and understanding of, Catholic moral theology today.

Notes

1. For the relative authority of different papal documents, see Francis A. Sullivan, *Creative Fidelity: Weighing and Interpreting Documents of the Magisterium* (New York: Paulist Press, 1996); and Francis G. Morrisey, *Papal and Curial Pronouncements: Their Canonical Significance in Light of the Code of Canon Law*, 2d ed. (Ottawa: St. Paul University Press, 1995).

2. For a collection of the first thirteen encyclicals of John Paul II with helpful introductions, see J. Michael Miller, ed., *The Encyclicals of John Paul II* (Huntington, Ind.: Our Sunday Visitor, 2001). Subsequent references in the text to these encyclicals will be to the initials followed by the paragraph number. In a similar way, references to all official Vatican documents will give the paragraph number of the document. John Paul II refers most often to the documents of the Second Vatican Council. The text will use his translation of these documents whenever he gives it. For a collection of these documents, see Walter J. Abbott, ed., *Documents of Vatican II* (New York: Guild, 1966). For a nonofficial inclusive-language translation, see Austin Flannery, ed., *Vatican Council II: The Basic Sixteen Documents: Constitutions, Decrees, Declarations* (Northport, N.Y.: Costello, 1996).

3. For a collection of John Paul II's postsynodal apostolic exhortations, see J. Michael Miller, ed., *The Post-Synodal Apostolic Exhortations of John Paul II* (Huntington, Ind.: Our Sunday Visitor, 1998).

4. Pope John Paul II, *The Theology of the Body: Human Love in the Divine Plan* (Boston: Pauline Books, 1997). Subsequent references in the text will be to *TB* followed by the page number or numbers.

5. For perspectives on Karol Wojtyla's philosophy, see Rocco Buttiglione, *Karol Wojtyla: The Thought of the Man Who Became Pope John Paul II* (Grand Rapids, Mich.: William B. Eerdmans, 1997); Kenneth L. Schmitz, *At the Center of the Human Drama: The Philosophical Anthropology of Karol Wojtyla / Pope John Paul II* (Washington, D.C.: Catholic University of America Press, 1993); and George Hunston Williams, *The Mind of John Paul II: Origins of His Thought and Action* (New York: Seabury Press, 1981).

6. For recent English biographies of John Paul II, see Jonathan Kwitny, *Man of the Century: The Life and Times of John Paul II* (New York: Henry Holt, 1997); Tad Szulc, *Pope John Paul II: The Biography* (New York: Scribner, 1995); and George Weigel, *Witness to Hope: The Biography of Pope John Paul II* (New York: Cliff Street Books, 1999).

7. John J. Conley and Joseph W. Koterski, eds., *Prophecy and Diplomacy: The Moral Doctrine of John Paul II: A Jesuit Symposium* (New York: Fordham University Press, 1999); and Charles E. Curran and Richard A. McCormick, eds., *John Paul II and Moral Theology: Readings in Moral Theology No. 10* (New York: Paulist Press, 1998).

THEOLOGICAL PRESUPPOSITIONS

THIS CHAPTER focuses on the theological presuppositions for John Paul II's moral theology as found primarily in his encyclicals, as well as in some other significant writings. For John Paul II, truth is the most important factor in considering morality, and the church teaches the truth about humankind.

The Truth about the Human Person and Its Denial

In *Dives in misericordia*, John Paul II describes his very first encyclical, *Redemptor hominis* (1979), as addressing the subject of "the truth about man" (*DM* 1.2). Thus, right from the very beginning of his service as the bishop of Rome, he insisted on the centrality of the truth about the human person. His encyclicals and major writings give a singular importance to the truth about the human person. His encyclical on moral theory and moral norms is titled *Veritatis splendor*—the splendor of truth. The answer to the basic questions, "What must I do? How do I distinguish good from evil?" comes from "the splendor of truth" (*VS* 2.1).

Redemptor hominis, with its emphasis on the truth about the human person, begins with John Paul II's insistence on "the key truth of faith"—the Incarnation, which the evangelist John described as "the Word became flesh and dwelt among us" (1.1). *Re-*

demptor hominis cites *Gaudium et spes* 22 to insist that "the truth is that only in the mystery of the Incarnate Word does the mystery of man take on light" (8.2). The second encyclical of Wojtyla's pontificate, *Dives in misercordia* (1980), deals with God the Father, seen especially in terms of God's great mercy. This revelation of the mystery of the Father and his love "fully reveals man to himself and brings to light his lofty calling" (1.2).

The third of John Paul II's three Trinitarian encyclicals deals with the Holy Spirit as the Lord and giver of life—*Dominum et vivificantem* (1986). The primary emphasis in this encyclical, despite its title, falls on the truth that the Spirit gives to us. The very first words of the first chapter, "The Spirit of the Father and of the Son, given to the Church," emphasize the Spirit of truth. The chapter begins with a citation of John 14:13–17—Jesus prays that the Father will give to the disciples the "Spirit of truth." This Spirit of truth will teach you all things. "The Holy Spirit then will ensure that in the church there will always continue *the same truth* which the Apostles heard from their Master" (3.1–4; italics here and in subsequent quotations are in the original). Truth is such an important concept for John Paul II that he discusses the persons of the Trinity in his three different encyclicals on the Redeemer, the Father, and the Holy Spirit precisely in the light of truth.

For John Paul II, the truth about the human person constitutes the basis for his understanding of morality. But he also points out the failure of so many people in the modern world, including some in the church, to recognize the truth.

His 1998 encyclical *Fides et ratio* clearly focuses on truth, as is evident from the very opening paragraph—"Faith and reason are like two wings on which the human spirit rises to the contemplation of truth; and God has placed in the human heart a desire to know the truth—in a word to know himself—so that, by knowing and loving God, men and women may also come to the fullness of truth about themselves." In this encyclical, John Paul II expresses the church's and his own understanding that sees in philosophy the way to come to know fundamental truths about human life. But unfortunately today in modern philosophy the search for ultimate truth seems to be neglected. Modern philosophy has so emphasized human subjectivity that it has forgotten objective truth and the fact that men and women are called to direct their steps toward a truth that transcends them. Rather than make use of the human capacity to know the truth, modern philosophy has preferred to accentuate the ways in which this capacity is limited and conditioned. This approach gives rise to different forms of agnosticism, relativism, and skepticism that despair of human beings' capacity for truth (5.1–3). For John Paul II, there is truly a crisis of meaning and truth in our world today (81.1).

Above all, John Paul II understands the problem of the modern world with regard to truth as the absolutization of freedom over truth. But in reality, true freedom exists only in obedience to the truth. In the very beginning of his pontificate, *Redemptor hominis* insists that the truth will make you free. These biblical words contain a fundamental requirement and a warning—"the requirement of an honest relationship with regard to truth as a condition for authentic freedom, and the warning to avoid every kind of illusory freedom, every superficial unilateral freedom, every freedom that fails to enter into the whole truth about man and the world" (12.3).

In practically all his writings, John Paul II seems to come back to this point—the attempt of the modern world to absolutize freedom and its failure to see that true freedom exists only in obedience to the truth. *Dives in misericordia* excoriates the modern permissiveness of our age and the crisis of truth in human relationships (12.4). Above all, in the encyclicals dealing with moral and social issues, John Paul II constantly emphasizes the need for freedom to be governed by truth. *Veritatis splendor* in its very first paragraph insists on the scriptural injunction of obedience to truth (1.1). This encyclical goes on to recognize that the moral issues frequently debated in contemporary moral reflection are all closely related to the crucial issue of human freedom. Here, John Paul II cites John 8:32—"You will know the truth and the truth will make you free" (31). He strongly opposes the moral autonomy and absolute sovereignty that come from an absolutization of freedom and a severing of its basic relationship to the truth. Freedom depends on truth. Even in the Catholic Church today, certain tendencies in moral theology under the influence of subjectivism and individualism lessen or even deny the fundamental dependence of freedom on truth (31–34). J. Michael

Miller maintains that "obedience of freedom to truth" is the first key theme of *Veritatis splendor* and appears as a central theme in many of John Paul II's writings.[1]

Evangelium vitae excoriates the culture of death in the modern world. One of the sources of the culture of death is a notion of freedom that denies freedom's essential link with truth. The culture of death as seen in the call for abortion and euthanasia betrays a completely individualistic concept of freedom that ends up by becoming the freedom of the strong against the weak (19). This view of freedom leads to a serious distortion of life in society (20.1). Majority vote can never make something right or wrong. The democratic ideal must acknowledge and safeguard the truth of the dignity of every human person (20.2).

At the beginning of *Centesimus annus,* Pope John Paul II cites Leo XIII's encyclical *Libertas praestantissimum,* which called attention to the central bond between human freedom and truth so that freedom that refuses to be linked to the truth falls into arbitrariness and even self-destruction. The origin of all evils in the social and economic orders detailed by Leo XIII in *Rerum novarum* comes from a concept of freedom that "cuts itself off from the truth about man" (4.5).

In the process of showing the centrality of truth and the subordination of freedom to truth, John Paul II often invokes the concept of martyrdom. *Veritatis splendor* discusses martyrdom in a number of paragraphs and describes martyrdom as "the high point of the witness to moral truth" (93.2). Even though not all are called to martyrdom, all are called to be witnesses to truth and to be faithful to the moral order (90–94). *Fides et ratio* sees martyrs as the most authentic witnesses to the truth about existence. The martyrs know that they have found the truth about life in their encounter with Jesus Christ, and nothing and no one could ever take this certainty from them (32.3). *Dominum et vivificantem* praises martyrdom as a "witness to divine Truth" that reveals the true meaning of Christian freedom (60.2). Thus John Paul II frequently invokes martyrdom as the best example of the centrality of truth and the subordination of freedom to truth. Martyrs are willing to die for the truth.

The truth about the human person forms the basis for morality. But the modern world does not often have that truth because modernity extols freedom and fails to see the subordination of freedom to truth. Where then can we find the truth about the human person? John Paul II points to Jesus Christ.

Jesus Christ as the Source of the Truth about the Human Person

Christians have emphasized different aspects about Jesus Christ and his role with regard to the moral life. Thus, some have spoken of Jesus as teacher, Jesus as model, Jesus as lawgiver.[2] Without doubt, John Paul II sees the role of Jesus Christ primarily as Redeemer, as is evident from the titles of his encyclicals—"the Redeemer of Man," "The Mother of the Redeemer," and "The Mission of the Redeemer." *Redemptor hominis* distinguishes the divine dimension of the mystery of the redemption from the human dimension of this mystery. The divine dimension focuses on Jesus Christ, the Son of the Living God, who becomes our Redeemer with the Father (9.1). According to John Paul II, "the human dimension" of the mystery of redemption consists in the fact that "Christ the Redeemer 'fully reveals man to himself'" (*RH* 10.1). John Paul II devoted his first encyclical "to the truth about man, a truth that is revealed to us in its fullness and depth in Christ" (*DM* 1.2). "In Christ and through Christ God has revealed himself fully to mankind and has definitively drawn close to it; at the same time, in Christ and through Christ, man has acquired full awareness of his dignity, of the heights to which he is raised, of the surpassing worth of his own humanity, and of the meaning of his existence" (*RH* 11.3). For John Paul II, Christ is the Redeemer who reveals the truth about human beings.

John Paul II often cites paragraph 22 of *Gaudium et spes*, the Pastoral Constitution on the Church in the Modern World—"The truth is that only in the mystery of the Incarnate Word does the mystery of man take on life. For Adam, the first man, was a type of him who was to come (Rom 5:14), Christ the Lord. Christ, the new Adam, in the very revelation of the mystery of the Father and his love, *fully reveals man to himself* and brings to life his most high calling" (*RH* 8.2). *Redemptor hominis* refers to "the penetrating analysis" found in *Gaudium et spes* (8.2). *Dives in misericordia* cites this passage from *Gaudium et spes* in its very first paragraph and refers to the fact that the linking of theocentrism and anthropocentrism, as shown in the fact that Christ reveals the human being to oneself, is "one of the basic principles, perhaps the most important one, of the teaching of the last Council" (1.4). Thus anthropocentrism and theocentrism are not opposed to one another. John Paul II links them up in a deep and organic way. The subsequent chapters of this book will often refer to this close connection between anthropocentrism and theocentrism with its grounding in the Incarnation, as found in *Gaudium et spes* 22, John Paul II's favorite text from Vatican II. For our purposes in this chapter, the pope insists that redemption tells us the truth about the human person.

The proper understanding of redemption and the truth about the human person comes to light in terms of the theological realities of creation and sin. God created us as good with the possibility of coming to the truth, but through sin human beings have been separated from God and consequently have lost the truth about themselves. In God's plan of creation, the human person is made in the image and likeness of God. Everything in creation is ordered to the human person and everything is subject to the human person. But then comes the sin of Adam and Eve that separates the human person from the love of God. The sin of Adam and Eve, which John Paul II sees especially in terms of disobedience, involves a turning away from God and God's love. But John Paul II also sees sin as the turning away from the truth. Through sin, the truth about God is falsified and consequently "the truth about man becomes falsified" (*DV* 36–37). In the beginning, it was from God the Creator that the human person could know what was good and evil. The blindness of pride deceived our first parents into thinking they could know and determine good and evil (*FR* 22). As a result of sin, the human being, the image of God, exchanged the truth about God for a lie (*EV* 36.1).

In keeping with his central focus on the truth about the human person, John Paul II sees the problem of contemporary human beings and society as a crisis of truth. According to a later encyclical, the whole thrust of *Veritatis splendor* was to show the rejection and denial of truth in the moral order today (*FR* 98.2). Modern philosophy, as mentioned above, is part of the problem of this crisis of truth and offers little or no help in the human search for the truth. "The development of a good part of modern philosophy has seen it move further and further away from Christian Revelation, to the point of setting itself quite explicitly in opposition. This process reached its apogee in the last century" (*FR* 46.1). Nihilism, idealism, atheistic humanism, and positivism are often found in modern philosophy. Instrumental reason, interested only in utilitarian ends, has rejected the wisdom of true philosophy that deals with the ultimate questions of human existence and meaning. Some philosophers have abandoned the search for truth and made their sole aim the attainment of a subjective certainty or a pragmatic sense of utility (*FR* 46–47).

John Paul II's negative assessment of contemporary humanity and society reaches its strongest point in the 1995 encyclical *Evangelium vitae*, which contrasts the culture of life with the culture of death. The ultimate root of this contradiction between the culture of death and the culture of life is sin. *Evangelium vitae* points out four specific roots of the culture of death, and all four are ultimately rooted in the lack of truth. The first root comes from a distorted view of human subjectivity that recognizes as a subject of rights only the person who enjoys full or at least incipient autonomy. Here and throughout the corpus of his encyclicals, John Paul II insists time and again that human dignity is not based on what we do or accomplish but on our being. Personal dignity cannot be equated with the capacity for verbal or perceptible communication (19.2).

The second root comes from a poor notion of human freedom that no longer recognizes and respects freedom's essential link to the truth—the thrust of the earlier encyclical *Veritatis splendor*. This view of freedom leads to a serious destruction of life in society. The absolute autonomy of the self leads to an absolute power over, and even against, all others with no place for human solidarity (19.3–20.3). The third root of the culture of death is the eclipse of the sense of God and of the human person (21.1). When the sense of God is lost, the human being no longer considers oneself something sacred, a splendid gift of God, but becomes a mere thing with no appreciation of the transcendent nature of one's existence and being. "By living 'as if God did not exist,' man not only loses sight of the mystery of God, but also the mystery of the world, and the mystery of his own being" (22.4). The eclipse of the sense of God and of the human person inevitably leads to practical materialism, individualism, utilitarianism, and hedonism (23.1).

The fourth root of the culture of death is the darkening of human conscience both in the individual and in society. This contemporary confusion about good and evil creates and consolidates "structures of sin" that encourage the culture of death. Conscience too often today calls evil good and good evil (24.1–2).

The major encyclicals of John Paul II dealing with matters of faith—redemption, God, the Holy Spirit, Mary, the church and its mission—without doubt emphasize that Jesus Christ has given us the truth about the human person. These encyclicals above all express the tension and even more the opposition between sin and Jesus Christ. There can be no doubt that in these encyclicals John Paul II stresses the dichotomy that emphasizes just the two terms—redemption through Jesus Christ or sin. His very negative assessment of contemporary human beings and their ability to come to the truth about the human person is in keeping with this dichotomy. One might maintain that in this context John Paul II is talking primarily about the truths of salvation and not moral truths. But when he speaks about the effects of sin in the world today, he often describes the moral realities of contemporary life both in the social and in the personal spheres. He is also very negative about contemporary philosophy and the use of human reason. These encyclicals addressing aspects of faith never explicitly develop the ability of human reason to come to the truth.

One would expect someone coming out of the Roman Catholic tradition to emphasize even in these encyclicals dealing primarily with matters of faith that human reason on the basis of the natural law can and does arrive at moral truth. But there is no development of this perspective in these encyclicals. In addition, the opposition between Christ and sin seems to leave little or no room for human reason to arrive at truth. Three factors, however, indicate that there is not a total opposition between Christ and truth, on the one hand, and sin and error, on the other.

First, there are sometimes qualifications about the truth that comes from Christ. According to John Paul II in *Dives in misericordia*, his first encyclical, *Redemptor hominis*, is devoted "to the truth about man, a truth that is revealed to us in its fullness and depth in Christ" (1.2). *Evangelium vitae* maintains that "through the words, the actions, and the very person of Jesus man is given the possibility of 'knowing' the *complete truth* concerning the value of human life" (29.3). The recognition that Christ gives the fullness of truth, the depth of truth, or the complete truth means that there can be some level of truth without Christ. Such a position has been the traditional understanding in Roman Catholicism.

Second, John Paul II recognizes what Catholic theology, even in its pre–Vatican II days, called the "universal salvific will of God." God calls all people to salvation. *Dominum et vivificantem* cites *Gaudium et spes* 22 in maintaining that the Holy Spirit, in a manner known only to God, offers to every person the possibility of being associated with the Paschal Mystery. For John Paul II, the Holy Spirit was active in the world even before Jesus Christ came into the world. Grace can also work in human hearts that do not explicitly accept Jesus Christ (*DV* 53.2–3).

John Paul II deals with this understanding of grace and the Holy Spirit working outside explicit Christian faith especially in his encyclical *Redemptoris missio*. "The universality of salvation means that it is granted not only to those who explicitly believe in Christ and have entered the Church." Here, too, the encyclical once again quotes *Gaudium et spes* 22. However, even this grace comes from Christ. It is the result of Christ's sacrifice and is communicated by the Holy Spirit (10.1). This encyclical insists that the Spirit is present and active in every time and place, affecting not only individuals but also society, history, cultures, people, and religions. However, all these activities of the Spirit are not an alternative to Christ but can only be understood in reference to Christ (29.1–2). Thus, grace and the truth that comes from it can be found outside the church and explicit Christianity.

Third, these encyclicals dealing primarily with matters of faith at times recognize, but certainly do not stress, the traditional Catholic understanding that sin has not completely destroyed the gift of creation and the God-given human quest for truth. *Dominum et vivificantem* insists on the opposition between truth and "antitruth" that comes from the fall and human sinfulness, but the opposition is somewhat nuanced. The fall and sin bring about "in a certain sense *the closing up* of human freedom in his regard. It also means a certain opening of this freedom . . . to the one who is the 'father of lies'" (37.2). Even though *Evangelium vitae* stresses the sharp opposition between the culture of life and the culture of death, it at least recognizes that human reason can know the Gospel of Life. "This is the Gospel which, already present in the revelation of the Old Testament and indeed written in the heart of every man and woman, has echoed in every conscience 'from the beginning,' from the time of creation itself, in such a way that, despite the negative consequences of sin, *it can also be known in its essential traits by human reason*" (29.3). *Redemptoris missio* recognizes in all human beings the quest for answers to the deepest questions of life (29.1). Despite their strong rhetoric of the opposition between Christ and truth on the one hand and sin and error on the other hand, the encyclicals of John Paul II that deal with faith recognize without any real development that aspects of truth can and do exist in our present world outside explicit Christian belief.

Human Sources of the Truth about the Human Person

In addition to the encyclicals considering primarily matters of faith, John Paul II's encyclicals touch on other areas—the relationship of faith and reason (*Fides et ratio*) and the social teachings of the church (*Laborem exercens*, *Sollicitudo rei socialis*, and *Centesimus annus*). *Veritatis splendor* considers moral theory. *Evangelium vitae*, although it deals with the Gospel of Life, also has some affinities with the other encyclicals mentioned here. These encyclicals just mentioned continue to emphasize the primacy of truth, but in various degrees recognize human sources for the truth about humankind that are not explicitly dependent on Christ. For the pope, reason is always informed by faith, but reason can be a source of truth for those who do not have Catholic faith. This section discusses how these three different types of encyclicals deal with these human sources of truth, especially reason and natural law.

Fides et ratio

The encyclical *Fides et ratio* (1998) deals in a traditional Catholic way with the issue of human reason and its relation to faith and theology. John Paul II explains the fundamental harmony between faith and reason in this way. Faith asks that its object be understood with the help of reason, and reason, at the summit of its searching, knows that it cannot do without what faith presents (42.2). The encyclical focuses primarily on the theological truth about God and faith, what it calls "the ultimate truth about human life" (2). In this context, John Paul II again speaks very negatively about contemporary philosophy, but there exists within all human beings a strong desire and searching for truth—a search deeply rooted in human nature (29.1). Revelation gives to us this "universal," "ultimate," and "absolute truth" (14.2, 15.1).

In considering the relationship between theology and philosophy, *Fides et ratio* discusses dogmatic theology, fundamental theology, and moral theology. Theology in general follows the twofold methodological principles of hearing the faith and understanding it. Philosophy contributes to both aspects (65–67). As for moral theology, the Gospel and apostolic writings set forth both the general principles of Christian conduct and specific teachings and precepts. To apply these to particular personal and social situations, "moral theology requires a sound philosophical vision of human nature and society as well as of the general principles of ethical decision making" (68).

Fides et ratio also points out how moral theology has to use philosophy understood in the sense of metaphysics, which is capable of transcending empirical data to achieve something absolute, ultimate, and foundational in its search for truth. Metaphysics is necessary for knowing the moral good that has its ultimate foundation in the supreme good, God himself. In keeping with his own philosophical interests, John Paul II in this encyclical sees the person as the privileged locus for the encounter with being and with metaphysics (83.1–3). He insists on the metaphysical element "in order to move beyond the crisis pervading large sections of philosophy at the moment and thus to correct certain mistaken modes of behavior now widespread in our society" (83.4). *Fides et ratio*, however, has only five references to human nature (3.1, 29.1, 68.1, 80.3, 102) and never uses the term "natural law." In light of the heavy use of natural law in the earlier *Veritatis splendor*, one would have expected his 1998 encyclical to be more explicit about natural law.

Social Encyclicals

The three social encyclicals of John Paul II—*Laborem exercens*, *Sollicitudo rei socialis*, and *Centesimus annus*—as would be expected, form a coherent whole. These encyclicals are concerned with justice and peace in our world—the area of social morality. They have some continuity with the encyclicals dealing primarily with faith but also show very significant discontinuity.

The continuity, above all, comes from the insistence on truth as primary, the truth about the human person as the basis for the teaching proposed, and the need for freedom to be subordinated to truth. *Centesimus annus*, for example, maintains that "the guiding principle of Pope Leo's Encyclical, and of all of the Church's social doctrine, is a *correct view of the human person* and of his unique value, inasmuch as man '. . . is the only creature on earth which God willed for itself.' God has imprinted his own image and likeness on man (cf. Gen 1:26), conferring upon him an incomparable dignity" (11.3). At the very beginning of this encyclical, John Paul II insists on the essential link between truth and freedom. "Indeed what is the origin of all the evils to which *Rerum novarum* wished to respond, if not a kind of freedom which, in the area of economic and social activity, cuts itself off from the truth about man?" (4.5). Catholic social teaching for John Paul II is thus based on the truth about the human person and the need for freedom to respect that truth.

But the significant discontinuity between these social encyclicals and those dealing primarily with faith comes through in the under-

standing of where truth is found. One does not see here the dichotomy and even the opposition between Christ and sin, life and death,
truth and antitruth, and the very negative assessment of the human
condition in general and of human reason in particular.

It is true that for John Paul II, Catholic social teaching is
grounded in the "Christian basis of truth which can be called ageless" (*LE* 3.1). But this truth is not found only in Jesus Christ and
only in scripture. In his discussion of labor, John Paul II insists that
the principle of the priority of labor over capital "is an evident truth
that emerges from the whole of man's historical experience" (*LE*
12.1). The fall of communism in 1989 "was accomplished almost
everywhere by means of peaceful protest, using only the weapons of
truth and justice" (*CA* 23.2). Thus "protests which led to the collapse
of Marxism tenaciously insisted on trying every avenue of negotiation, dialogue, and witness to the truth, appealing to the conscience
of the adversary and seeking to reawaken in him a sense of shared
human dignity" (23.2). In discussing the state and culture, *Centesimus
annus* maintains about the Christian person that, "while paying heed
to every fragment of truth which he encounters in the life experience
and in the culture of individuals and of nations, he will not fail to
affirm in dialogue with others all that his faith and the correct use
of reason have enabled him to understand" (46.4). Note from these
quotations the multiple sources for truth—faith, reason, experience,
culture, even the conscience of the adversary.

In these encyclicals, John Paul II calls for the cooperation and
working together of all for the common good. *Sollicitudo rei socialis*
concludes with a ringing call to all humanity to work together
(47.5–9). The conclusion of *Centesimus annus* recognizes that "openness to dialogue and to cooperation is required of all people of good
will, and in particular of individuals and groups with specific responsibilities in the areas of politics, economics, and social life, at both
the national and international levels" (60.4). Grave problems facing
society can be solved only by cooperation among all forces (60.1).
John Paul II explicitly points out that Pope John XXIII addressed
his encyclical on peace to "all men of good will" (*CA* 60.1). John Paul
II follows this same inclusion of all people of goodwill in those addressed by his three social encyclicals.

The social encyclicals, however, still recognize the presence of sin in the world and even the structures of sin. In a four-paragraph section of *Sollicitudo rei socialis*, John Paul II uses the term "structures of sin" nine times (36–39). In these encyclicals, the pope still proposes serious criticisms of the many negative aspects in our contemporary world and calls for eradicating the evils that stand in the way of a greater justice and peace as well as the common good of all. In this context, however, the social encyclicals do not see non-Christians or even the world itself in light of the dichotomy or opposition between Christ and sin or between life and death. Overcoming the injustices and evils of our world requires the cooperation of all people of goodwill for the common good.

Anyone familiar with the Catholic tradition might expect the social encyclicals of John Paul II dealing with justice in society and addressed to all people of goodwill to develop or at least refer to the concept of natural law. Catholic social teaching has traditionally appealed to the natural law that is common to all human beings to develop its positions on social justice and the demands of the common good.[3] The pope obviously continues to support and develop the older teachings based on the natural law approach. But his social encyclicals do not develop the theory of natural law and do not even explicitly mention natural law as such.

Veritatis splendor *and* Evangelium vitae

Two encyclicals, *Veritatis splendor* (1993) and *Evangelium vitae* (1995), deal with moral theology and issues of personal morality as distinguished from the subject matter of the social encyclicals. *Veritatis splendor* is in continuity with the encyclicals dealing primarily with matters of faith with its emphasis on the importance of truth. Obedience to the truth is not always easy because of original sin. The human capacity to know the truth is also darkened, and the will to submit to it is weakened with the consequent searching for an illusory freedom apart from truth itself. "But no darkness of error or of sin can totally take away from man the light of God the Creator. In the depths of his heart there always remains a yearning for absolute truth and a thirst to attain full knowledge of it" (1.1–3). The encyclical deals with "the crisis of truth" (32.2). Many modern tendencies, such as subjectivism, individualism, and erroneous notions of conscience, "are at one in lessening or even denying the dependence of freedom on truth" (34.2).

However, *Veritatis splendor* strongly contrasts with the earlier encyclicals in the nature of the truth that it defends and promulgates. Here, John Paul II extols the truth of natural law. The words "natural law" appear more than thirty times in this document, to say nothing of related terms such as "human nature." At the beginning of the encyclical, the pope clearly states its purpose. A new situation has arisen within the church itself—"an overall and systematic calling into question of traditional moral doctrine . . . regarding the natural law, and the universality and permanent validity of its precepts" (4.2).

In the encyclical itself, John Paul II goes into a somewhat detailed description of how natural law can arrive at the truth of God's law. As he explains, from a theological perspective, natural law avoids both autonomy and heteronomy (i.e., the human person is governed by some outside force that does not accept human self-determination) by embracing theonomy (i.e., the human person is governed by God) or participated theonomy. Autonomy makes the human person absolute and leads to subjectivism, individualism, and the human being as the ultimate source of morality. Heteronomy sees morality as imposed on the passive subject from an outside source. John Paul II employs the Thomistic notion of law to illustrate the participated theonomy of natural law. Natural law is the participation of eternal law in the rational creature. Eternal law is the plan of God for all creation that comes from God's reason and wisdom. Human reason, reflecting on the human nature that God has given us, can discern then how God wants us to act. But in so doing, human beings fulfill their very nature and find their true humanity and happiness. Human freedom is called to respond to the truth of natural law and thus find its true humanity (40–46). In this comparatively long discussion of natural law, John Paul II also develops the scriptural basis for natural law, the law written in our hearts in Romans 2:15, and illustrates his point that the church has often made reference to this classical teaching by citing Augustine, Thomas Aquinas, Leo XIII, and Vatican II (43). *Veritatis splendor* not only strongly defends and supports the natural law method but also "the universality and permanent validity of its precepts" (4.2).

In light of the earlier encyclicals, one is surprised to find the centrality of natural law in *Veritatis splendor*. But anyone familiar with the tradition of Catholic moral theology is not surprised by the insistence of *Veritatis splendor* on natural law. A very important question of moral theology and Christian moral teaching concerns where the Christian finds moral wisdom and knowledge. Do we find moral wisdom only in scripture, in Jesus Christ, and in Christian tradition? Or do we share some moral wisdom and knowledge with all humankind?

The historical and traditional Roman Catholic approach has recognized that we share some moral wisdom with all others. The specific Catholic answer to this question has been "natural law." There are two different aspects to the natural law issue. The theological aspect, which is the one considered here, is the response to the question of whether the Christian shares some moral wisdom and knowledge with all others. Natural law maintains that Christians and all others, reflecting on what God has created and using the human reason given to us by God, can arrive at true moral wisdom and what God requires of us in our lives. The philosophical aspect of the natural law issue involves what one means by human reason and human nature. In chapter 3, I will discuss this philosophical aspect of natural law. The insistence on the importance of human reason in general and of natural law in the area of moral theology has been characteristic of the Catholic theological approach.[4]

The historical circumstances occasioning the encyclical also help to explain the emphasis on natural law. *Veritatis splendor* recognizes the widespread disagreement and dissent even among Catholic theologians regarding the moral teaching of the hierarchical magisterium (4.2). Most of these newer Catholic approaches have attacked various aspects of natural law, but not the theological aspect of natural law asserting that human reason can arrive at moral truth. As a result, John Paul II had to explain and defend the natural law theory—a point explicitly recognized in the encyclical. "This is the first time, in fact, that the Magisterium of the Church has set forth in detail the fundamental elements of this teaching" (115.1). Although

Veritatis splendor primarily develops the philosophical aspect of natural law, it also deals with the theological aspect of natural law.

Evangelium vitae (1995), as mentioned above, continues to emphasize the basic themes found in the encyclicals about matters of faith—Jesus Christ reveals the truth about the human person. "Through the words, the actions, and the very person of Jesus, man is given the possibility of 'knowing' the complete truth concerning the value of human life" (29.3). This encyclical also insists on the primacy of truth and the need for freedom to be seen in the light of truth. The encyclical focuses on "a dramatic conflict" between the culture of death and the culture of life (50.2). The culture of death is associated with evil and sin, whereas the culture of life comes from Christ and the Gospel of life. Such an approach would seem logically to have no place for natural law as a source of moral truth.

However, *Evangelium vitae*, following chronologically and also logically in the footsteps of *Veritatis splendor*, recognizes natural law. The Gospel of life "has a profound and persuasive echo in the heart of every person—believer and nonbeliever alike. . . . Every person sincerely open to truth and goodness can, by the light of reason and the hidden action of grace, come to recognize in the natural law written in the heart (cf. Rom 2:14–15) the sacred value of human life from its very beginning until its end. . . . Upon the recognition of this right, every human community and the political community itself are founded" (2.2).

Evangelium vitae, in a very solemn way, condemns direct killing (57.4), direct abortion (62.3), and euthanasia (65.4). All these three solemn condemnations insist on the natural law basis for the teaching and use a very similar wording. Thus, in the case of abortion— "This doctrine is based upon the natural law and upon the written word of God, is transmitted by the Church's Tradition and taught by the ordinary and universal Magisterium" (62.3).

Another significant reason for John Paul II's insistence on the natural law basis for these three condemnations comes from his strong support for civil laws against abortion and euthanasia. All recognize that civil law in pluralistic societies cannot be based simply on the teaching of a particular religion. The natural law basis for abortion and euthanasia means that civil law should not go against natural law.

The right to life is a "fundamental right and source of all other rights . . . . Consequently, laws which legitimize the direct killing of innocent human beings through abortion or euthanasia are in complete opposition to the inviolable right to life proper to every individual; thus they deny the equality of everyone before the law" (72.2).

Tensions within the Encyclical Corpus

John Paul II's encyclicals consistently emphasize the primacy of truth about the human person as the most important consideration for morality. Too often the modern world has absolutized freedom and failed to see that freedom must always be subordinated to truth.

But, at the minimum, there is tension and, at the maximum, there is inconsistency within and among these encyclicals. The encyclicals dealing with matters of faith stress Christ as the truth about the human person. Not only are human sources of truth about the human person not developed, but the theology proposed tends to exclude human sources of truth. Sin has distorted our understanding of the truth. The pope is often quite negative about what is happening in our world. Conversely, the social encyclicals, because they are addressed to all people of goodwill and call for all to work together for the common good, recognize a human truth that all, including non-Christians, share. *Veritatis splendor*'s basic thrust is to defend natural law that is open to all human beings. *Fides et ratio* insists on a proper place for both faith and reason.

One might explain the tension or the inconsistency about common human sources of truth by the occasional nature of the encyclicals dealing with particular topics. In dealing with a particular aspect or issue, an individual encyclical will stress what is pertinent. But still one would expect documents coming from the Catholic tradition to explicitly recognize and develop both faith and reason as sources for the truth about the human person in every issue and aspect treated.

The one encyclical in which the tension or inconsistency is most felt is *Evangelium vitae*. Here the pope insists on the tectonic struggle between truth and error, between the culture of life and the culture of death. But the encyclical then claims that its teachings opposing direct killing, direct abortion, and euthanasia are based on natural law with its emphasis on human reason common to all.

The Church Teaches the Truth about the Human Person

Redemptor hominis, the first encyclical of John Paul II, sets the tone for much of his pontificate. The church continues in time and space the mission of Jesus the Redeemer by fully revealing the meaning of the human and teaching the truth about the human person. "By Christ's institution the Church is its [truth's] guardian and teacher, having been endowed with a unique assistance of the Holy Spirit in order to guard and teach it [truth] in its most exact integrity" (12.2).

The 1986 encyclical *Dominum et vivificantem* spells out in greater detail the role of the Holy Spirit whereby the church continues the mission of Jesus. "The supreme and complete self-revelation of God, accomplished in Christ and witnessed to by the preaching of the Apostles, continues to be manifested in the Church through the mission of the invisible *Counselor*, the Spirit of truth" (7.1). "The Holy Spirit, then, will insure that in the Church there will always continue *the same truth* which the Apostles heard from their Master" (4). Thus, we see here the Trinitarian dimension of the church, which, through the assistance of the Holy Spirit, carries on the work of Jesus of teaching God's truth about the human person.

Three times paragraph 14 of the first encyclical, *Redemptor hominis,* refers to humanity as "the way for the Church." *Redemptor hominis*'s insistence that humanity is "the primary and fundamental way for the church" (14.1) becomes a central point, if not the central point, in the encyclicals of John Paul II, despite their dealing with a variety of subjects. The beginning of *Dives in misericordia* insists "that every individual human being is, as I said in my Encyclical *Redemptor hominis,* the way for the Church. . . . In Jesus Christ, every path to man . . . has been assigned once and for all to the Church" (1.3). *Dominum et vivificantem,* the third of the Trinitarian encyclicals, also cites *Redemptor hominis* that humanity is the way for the church (58.2, 59.3).

In this context, it is no surprise that the three social encyclicals and the two encyclicals on moral teaching stress and develop the fundamental theme of *Redemptor hominis* that "man is the way for the church." In the very opening paragraph of *Laborem exercens*, John Paul II justifies his devoting this document to human work and, even more, to the human person in the vast context of the reality of work by citing his insistence in *Redemptor hominis* that "man 'is the primary and fundamental way for the Church'" (1.1). Consequently, "it is necessary to return constantly to this way and to follow it ever anew in the various aspects in which it shows us all the wealth and at the same time all the toil of human existence on earth" (1.1).

The sixth chapter of *Centesimus annus*, the document written on the hundredth anniversary of *Rerum novarum*, bears the title, "Man is the Way of the Church" (53). Why has the church developed its Catholic social teaching in the one hundred years since *Rerum novarum*? "Her sole purpose has been *care and responsibility* for man, who has been entrusted to her by Christ himself" (53.1). "This, and this alone, is the principle which inspires the Church's social doctrine" (53.2).

Veritatis splendor, according to the pope's own recognition, is the first papal encyclical to deal in depth with moral theology (115.1). Here, as is his wont, John Paul II often cites Vatican II to make his point: "*The task of authentically interpreting the word of God, whether in its written form or in that of Tradition, has been entrusted only to those charged with the Church's living Magisterium, whose authority is exercised in the name of Jesus Christ*" (27.3). But notice that this citation does not deal specifically with moral issues, so the pope goes on to support this with a citation from canon law (canon 747.2) to make the point. "The Church, in her life and teaching, is thus revealed as 'the pillar and bulwark of truth' (1 Tim 3:15), including the truth regarding moral action. Indeed, 'the Church has the right always and everywhere to proclaim moral principles, even in respect to the social order, and to make judgments about any human matter insofar as this is required by fundamental human rights or the salvation of souls'" (27.3).

As he often does, John Paul II begins this encyclical by reflecting on a biblical passage—in this case the story of the rich young man who came to Jesus with the question: "Teacher, what good must I do to have eternal life?" (Mt 19:16). Papal commentary on this passage of scripture serves as the introduction to and the justification for the whole body of the encyclical that defends the church's moral teachings, especially with regard to universal and immutable moral commandments. "This 'answer' to the question about morality has been entrusted by Jesus Christ in a particular way to us, the Pastors of the Church; we have been called to make it the object of our preaching, in the fulfillment of our *munus propheticum*" (114.3). The whole structure of this encyclical with its insistence on "the reaffirmation of the universality and immutability of the moral commandments, particularly those which prohibit always and without exception intrinsically evil acts" (115.3) builds on the understanding that Jesus, who answered the question of the rich young man about what is good, has now given that power and authority to the church to continue down through the centuries the function of teaching the moral commandments.

Evangelium vitae appeals to *Redemptor hominis* to justify the church's need to teach the truth of the Gospel of life—"man—living man—represents the primary and fundamental way for the Church" (2.5). *Evangelium vitae* then solemnly condemns direct killing, direct abortion, euthanasia, and suicide.

The papal insistence on the fact that the church teaches the truth about the human person raises the two obvious questions about the understanding of truth and the understanding of the church as found in these encyclicals. The encyclicals by their very nature do not aim at providing an in-depth understanding of either truth or the church, but some things are said about each of these two important realities.

Truth

The many statements that the church teaches the truth about the human person make no distinctions about different kinds of truth. Truth appears as a simple and univocal concept. There are no grades or levels of truth. This truth is obviously opposed to all that is false. But in reality, John Paul II does make distinctions about different types and levels of truth.

Distinctions and Limitations with Regard to Truth

Fides et ratio recognizes "the different faces of human truth" (28) and "the different modes of truth" (30.1). There is a mode of truth proper to everyday life and to scientific research. At another level, there exists philosophical truth attained by means of the speculative powers of the human intellect. Finally, there are religious truths, which are to some degree grounded in philosophy and which we find in the answers that the different religious traditions offer to the ultimate questions (28–30.1).

This section, however, deals only with truths taught by the church. *Redemptor hominis* refers to "divine truth" and "revealed truth" (19). Often these encyclicals refer to the truths of revelation and the truths of faith. Even with regard to the general category of revealed truth or truths of faith, the encyclicals recognize some limitations. The most frequent limitation is the distinction between truth and its expression that is often supported by a reference to *Gaudium et spes* 62. Thus, for example, *Veritatis splendor* notes that "there is a difference between the deposit or the truths of faith and the manner in which they are expressed, keeping the same meaning and the same judgment" (29.2). *Ut unum sint* cites the 1973 declaration *Mysterium fidei*: "Even though the truths which the Church intends to teach through her dogmatic formulas are distinct from the changeable conceptions of a given epic and can be expressed without them, nevertheless it can sometimes happen that these truths may be enunciated by the sacred Magisterium in terms that bear traces of such conceptions" (38.2). In this context, John Paul II points out: "One of the advantages of ecumenism is that it helps Christian Communities to discover the unfathomable riches of the truth" (38.3). *Ut unum sint* also refers in the same context to the famous opening address of John XXIII at Vatican II in recalling "the distinction between the deposit of faith and the formulation in which it is expressed" (81.3).

The basis for John Paul II's often-recalled distinction between the truths of faith and their expression comes from the fact that "revealed truth, to be sure, surpasses our telling. All our concepts fall short of its ultimately unfathomable grandeur (cf. Eph 3:19)" (*VS*

109.2). This distinction between the truths of faith and their expression also stands behind the recognition of the development of dogma with regard to the truths of faith (*VS* 28.2, 53.3).

In addition to the truths of faith, John Paul II, especially in his encyclicals on moral matters, recognizes the truths of the moral life and especially truths of moral norms based on natural law, which are universal and unchanging. Such truths by their very nature differ somewhat from the truths of faith. In this context, John Paul II fears that many contemporary thinkers so stress historicity and cultural diversity that they call into question the universality of the natural law. But human nature transcends all cultures. "This nature is itself the measure of culture and the condition ensuring that man does not become the prisoner of any of his cultures, but asserts his personal dignity by living in accordance with the profound truth of his being" (53.2). There is a need "to seek out and discover *the most adequate formulation* for universal and permanent moral norms in the light of different cultural contexts. . . . This truth of the moral law . . . must be specified and determined . . . in the light of historical circumstances by the Church's Magisterium, whose decision is preceded and accompanied by the work of interpretation and formulation characteristic of the reason of individual believers and of theological reflection" (53.3). Thus, the formulation of universal and unchanging moral norms depends on natural law and a reasonable power of interpretation and formulation.

John Paul II, in these encyclicals, admits another type of Catholic truth—the truth involved in the social teaching of the church. According to *Centesimus annus*, the church's social teaching focuses on the human person involved in a complex web of relationships and societies. "The human sciences and philosophy are helpful for interpreting *man's central place within society* and for enabling him to understand himself better as a 'social being.' However, a man's true identity is only fully revealed to him through faith, and it is precisely from faith that the Church's social teaching begins. While drawing upon all the contributions made by the sciences and philosophy, her social teaching is aimed at helping everyone on the path of salvation" (54.1). *Centesimus annus* thus explicitly recognizes that "the Church's social teaching has an important interdisciplinary dimension. In order better to incarnate the one truth about man in different and constantly changing social, economic, and political contexts, this teaching enters into dialogue with various disciplines concerned with man. It assimilates what these disciplines have to contribute" (59.3). The encyclicals of John Paul II thus expressly recognize that they are dealing with different types of truth—truths of faith, truths of moral norms, and truths of social teaching. Although the pope has recognized the differences among these three types of truth, the impression from the encyclicals seems to be that they all fall under the same general understanding of truth and its certitude precisely because they are all proposed by the church as authentic teaching due to the assistance of the Holy Spirit.

It might be helpful to inquire in greater detail about the different kinds of truth and the certitude claims involved in these encyclicals. Even on the level of truths of faith, John Paul II recognizes the need for doctrinal development and even for the reformulation of truth. But the historical reality of such developments that have occurred in the truths of Catholic faith includes more discontinuity than John Paul II explicitly admits. Think of developments with regard to the Trinity, Christology, sacraments, and the papal office itself.

With regard to the truths of absolute moral norms, John Paul II has recognized that these truths rest on natural law and the interpretation of reason. However, the effect of these factors on moral truths and the claim to certitude are more significant than the pope explicitly recognizes. Take, for example, the universal and unchangeable moral norm on abortion found in *Evangelium vitae*. The pope, in a very solemn way, reasserts the teaching of the church condemning direct abortion (62.3). Notice that the condemnation does not include all abortion but only direct abortion. The pope thus invokes the philosophical distinction between direct and indirect to distinguish right from wrong with regard to abortion. This distinction is obviously based on a particular philosophical view and is far removed both from the core of faith and from more general ethical norms, such as the respect due to all life including nascent life. One cannot claim the same certitude on this level as one can regarding the more general ethical principles of respecting life or doing good.

When the universal moral norm is applied in concrete cases, one cannot always claim a certitude that excludes the possibility of error. Long ago, Thomas Aquinas recognized that the secondary principles of the natural law oblige as generally occurs but not always precisely because of the more circumstantial elements that can occur and change the case. He illustrates this point with the moral norm that goods being held for another should be returned when the owner requests them. However, this is not true when the owner has left a sword with you and now comes back and wants the sword back but is raving drunk and threatening to kill people.[5] Thus, the truth claims about direct and indirect abortion are limited by the very nature of the complex philosophical theory proposed to solve conflict situations.

With regard to the truths of social teaching, John Paul II correctly recognizes the interdisciplinary nature of that teaching and its dependence on sources other than faith. Here, too—as in the area of the truth of universal and unchangeable moral norms—one can only claim a limited certitude with regard to the teaching proposed. The social teaching of the church has undergone significant changes as well, for instance in its acceptance only in 1965 of religious freedom after a long denial of such freedom. With regard to human rights in general, official Catholic teaching has moved from reluctance and even opposition to strong support. The church has also changed its social teaching on the best form of government with significant support for democracy only beginning in the middle of the twentieth century.[6] In *Veritatis splendor*, John Paul II points out some "principles which are primarily rooted in, and in fact derive their singular urgency from, the transcendent value of the person and the objective moral demands of the functioning of States" (101.1). Among these principles are "respect for the rights of political adversaries, safeguarding the rights of the accused against summary trials and convictions" (101.1). But there has been significant change in church teaching and practice. For many centuries, the Catholic Church did not respect the rights of political adversaries. In addition, the church has changed its own teaching with regard to the rights of the accused to keep silent and not reveal their crimes.[7]

Three Difficulties

Three difficulties arise from the understanding of the truth about humankind found in the encyclicals of John Paul II. First, the generic use of truth insinuates that truth is a univocal term, but such is not the case. The beginning of *Veritatis splendor* well illustrates the problem. The introduction to the encyclical refers to the fundamental questions about human existence. Here Jesus Christ, who is the way, the truth, and the life, gives "the decisive answer to every one of humankind's questions, his religious and moral questions in particular" (85). But there exists a significant difference between the truths of faith regarding the ultimate questions of human existence and decisive answers to every one of humankind's questions, especially religious and moral questions.

The Catholic tradition has consistently recognized that the truth about specific moral questions differs considerably from the truth about the ultimate meaning of human existence. To its great credit, the Catholic theological tradition has insisted on the importance of mediation—the divine is mediated in and through the human. In the area of moral theology and dealing with moral questions, one must examine in great detail all aspects of the complex human reality before coming to an answer to a complex moral question about what should be done in a particular situation.[8] The Catholic tradition has argued against going immediately from a truth of faith or a scriptural citation (e.g., love of neighbor or concern for the poor) to a specific conclusion, such as that multinational corporations are immoral. One must consider all the complex human realities before coming to a specific moral conclusion. The Catholic tradition has often used casuistry as a way of trying to deal with specific moral issues, thus showing how important it is to consider all the details of the situation.[9] Too often the papal encyclicals employ truth in a univocal sense that fails to recognize that truth is an analogous concept.

Second, problems also arise when the encyclicals recognize the analogous nature of truth and describe the different kinds of truth. In their descriptions of truths of faith, moral truths, and truths of social teaching, they do not explicitly recognize the significant limitations involved in some types of truth and also fail to appreciate the different levels of certitude involved. On the level of moral truth, the Catholic tradition has consistently recognized a difference between moral truth and speculative truth. Moral truth deals with practical matters. As Thomas Aquinas pointed out, speculative truths are always true. Thus, for example, a triangle always has 180 degrees even if some people, because of their poor background or knowledge, do not always recognize this fact. However, though secondary precepts of the moral law oblige generally, they admit of exceptions precisely because of the myriad circumstances that can enter in.[10] Thus, John Paul II needs to recognize explicitly the limits on truth and certitude, especially in the moral area that is the proper concern of this book.

Third, a discussion of truth in these documents raises the age-old epistemological problem: What is truth and how do we know truth? A detailed examination of this question lies beyond the scope of this book. But the papal documents seem to have a classicist notion of truth as something out there, which is then knowable by all. A more historically conscious understanding of truth sees it always in relation to persons seeking truth and imbedded in the historical and cultural circumstances of time and place.

Such a historically conscious understanding of epistemology coheres with the recognition that papal and hierarchical teaching on some moral issues has changed over the years. Today, John Paul II insists that slavery is intrinsically evil (80.1). But the Hebrew Bible and the New Testament accepted and did not condemn slavery. In theory and practice, the Catholic condemnation of slavery as evil really begins only in the last half of the nineteenth century. Apostles, Fathers of the church, theologians, bishops, and popes in general did not condemn slavery for more than 1,800 years! Reason illumined by faith and assisted by the Holy Spirit for all those centuries did not see slavery as intrinsically evil. Precisely because of this long history going back to scripture itself, John Henry Newman in the nineteenth century could not condemn slavery as intrinsically evil.[11]

Thus, the concept of truth in the papal encyclicals is overly simplistic and suffers from significant deficiencies in light of the Catholic tradition itself and of many contemporary Catholic approaches.

The Church

The encyclicals of John Paul II address the understanding of the church in many different contexts, with *Redemptoris missio* and *Ut unum sint* concentrating on the church as such. Our focus here is on a general understanding of the church as it relates to the church's teaching the truth about the human person and does not involve a detailed study of the hierarchical magisterium, which is a principal way for the Catholic Church to carry out its teaching function.

The basic role and mission of the church for John Paul II is very clear, as has already been pointed out. Thanks to the gift of the Holy Spirit, the church continues in time and space the mission of Christ the Redeemer in teaching the truth about the human person. But more specific aspects help to flesh out this understanding of the role and mission of the church.

Grace and Truth Outside the Catholic Church

Yes, the church carries on in time and space the redemptive message of Jesus, but God's grace also exists outside the boundaries of the church. The church remains distinct from both Christ and the Kingdom, but "the Church is indissolubly united to both. . . . The result is a unique and special relationship which, while not excluding the action of Christ and the Spirit outside the Church's visible boundaries, confers upon her a specific and necessary role; hence the Church's special connection with the Kingdom of God and of Christ which she has 'the mission of announcing and inaugurating among all peoples'" (*RM* 18.3). This basic understanding grounds the necessity for the evangelizing mission of the church as developed especially in the encyclical *Redemptoris missio*. Yes, the Spirit exists and works outside Christ and the church, but this work of the Spirit is linked both to Christ and to the church. The Spirit develops gifts in all peoples but also works "guiding the Church to discover these gifts, to foster them, and to receive them through dialogue. Every form of the Spirit's presence is to be welcomed with respect and gratitude, but the discernment of this presence is the responsibility of the Church, to which Christ gave his Spirit in order to guide her into all the truth (cf. Jn 16:13)" (29.3). The Spirit, grace, and even religious truths exist outside the boundaries of the Catholic Church, but they are related to Christ and to the Catholic Church, who has the God-given responsibility to discern their truth. The recognition of the Spirit, grace, and even religious truth outside the Catholic Church does not take away from the church's mission to teach the truth about the human person to all.

What about the Catholic Church's relationship with other churches? *Ut unum sint* deals precisely with the question of ecumenism, to which John Paul II is definitely committed. In this context, he cites the position enunciated in Vatican II that "the Church of Christ 'subsists in the Catholic Church . . .' and at the same time acknowledges that 'many elements of sanctification and of truth can be found outside her visible structure'" (*UUS* 10.2).

In ecumenical dialogue, according to *Ut unum sint*, truth remains the ultimate principle. Ecumenical dialogue rests on "a common quest for the truth" (33). "The obligation to respect the truth is absolute" (79.3). The famous distinction between the truths of faith and their expression opens the door for ecumenical dialogue. John Paul II cites his own previous documents, pointing out that "we are aware as the Catholic Church, that we have received much from the witness borne by other Churches and Ecclesial Communities to certain common Christian values" (87).

As an example of the need for dialogue to be connected to the truth, the pope recognizes that the office of papacy and its concomitant gift of infallibility constitute a difficulty for many other Christians. John Paul II clearly insists on the need for papal primacy and infallibility as a part of the papal office but also recognizes that the papal office must be carried out in a theology of communion. He then asks non-Catholics to help him find ways of exercising his office that will not be an obstacle to Christian union (88–97).

John Paul II has admitted that the Catholic Church has learned from the ecumenical dialogue, but some passages seem to play down this learning by implying that the Catholic Church learns from other churches something that the Catholic Church in its fullness already has. The pope explicitly recognizes that there is not an ecclesiastical vacuum outside the boundaries of the Roman Catholic community, but then goes on to say: "Many elements of great value, which in the Catholic Church are part of the fullness of the means of salvation and of the gifts of grace which make up the church, are also found in the other Christian communities" (13.2). His recognition that the Catholic Church has learned from other churches in no way modifies or denies his basic understanding of the Catholic Church as called by God to teach the truth about the human person and the role of the Catholic Church in discerning truth.

The Nature of the Church

What precisely is the nature of the Catholic Church? John Paul II sees both a divine and a human element in the church—"the very essence of her divine-human constitution" (*DV* 61.1). In the light of this understanding of the "divine–human constitution" of the church, the shortcomings, failures, and even sins come from the human element in the church but not from the church itself, which also includes the divine element. In his very first encyclical, John Paul II inveighs against an overly critical attitude toward the church that often existed immediately after Vatican II. But he quickly recognizes the need for some criticism in the church: "The church also should have humility as her foundation, that she should have a critical sense with regard to all that goes to make up her human character and activity, and that she should always be very demanding on herself, nevertheless criticism too should have its just limits" (*RH* 4.1). The church knows trials and tribulations but is sustained and *"strengthened by the power of God's grace promised to her by the Lord"* (*RMA* 35.1). "The Catholic Church acknowledges and confesses *the weaknesses of her members*, conscious that their sins are so many betrayals of and obstacles to the accomplishment of the Savior's plan. . . . At the same time she acknowledges and exalts still more *the power of the Lord*, who fills her with the gift of holiness, leads her forward, and conforms her to his Passion and Resurrection" (*UUS* 3.1). Notice here how the human and the divine elements in the church work. Such an approach prevents John Paul II from saying that the church itself has sinned or done wrong. Only the human part or the members of the church do wrong and sin. The church itself precisely because of the divine element cannot do wrong or be sinful.

But many Catholic theologians take a different tack. The church is a sinful church—always in need of reform and repentance. John Paul II's ecclesiology sees the divine element as a separate element in the church and never completely merging with the total reality of the church. John Paul II, however, more than any other pope, has often called attention to the sins and injustices committed by members of the church and asked for forgiveness, even though his ecclesiology prevents him from saying that the church itself has done wrong or is a sinful church.[12]

Metaphors for the Church

John Paul II's metaphors for the church also cohere with his understanding of the church as having a divine element and a human element. Those who recognize a sinful church often use the metaphor of the people of God on pilgrimage. There can be no doubt that the pilgrim people of God have done wrong and are in need of repentance and reform. John Paul II's favorite metaphors for the church tend to highlight the divine element of the church as something always present. In his writings before becoming pope, his primary metaphor for the church was the mystical body of Christ.[13] His very first encyclical includes three references to the church as the body of Christ (*RH* 7.3, 18.1, 21.2). The church as the mystical body of Christ "makes the church as a body, an organism, a social unit perceive the same divine influences, the light and strength of the Spirit that come from the crucified and risen Christ, and it is for this very reason that she lives her life. The Church has only one life: that which is given her by her Spouse and Lord" (*RH* 18.1).

John Paul II as pope mentions many of the metaphors for the church found in *Lumen gentium*, Vatican II's Constitution on the Church, including the church as the people of God, but the encyclicals prefer the understanding of "the Church as a kind of sacrament or sign and means of intimate union with God, and of the unity of all mankind" (*RH* 7.3). Such an understanding of the church fits in very well with his basic thesis of the church as continuing the mission of Jesus to teach the truth about man. The very beginning of *Redemptor hominis* describes the church as the body of Christ and then goes on to develop this concept in light of *Lumen gentium*'s understanding of the church as the sacrament or sign of two realities—intimate union with God and of the unity of all humankind (7.3). Later on, *Redemptor hominis* again quotes *Lumen gentium* on the church as sacrament (18.4). *Redemptoris missio*, which deals especially with the role of the church in redemption, devotes an entire paragraph to "the Church as sign and instrument of salvation" citing *Lumen gentium* 48 and *Gaudium et spes* 43 (9). Later the same encyclical refers to the church as "the sacrament of salvation for all mankind" (20.4). *Dominum et vivificantem* devotes an entire section of three paragraphs to "the Church as the sacrament of intimate union with God" (61–64). But John Paul II never mentions or develops the possibility that the sign falls short of the reality it signifies.

Other Vatican II metaphors of the church stress more the lack of complete identification between the church and the Risen Jesus and also do not identify the church with the divine element in the church. Perhaps the most popular metaphor of the church in the post–Vatican II era has been the church as the people of God. This metaphor is used as the title for chapter 2 of *Lumen gentium*, the Constitution on the Church. Such a metaphor, as mentioned above, does not support a sharp distinction between the divine and human elements in the church that would restrict sins and shortcomings to the members of the church. The church, as the people of God on earth, cannot be separated from the members of the church.

The encyclicals of John Paul II do not neglect the metaphor of the people of God. In fact, *Redemptor hominis* uses the term "people of God" about twenty times. But the encyclicals of John Paul II do not develop this metaphor and fail to adopt it in dealing with the sins and shortcomings of the church.

The metaphor of the church as the pilgrim people of God recognizes the tension between the imperfect and sinful church of the present and the eschatological fullness of the reign of God. Chapter 7 of *Lumen gentium* of Vatican II is titled "The Eschatological Nature of the Pilgrim Church and Her Union with the Heavenly Church." The metaphor of the pilgrim church serves as the basis for

Vatican II's recognition that the church is always in need of change and reform. The pilgrim church is in constant need of conversion and forgiveness and never possesses the fullness of sanctity and truth.

John Paul II develops the metaphor of the pilgrim church in chapter 2 of *Redemptoris mater* with its title, "The Mother of God at the Center of the Pilgrim Church." But in this section the description of the pilgrim church does not include a recognition of the church either as a sinful church in need of conversion or of the church growing in grace and in its understanding of the truth. Mary and her *Magnificat* serve as a model for the pilgrim church because Mary like the church lives by faith. Mary boldly proclaimed "the *undimmed* truth about God" (37.1). "The Church, which even 'amid trials and tribulations' does not cease repeating with Mary the words of the *Magnificat,* is sustained by the power of God's truth, proclaimed on that occasion with such extraordinary simplicity. At the same time *by means of this truth about God*, the Church *desires to shed light upon* the difficult and sometimes tangled paths of humankind's earthly existence" (37.2).

The metaphor of the church as the herald or servant of the reign of God also recognizes eschatological tension. The church is not the reign of God but points to the reign of God. The tension between the church at present and the fullness of the reign of God will always be present and felt. In *Redemptoris missio* (12–20), John Paul II deals in some depth with the relationship of the church and the Kingdom. He chides those who have separated the Kingdom both from Jesus and from the church. "It is true that the Church is not an end unto herself, since she is ordered toward the Kingdom of God of which she is the seed, sign, and instrument. Yet, while remaining distinct from Christ and the Kingdom, the Church is indissolubly united to both" (18.3). John Paul II thus tends to downplay somewhat the eschatological tension between the church and the reign of God.

Fides et ratio recognizes some eschatological tension between the fullness of truth and the truths taught at the present time. The encyclical acknowledges that the church is on a "pilgrim way" and that the believing community is "a partner in humanity's shared struggle to arrive at truth." But, conversely, the church has "received the gift of the ultimate truth about human life" and has "her duty to serve humanity" as "the *diakonia* [servant] *of the truth.*" This service "obliges the believing community to proclaim the certitudes arrived at, albeit with a sense that every truth attained is but a step toward the fullness of truth which will appear with the final revelation of God" (2). Here there seems to be some tension between the recognition of humanity's shared search for the truth and the role of the church as the *diakonia* (servant) of truth for humankind. However, the eschatological tension based on the fullness of truth as coming only at the end of time does not take away from the certitude of the truth that the church teaches humanity today.

The understanding of the church found in John Paul II's encyclicals thus fits in very well with his thesis that the church continues in time and space the work of the Risen Jesus in teaching the truth about humankind without explicit recognition of the shortcomings and limitations of both the church and the truth it teaches about humankind during the journey toward the fullness of the reign of God.

The Church as Learner of the Truth

John Paul II's encyclicals never explicitly address a basic question: How does the church learn or acquire the truth? The encyclicals frequently refer to the deposit of faith. Especially in the nineteenth century, this term signified the propositional truths of faith that were handed over to the church and that the church preserves. Thus the church has the deposit of truth and simply draws on these truths when needed. But even with regard to the truths of faith, John Paul II himself has recognized the difference between truth and the expression of truth. For that reason and many others, including historical consciousness and the recognition of the development of doctrine, the deposit of faith cannot be conceived as a deposit of verbal propositions handed over to the church that it preserves and applies.[14] Thus, even with regard to the truths of faith, the church itself has to learn these truths. Take, for example, the Trinitarian (three persons in one God) and Christological (two natures in one person) doctrines. The church came to a knowledge of these truths as expressed this way in the course of history. Likewise, as has been mentioned, only in the second millennium did the church learn the existence of seven sacraments.

In the area of specific moral issues, we usually are not dealing with truths that can be said to belong to the deposit of faith or with truths of faith at all. These truths, by John Paul II's own recognition, are often based on natural law. So here it is obvious that the church has to learn these truths before it can teach them. But how does the church learn these truths? One can appeal to the assistance of the Holy Spirit, but how does the Spirit work? In keeping with the Catholic notion of mediation and God working in and through the human, though the assistance of the Holy Spirit means assistance in the human ways of acquiring truth, that assistance does not substitute for the human process.[15] As has been noted, the truth about the condemnation of direct abortion or direct killing depends on a philosophical distinction between direct and indirect that arose in the late nineteenth century and that, at the very minimum, is somewhat controversial.

History reminds us that over the centuries and the years the church has changed its teaching on a number of significant issues—such as slavery, usury, freedom, religious freedom, human rights, democracy, torture, the right of the defendant to remain silent, the death penalty, the intention and role of procreation in marital sexuality, the nature of the family, and the role of women in society.[16] Such changes remind all that the church has learned its moral teaching and moral truths from a multitude of different human sources while helped by the assistance of the Holy Spirit.

To explore thoroughly how the church learns the truth that it teaches goes well beyond the scope of this book. For our purposes, it is sufficient to point out that John Paul II's encyclicals fail to recognize that the church not only teaches the truth about humankind but must also learn it. The church is both learner and teacher.

This chapter has examined the understanding of Pope John Paul II in his encyclicals that the church teaches the truth about humankind. Such an understanding needs to be nuanced. Thus, the church should strive to teach the "truth about humankind," but in reality there are different types of truths with different types of certitude connected with them, and, above all, the church itself must learn these truths, especially moral truths, before it teaches them.

Notes

1. J. Michael Miller, ed., *The Encyclicals of John Paul II* (Huntington, Ind.: Our Sunday Visitor, 2001), 575.

2. James M. Gustafson, *Christ and the Moral Life* (New York: Harper & Row, 1968).

3. Charles E. Curran, *Catholic Social Teaching 1891–Present: A Historical, Theological, and Ethical Analysis* (Washington, D.C.: Georgetown University Press, 2002), 23–37, 53–96.

4. See, for example, Josef Fuchs, *Natural Law: A Theological Investigation* (New York: Sheed & Ward, 1965).

5. Thomas Aquinas, *Summa theologiae*, 4 vols. (Rome: Marietti, 1952), Ia IIae, q. 94, a. 4.

6. For these and other examples of change in hierarchical teaching on specific moral issues, see Charles E. Curran, ed., *Change in Official Catholic Moral Teachings: Readings in Moral Theology No. 13* (New York: Paulist Press, 2003).

7. Patrick Granfield, "The Right to Silence: Magisterial Development," *Theological Studies* 27 (1966): 401–20.

8. For my understanding of the role of mediation in Catholic moral theology, see Charles E. Curran, *The Catholic Moral Tradition Today: A Synthesis* (Washington, D.C.: Georgetown University Press, 1999), 11–13, passim.

9. James E. Keenan and Thomas A. Shannon, eds., *The Context of Casuistry* (Washington, D.C.: Georgetown University Press, 1995).

10. Aquinas, Ia IIae, q. 94, a.4.

11. For the Catholic approach to slavery, see John T. Noonan Jr., *A Church That Can and Cannot Change: The Development of Catholic Moral Teaching* (Notre Dame, Ind.: University of Notre Dame Press, 2004); for Newman's understanding, see Noonan, *Church That Can and Cannot Change*, chap. 1.

12. Pope John Paul II, *Tertio millennio adveniente*, nn. 133–36, in *Origins* 24 (1994): 401 ff.; *Incarnationis mysterium*, n. 11, in *Origins* 28 (1998): 450–51; "Jubilee Characteristic: The Purification of Memory," *Origins* 29 (2000): 649–50. See also John Ford, "John Paul II Asks for Forgiveness," *Ecumenical Trends* 27 (December 1998): 173–75; Francis A. Sullivan, "The Papal Apology," *America* 182, no. 12 (April 8, 2000): 17–22; and Aline H. Kaliban, "The Catholic Church's Public Confession:

Theological and Ethical Implications," *The Annual of the Society of Christian Ethics* 21 (2001): 175–89.

13. Kenneth L. Schmitz, *At the Center of the Human Drama: The Philosophical Anthropology of Karol Wojtyla* (Washington, D.C.: Catholic University of America Press, 1993), 110.

14. Nancy C. Ring, "Deposit of Faith," in *New Dictionary of Theology*, ed. Joseph A. Komonchak, Mary Collins, and Dermot Lane (Wilmington, Del.: Michael Glazier, 1987), 277–79.

15. Richard R. Gaillardetz, *Teaching with Authority: A Theology of the Magisterium in the Church* (Collegeville, Minn.: Liturgical Press, 1997), 131–58.

16. Curran, *Change in Official Catholic Moral Teachings*.

THEOLOGICAL
METHODOLOGY

IN THIS CHAPTER on theological methodology, I consider the theological sources of moral theology, the general theological approach, Christology, and eschatology. From a theological perspective, most Christians would agree in general with the Catholic insistence on the two sources of scripture and tradition that is also found in the writings of John Paul II. But how does he use these two sources?

Scripture

All today recognize the importance of scripture for moral theology. Both implicitly and explicitly, John Paul II emphasizes scripture as a primary source for moral theology. His references to scripture in his encyclicals far outnumber any of the other references made within these documents. The encyclical *Veritatis splendor* explicitly invokes the importance of scripture for moral theology: "The specific purpose of the present Encyclical is this: To set forth, with regard to the problems being discussed, the principles of a moral teaching based upon Sacred Scripture and the living Apostolic Tradition" (5.3). Here he footnotes the teaching of *Dei verbum* 10, the Dogmatic Constitution on Divine Revelation of Vatican II, on this point. At the beginning of chapter 2, which constitutes the bulk of the encyclical dealing with certain present-day tendencies in moral theology, the pope insists that "Sacred Scripture remains the living and fruitful source of the Church's moral doctrine; as the Second Vatican Council recalled, the Gospel is 'the source of all saving truth and moral teaching'" (28.2). The church's moral reflection is developed in the theological science called moral theology that recognizes both revelation and reason as sources of moral wisdom and knowledge (29.1). In this context, John Paul II cites Vatican II's call for the renewal of moral theology "increasingly based on the teaching of Scripture" (29.2).

John Paul II's Basic Approach

How precisely does the pope use scripture in developing moral theology in his encyclical writings? Two questions come to the fore. First, how does the pope use the contemporary critical understanding of the Bible? In the mid–twentieth century, Catholic biblical scholars began to develop and employ a more critical approach to the scriptures. Thus, for example, scholars recognized different sources that are found and used in the books of both the Hebrew Bible and the New Testament that were ultimately put together by a redactor. New Testament critical scholarship distinguishes different levels, such as what was said by the historical Jesus, how it was understood by the early church, and how it was used by the evangelist to achieve his own purposes.[1]

Generally speaking, the pope does not allude to the findings of critical biblical scholarship. His footnotes never mention contemporary biblical scholars, nor do they mention any contemporary scholars of any type. John Paul II, however, does recognize two different sources in the accounts of creation in Genesis (*TB* 27–29). Likewise, in discussing the prodigal son and the mercy of God, he refers to the fact that Luke's Gospel "has earned the title of the 'Gospel of Mercy'" (*DM* 3.5).

In fairness to the pope, many Catholic moral theologians themselves do not employ critical biblical scholarship in their use of scripture in moral theology.[2] There exist some inherent difficulties in trying to use the critical approach to the scriptures in moral theology. As mentioned, critical biblical scholarship emphasizes the unique approach of each biblical author. But in that light, it is very difficult to develop a unified moral theology. Critical historical scholarship reminds us that there is no such thing as a biblical moral teaching, but there are the moral teachings of individual authors. Moral theologians today by their very nature are trying to develop an approach calling for how Christians should exist and live in this world. Therefore, moral theologians must move from the different approaches of different biblical authors to their own somewhat unified understanding of how Christians should live today. Thus, there exist certain inherent tensions between the results of critical biblical scholarship and the need for moral theologians to develop a systematic theological ethic.

If John Paul II does not use a critical approach to scripture, how does he employ scripture in his moral theology? He tends to consider scripture as a unified whole but never explicitly appeals to the canon of scriptural books as the basis for the unified whole. He often develops his teaching on the basis of a meditative and even homiletical reflection on scripture. This approach is somewhat similar to that used by the writers in the so-called Patristic Age of the early church. *Dives in misericordia,* dealing with the God who is rich in mercy, devotes one chapter to the Old Testament understanding of mercy, using many different texts from many different genres. Then the encyclical moves to the New Testament and especially the parable of the prodigal son. "*In the teaching of Christ himself,* this image inherited from the Old Testament becomes at the same time simpler and more profound. This is perhaps most evident in the parable of the prodigal son" (5.2). Meditating on this parable, the pope draws out meaning for us today. Love is transformed into mercy when it goes beyond the precise and narrow norm of justice (5.6). The father in the parable is faithful to his fatherhood and faithful to his love, thus illustrating the mercy of God (6.1). The parable expresses in a profound and simple way the reality of conversion, the most concrete expression of the working of love and of the response of mercy in the human world (6.5). A subsequent chapter describes this merciful love as revealed in the Paschal Mystery of Jesus (7.1–9.6).

Another example of using scripture in a homiletical and catechetical way but not recognizing critical biblical scholarship is the use of a scripture text to begin each chapter in the encyclical *Veritatis splendor*. Thus, "Teacher, What Good Must I Do . . . ?" (Mt 19:16) is the text for chapter 1, "Christ and the Answer to the Question about Morality." "Do Not be Conformed to This World" (Rom 12:2) is the text for chapter 2, "The Church and the Discernment of Certain Tendencies in Present-Day Moral Theology." "Lest the Cross of Christ Be Emptied of Its Power" (1 Cor 1:17) is the text for chapter 3, "Moral Good for the Life of the Church and of the World." Another example of a homiletic and catechetical use comes in *Evangelium vitae* when the subheadings of all three chapters involve a scripture text followed by a theme. Thus, for example, "'*You have come to the sprinkled blood*' (*cf. Heb 12:22, 24*): signs of hope and invitation to commitment" (25.1). "'*It is I who bring both death and life*' (*Dt 32:39*): the tragedy of euthanasia" (64.1). At the very minimum, there is no logical or necessary connection between the scripture text and the enunciated theme.

The encyclicals have different genres that influence how scripture is used. *Dives in misercordia* is a more contemplative and meditative document that heavily rests on scripture. Conversely, *Centesimus annus* commemorates the one hundredth anniversary of *Rerum novarum* and devotes one of its chapters to the political changes of 1989. By its very nature, such a document makes comparatively few appeals to scripture.

The Hermeneutical Issue

The major issue in using scripture in moral theology involves dealing with the problem of how one moves from the time and place of scripture (and recognizing that there are different times and places for the different scriptural books) to the time, culture, and place today. Most contemporary theologians recognize that there is no presuppostionless way to approach scripture. Scriptural interpretation involves a fusion of two different horizons—the horizon of the scriptural author and the horizon of the contemporary person. According to David Kelsay, the theologian brings to scripture an imaginative judgment or metaphor for understanding it. He calls this metaphor the *discrimen*, according to which the individual theologian tries to understanding the meaning of scripture.[3] Many scholars writing after Kelsay have developed the same fusion-of-horizons approach.[4] Contemporary biblical scholars have applied to the New Testament many different forms of literary criticism, such as structuralism, deconstruction, rhetorical, sociological, psychoanalytic, and advocacy criticisms.[5] William Spohn emphasizes that such a hermeneutics or interpretation is not the work of individuals but of communities. The original scriptural books were produced by communities and addressed to communities and are now speaking to the communities of the disciples of Jesus.[6] The great danger here is that of *eisegesis*, of reading into scripture the contemporary viewpoint of the theologian. One uses scripture to support one's own presuppositions and this to a great extent distorts scripture itself. The use of scripture as a proof text to give support to something proved or asserted on other grounds is similar to this problem of *eisegesis*.

The concerns and horizon of the author are bound to affect the scripture texts that are used. John Paul II uses the Gospel of John more than any other Gospel, despite the fact that two of the encyclicals develop at length the parable of the prodigal son from Luke and the story of the rich young man in Matthew.[7] The emphasis on John fits in very well with the pope's emphasis on a Christology from above, which will be discussed below. The pope stresses that Jesus is the Incarnate Word of God who redeems us and brings about the new creation. John's Gospel stresses that the Word became flesh and dwelt among us. "God so loved the world that he gave his only Son." This passage from John 3:16 is cited by the pope in his first encyclical, *Redemptor hominis* (8.1). A high Christology or a Christology from above starts with the preexisting Word of God who becomes flesh in Jesus for the salvation and redemption of the world.

John Paul II cites Genesis 1 and 2 more often than any other texts in the Hebrew Bible.[8] The pope in his encyclicals insists in a special way on Genesis 1:26 (the human being made in the image of God) and Genesis 1:28 (the human being given dominion over all of creation). These two texts cohere with John Paul II's emphasis on the dignity of the human person, which he has consistently made the center of his thought and writing on ethics. Every encyclical dealing with the human person cites these verses from Genesis (*RH* 16.1;

DM 2.3; *LE* 4.2–3, 6.2–3, 9.1–2; *SRS* 29.2–4, 30.5; *CA* 11.3, 31.2; *VS* 38.2; *EV* 34.2–3; 42:1–2, 52.3, 53.3). It is obvious that the pope uses these particular texts because they support the central points that he is making, but he is not distorting the texts themselves. At times, John Paul II draws inferences from the biblical text that are creative and appear very apropos in the contemporary situation, even if they might not be absolutely present in the original texts themselves. For instance, in discussing the parable of the prodigal son, he is concerned that the person who is the object of mercy does not feel humiliated, as so often happens in our world. The very essence of fatherhood in the story calls for the father to be concerned about his son's dignity. In keeping with his understanding of scripture as a whole, the pope here cites Paul's praise of agape in 1 Corinthians 13. Such a love does not humiliate its receiver. The father has always recognized that the prodigal son has remained his son even when he went away (*DM* 6.3).

Evangelium vitae begins with a meditation on the story of Cain and Abel to show how death and killing came into the world through sin (7–28). The pope also supports the theory of killing coming into the world through sin by citing the Gospel of John (8:44) and the First Letter of John 3:11–12 (8.4). In Cain's question, "Am I my brother's keeper," the pope sees the tendency of so many people today to refuse to accept responsibility for their sisters and brothers (18–20). Cain is punished by God because God cannot leave this crime of killing unpunished. The encyclical finds scriptural support for this punishment in Genesis 37:26, Isaiah 26:21, and Ezekiel 24:7–8 (9.1). (However, we know of many instances where God leaves even the crime of murder unpunished.) The pope goes on to say that God is always merciful, even when he punishes. Thus, he puts a mark on Cain, lest anyone who came across him should kill him (Gen 4:15). *Evangelium vitae* draws the conclusion, "*Not even a murderer loses his personal dignity*, and God pledges to guarantee this" (9.3). Thus, John Paul II prepares the way for his own position of practically opposing capital punishment today. All have to recognize that one really cannot use this text to argue against capital punishment, but nonetheless in a homiletic way the pope makes a point.

Theologians recognize a greater role for scripture on the more general level of moral realities that are not so much subject to historical and cultural change, but they see a greater problem on the level of specifics, where historical and cultural circumstances are so intertwined. There can be no doubt that John Paul II often invokes scripture when referring to the very general responses and attitudes that should characterize the Christian life, such as discipleship, covenant, love, conversion, mercy, and forgiveness. But on certain specific issues, he seems to find unwarranted support in scripture. Take, for example, the question of abortion—which, as is well known, he severely opposes. The pope explicitly recognizes that the texts of scripture do not address the question of deliberate abortion and do not directly and specifically condemn it (*EV* 61.1). But then *Evangelium vitae* goes on to maintain that the great respect scripture shows for human life in the mother's womb requires as a logical consequence the condemnation of abortion. The references to respect for life in the womb tend to be somewhat general and do not prove that direct abortion, as distinguished from indirect abortion, is always wrong. Also, the biblical authors did not have the same kind of scientific knowledge that we have today about the early development of the embryo. In his solemn proclamation, the pope maintains the condemnation of direct abortion "is based upon the natural law and upon the written word of God" (*EV* 61.3).

The Use of Scripture in Veritatis splendor

Veritatis splendor heavily relies on scripture to develop its message.[9] The first chapter is a long meditation on the story of the rich young man in Matthew 19. In the words of the encyclical itself, the basic thesis of the entire document is "the *reaffirmation of the universality and inviolability of the moral commandments*, particularly those which prohibit always and without exception intrinsically evil acts" (115.3). Pastors and bishops of the church have the duty to lead the faithful to God, just as the Lord Jesus did with the rich young man. In response to the question, "What good must I do to have eternal life?" Jesus "reminded him of the moral commandments already revealed in the Old Testament and he indicated their spirit and deepest meaning by inviting the young man to follow Him. . . . This 'answer' to the question about morality has been entrusted by Jesus Christ in a special way to us, the Pastors of the Church" (114.2–3). Thus the encyclical uses scripture to prove that Jesus saw the moral life in terms of obedience to the commandments and claims that the magisterium is following Jesus today by insisting on commandments prohibiting actions that are always and everywhere wrong.

This encyclical thus relies very heavily on scripture to defend its thesis, but in the process, it reads into scripture and distorts it. First, it distorts the meaning of the story of the rich young man as found in Matthew 19. The parable does not deal with every person in general but deals in particular with a rich young man. In fact, the rich young man has acknowledged that he has already obeyed all the commandments mentioned by Jesus. He then turns down the invitation of Jesus to sell what he has, give it to the poor, and follow Jesus. He was sorrowful and went away sad precisely because he could not accept the invitation of Jesus to sell all that he had and follow him. Thus, the thrust of the story of the rich young man is the question of riches and not the question of all Christians being called to obey the commandments found in the Old Covenant.

Second, the encyclical distorts the meaning of Christian morality as found in scripture. The encyclical makes primary the insistence on obedience to the commandments. But morality, as portrayed throughout scripture, involves much more than just obedience to commandments. Morality involves a change of heart, conversion, response to the loving God, and the virtues, attitudes, and dispositions that characterize the Christian person. Obedience to commandments is not the primary aspect of the morality found in scripture. In this context, it is interesting that in the same Gospel (Mt 25), a different answer is given to the same basic question of what is required to gain eternal life: When I was hungry, naked, thirsty, and in prison. But when did we see you in these circumstances? Whatever you did to the least of my sisters and brothers, you did to me. Thus, the love of neighbor, revealed especially in taking care of the neighbor in need, is proposed here as the criterion for entry into eternal life.

According to *Veritatis splendor*, Jesus "himself becomes a living and personal Law, who invites people to follow him" (15). But Jesus cannot be reduced only to a living and personal law. Jesus is also the eschatological prophet, the proclaimer of the reign of God, the one whose love and life we are to imitate, the one who came not to be served but to serve and to give his life as a ransom for many, the one who preached good news to the poor.

The encyclical has distorted the meaning of Christian morality by putting primary emphasis on obedience to the Ten Commandments and laws prohibiting certain actions as always and everywhere wrong. In fairness, however, the encyclical tries to put the commandments of the Decalogue into a bigger picture. The pope mentions the invitation to be perfect, the following of Jesus, commitment to the very person of Jesus, and the new law of love proposed by St. Paul. But the encyclical proposes all these as illustrations of obedience to God's will and law (14–24). Thus, the conclusion to the long meditation on the rich young man maintains: "The moral prescriptions which God imparted in the Old Covenant, and which attain their perfection in the New and Eternal Covenant in the very person of the Son of God made man, must be *faithfully kept and continually put into practice.* . . . The task of interpreting these prescriptions was entrusted by Jesus to the Apostles and their successors with a special assistance of the Spirit of truth: 'He who hears you hears me' (Lk 10:16)" (25.2).

A third distortion concerns the attempt to use scripture to support what the pope is proposing today based on philosophical and ethical concepts that were not known in biblical times. The last paragraph showed at least an implicit identification of the commandment proposed by Jesus with the specific norms prohibiting always and everywhere certain actions proposed by the hierarchical magisterium. *Veritatis splendor* explicitly uses scripture to support the notion of intrinsic evil proposed by the contemporary hierarchical magisterium in its arguments against proportionalism and consequentialism. But scripture does not know any of these concepts. The heading before the discussion of intrinsic evil is: "*'Intrinsic evil': it is not licit to do evil that good may come of it (cf. Rom 3:8)*" (79.1). The text itself, in a paragraph discussing intrinsic evil, cites the reference to Romans 3:8 in a quotation taken from Pope Paul VI's encyclical *Humanae vitae*. "It is never lawful, even for the gravest reasons, to do evil that good may come of it (cf. Rom 3:8)" (80.2). But this biblical text does not necessarily support the papal concept of intrinsic evil. Consequentialists and proportionalists could readily accept the text. The real problem is how to determine what is evil. On this basic point, the text from Romans offers no help whatsoever.

Veritatis splendor goes on to assert, "In teaching the existence of intrinsically evil acts, the Church accepts the teaching of Sacred Scripture. The Apostle Paul emphatically states: 'Do not be deceived: Neither the immoral, nor idolaters, nor adulterers, nor sexual perverts, nor thieves, nor the greedy, nor drunkards, nor revilers, nor robbers will inherit the Kingdom of God' (1 Cor 6:9–10)" (81.1). But 1 Corinthians 6:9–10 talks about persons and not about intrinsically evil acts. Paul is speaking here about the vices of persons and not about intrinsically evil acts, to say nothing of the understanding of intrinsically evil acts as proposed in the encyclical. Thus, *Veritatis splendor* does not avoid the distortion of using scripture to support contemporary understandings that were not known by the biblical authors.

Ephesians 5:21–32

In his writings on marriage and sexuality, John Paul II often develops his teaching as a meditation on scripture. In chapter 5, I will discuss sexuality. Here, I concentrate on the fascinating way in which the pope deals with a famous passage in Ephesians 5 about the relationship between husband and wife. Both the apostolic letter *Mulieris dignitatem*[10] (On the Dignity and Vocation of Women) and his general audience address of August 11, 1982,[11] discuss this text.

Most have seen in this text the subordination of wives to husbands, as was the commonly accepted ethos of the time. This passage in Ephesians, like similar New Testament passages, belongs to the category of "household codes," which express how households at that time were structured. As is customary in such a genre, Ephesians 5:21–33 refers to the male head of the household and the relationship of husband and wife, parents and children, masters and slaves. The subordination of the wife to the husband is obvious in this passage that the pope cites. "Wives, be subject to your husbands, as to the Lord. For the husband is the head of the wife as Christ is the head of the Church, his body, and is Himself its Savior. As the Church is subject to Christ, so let wives also be subject in everything to their husbands. Husbands, love your wives as Christ loved the Church and gave Himself up for her" (Eph 5:22–25, as cited in *TB* 304).

But despite this, the pope sees a Gospel "innovation" in this text (*MD* 24). Ephesians 5:21 begins by calling for a mutual subjection out of reverence for Christ. This mutual subjection is an innovation of the Gospel resulting from redemption. But this mutual subjection of the spouses out of reverence for Christ and not just that of the wife to the husband "must gradually establish itself in hearts, consciences, behavior, and customs. This is a call which from that time onward does not cease to challenge succeeding generations; it is a call which people have to accept ever anew." The pope goes on to cite Galatians 3:20, asserting that in Christ Jesus there is neither male nor female, free nor slave. Yet how many generations were needed for such a precept to be realized in the history of humanity with the abolition of slavery! "But the challenge presented by the 'ethos' of the redemption is clear and definitive" (*MD* 24). But this is not just John Paul II's interpretation. He claims this was the meaning of the author of Ephesians. "The author knows that this way of speaking [subordination of wife to husband], so profoundly rooted in the customs and religious tradition of the time, is to be understood and carried out in a new way: as a 'mutual subjection out of reverence for Christ'" (*MD* 24).

Thus the pope's interpretation of the meaning proposed by the author of Ephesians 5 comes down squarely on the side of the basic equality of husbands and wives as determined by the innovation of the Gospel. Such an interpretation seems to go against the very words used by the biblical author. But John Paul II wants to insist that not only he but the scriptural author denies any subordination of the wife to the husband. He definitely seems to be reading his understanding of equality into the biblical text that explicitly says the opposite. Here a liberal interpretation distorts the scriptural meaning.

In summary, John Paul II in his encyclicals deserves great credit for trying to make his approach based on scripture. He does not employ a critical understanding of scripture, as certainly many other people writing on Christian morality have not done. His meditative and reflective use of scripture rightly insists on the basic moral realities of conversion, covenant, discipleship, the twofold commandment, the imitation of Christ, and many such concepts as basic and fundamental to the Christian life. Like everyone else, John Paul II brings his own perspective and horizon to understand what is going on in scripture. However, at times, his horizon distorts the meaning of scripture.

Tradition and Hierarchical Teaching

Tradition constitutes another significant source for theology. Tradition refers to that which has been handed down under the inspiration of the Spirit with regard to the teaching, life, and worship of the Catholic Church. Tradition includes the teaching of ecumenical councils, past official teachings, and major figures in the historical development of the church. Roman Catholicism has traditionally recognized the role of tradition in addition to scripture because the church strives to live out and be faithful to the word and work of Jesus in changing historical and cultural circumstances. *Veritatis splendor* refers to this as "*living Tradition.*" "This tradition which comes from the Apostles progresses in the Church under the assistance of the Holy Spirit" (27.1). *Centesimus annus* refers to "*the Church's Tradition*" as "ever living and vital" (3.2).

Moral theology in its development beginning after the sixteenth century Council of Trent has not put great emphasis on tradition. Two reasons help to explain this fact. The ecumenical councils seldom spoke about specific moral matters as such. In addition, many of the practical issues and problems facing moral theology came to the fore in the light of newer realities. John Paul II, in these encyclicals, likewise does not frequently invoke tradition in general. He does, however, in his solemn condemnations of direct killing, direct abortion, and euthanasia insist that this teaching is "transmitted by the Tradition of the Church" (*EV* 57.4, 62.3, 65.4). *Evangelium vitae* devotes one paragraph to the condemnation of abortion in the Christian tradition, citing the *Didache*, one author representative of the Greek fathers (Athenagoras), and one Latin father (Tertullian) (61). Obviously, this argument from tradition does not pretend to be exhaustive.

In the Roman Catholic Church, a special and significant form of tradition comes from the teaching of the hierarchical magisterium, especially papal teaching. Authoritative papal teaching in the moral area has developed radically in the past 150 years. John Paul II frequently cites the papal magisterium. The most prominent source in these papal encyclicals, outside scripture itself, is the Second Vatican Council. The first thirteen encyclicals contain about 170 citations and references to *Lumen gentium* and 130 to *Gaudium et spes*.[12] Three of the encyclicals deal specifically with Catholic social teaching and frequently cite earlier encyclicals of Catholic social teaching. In fact, these three encyclicals were written to commemorate the anniversaries of earlier papal documents—*Laborem exercens* in 1981, on the ninetieth anniversary of *Rerum novarum*; *Sollicitudo rei socialis* in 1987, on the twentieth anniversary of Paul VI's *Populorum progressio*; and *Centesimus annus* in 1991, on the hundredth anniversary of Leo's *Rerum novarum*.

Vatican II

John Paul II in his encyclicals refers to Vatican II documents more than to any other nonbiblical source. In addition, in these documents, he explicitly calls attention to his commitment to the implementation of Vatican II. Vatican II was the most significant Catholic event in the twentieth century, and John Paul has identified himself with the work of the council. "In the present phase of the Church's history we put before ourselves as our primary task *the implementation of the doctrine* of the great *Council*" (*DM* 1.4). *Dominum et vivificantem* states, "The Encyclical has been drawn *from the heart of the heritage of the Council*" (2.3).

But John Paul II is conscious that Vatican II has been interpreted in different ways. *Redemptor hominis* refers to the difficult postconciliar period in the life of the church. He mentions "the excess of self-criticism" in the church after the council (3.1). Without doubt, the greatest discussion in the Roman Catholic Church in the past forty years has been what is the true understanding of the council. An extended study of the way in which John Paul II implemented Vatican II goes well beyond the narrow perspectives of this study. However, there is no doubt that many people in the Catholic Church feel that John Paul II has not followed the spirit of Vatican II.[13]

As in the case of scripture, there is no presuppositionless reading of Vatican II. Once again, all recognize the need for a merger of the different horizons involved. Without doubt, John Paul II has emphasized those aspects of the conciliar documents that are most in accord with his own approach. In his encyclicals, the pope often quotes *Gaudium et spes* 22—the theological principle that only in the mystery of the Incarnate Word does the mystery of man take on light.[14] The first encyclical *Redemptor hominis* cites this passage on three different occasions (8.2, 13.1, 18.1). The first footnote in *Veritatis splendor* refers to the teaching of *Gaudium et spes* 22 that only in the mystery of the Word Incarnate is light shed on the mystery of humanity. The first footnote reference in *Evangelium vitae* (23) is to *Gaudium et spes* 22. The teaching of *Gaudium et spes* here obviously supports a central concept in the Christology of John Paul II. It brings together both Christology and anthropology. I doubt if most people would choose this as the most significant text from *Gaudium et spes*, but one can see where it readily serves that purpose for John Paul II.

Another important text for John Paul II is *Gaudium et spes* 24— "Man who is the only creature on earth which God willed for itself, cannot fully find himself except through a sincere gift of himself." *Redemptor hominis* (13.3) cites this text. The apostolic letter *Mulieris dignitatem* three times refers to *Gaudium et spes* 24 (7, 18, 20). One author develops the pope's new feminism on the basis of this notion of the sincere gift.[15] One can readily see why this text appeals to John Paul II with his emphasis on personalism, the dignity of the person, and the fulfillment of the person through the free loving gift of self.

This text not only has meaning for personalism but also for his understanding of marriage and virginity. Thus John Paul II often uses *Gaudium et spes* without any significant distortion but to support positions that are greatly in accord with his own perspective.

However, just as in the case of scripture, John Paul II occasionally uses *Gaudium et spes* in an unjustified way to support his emphases on the primacy of law, its universal and inviolable characteristics, and the concept of intrinsic evil. *Veritatis splendor* expressly cites *Gaudium et spes* 10 to support the contention that positive precepts such as to render due worship to God and to honor one's parents are universally binding and unchanging (53). *Gaudium et spes* 10 insists that "there are many realities which do not change and which have their ultimate foundation in Christ." But *Gaudium et spes* never mentions law or positive precepts in this passage.

Veritatis splendor holds that some actions are intrinsically evil, always and per se, because of their object. The pope then cites *Gaudium et spes* 27:

> Whatever is hostile to life itself, such as any kind of homicide, genocide, abortion, euthanasia, and voluntary suicide; whatever violates the integrity of the human person such as mutilation, physical and mental torture and attempts to coerce the spirit; whatever is offensive to human dignity, such as sub-human living conditions, arbitrary imprisonment, deportation, slavery, prostitution and trafficking in women and children; degrading conditions of work which treat laborers as mere instruments of profit and not as free responsible persons; all these and the like are a disgrace and so long as they infect human civilization they contaminate those who inflict them more than those who suffer injustice, and they are a negation of the honor due to the Creator. (80.1)

From the perspective claimed by the pope, however, there are some problems here. The first is the word "homicide." This could very well be a translation problem, but, at the very minimum, it shows that the official translation does not understand what the pope is trying to say. Murder is intrinsically evil but not homicide. Second, three of the aspects mentioned by the pope have not always been condemned by the church and have been accepted—slavery, torture, and attempts to coerce the spirit. Not only the Hebrew Bible but also the New Testament accepted slavery. Does John Paul II want to say that the Apostle Paul accepted what is intrinsically evil? Third, many of the categories mentioned here include much more than the "object of the human act"—for example, "whatever is offensive to human dignity." Fourth, note that the quote from *Gaudium et spes* uses the term abortion but not "direct abortion." Recall that indirect abortion can be justified in accordance with traditional Catholic teaching. Thus the list of actions in *Gaudium et spes* does not totally prove the point being made in *Veritatis splendor*.

Mary Elsbernd has argued that *Veritatis splendor* has reinterpreted *Gaudium et spes* in light of an older Catholic moral theology that insisted on a legal framework, an individualist anthropology, and a downplaying of human initiative.[16] In one sense, this analysis is correct. *Veritatis splendor* does interpret *Gaudium et spes* to justify its legal model and conclusions about individual human acts. Elsewhere, however, John Paul II stresses the social dimension of the human person especially with his emphasis on solidarity. Certainly *Veritatis splendor* emphasizes the legal model for ethics, but in other places the pope recognizes the importance of human initiative and creativity as well as obedience to law. *Gaudium et spes* is a broad inclusive document that in its own way was a product of compromise and thus by definition is open to different interpretations. Without doubt, *Veritatis splendor* insists on a legal model, whereas *Gaudium et spes* recognizes other models and might even give primacy to them. Yes, Pope Wojtyla does cite those parts that agree with his long-held perspectives and occasionally overreaches and even distorts *Gaudium et spes* in using citations to prove his points.

The other document of Vatican II dealing with moral issues is *Dignitatis humanae* (The Declaration on Religious Freedom). Without doubt, John Paul II has been a strong defender of religious freedom throughout the world. In comparison with *Gaudium et spes*, *Dignitatis humanae* is comparatively short and narrowly focused on a specific issue. Thus, it is much easier to say that one agrees or disagrees with this declaration. John Paul II in his writings on religious freedom frequently cites this declaration of Vatican II and obviously agrees with it.

However, in his discussion of civil law in *Evangelium vitae* (68–77), the pope refers to the approach to civil law and the proper role of the coercive force of government as found in the declaration. He cites *Dignitatis humanae* only twice. The second citation, to paragraph 7, supports the position that society has the right to protect itself against the abuse of freedom. All would agree with that as a principle. The first citation, again to paragraph 7, supports the position, asserting "the purpose of civil law" as "ensuring the common good of people through the recognition and defense of their fundamental rights, and the promotion of peace and of public morality" (71.3). But *Dignitatis humanae* 7 refers to these three aspects of fundamental rights, peace, and public morality as "public order," not "common good." Public order is a narrower concept than common good. In discussing civil law in *Evangelium vitae*, the pope never refers to public order, the term used in *Dignitatis humanae*. By emphasizing the common good as the purpose of civil law, he proposes a criterion that gives a greater scope to law and a lesser scope to freedom. As will be discussed in chapter 6 in the context of civil law, the pope gives more emphasis to truth and less to freedom than does the Vatican II declaration. Without doubt, the pope fully endorses the fundamental position of *Dignitatis humanae* on religious freedom, but he is unwilling to accept the narrower criterion for civil law as proposed in that document. He insists on the broader concept of common good, thus giving a greater scope to the role of civil law and restricting somewhat the role of freedom. Without explicitly saying so, here he does not follow what was proposed in Vatican II.

Social Encyclicals

Because three of the encyclicals deal with Catholic social teaching, it is natural that they would frequently cite the encyclical documents of Catholic social teaching, beginning with Leo XIII's *Rerum novarum* of 1891. Recall that *Sollicitudo* was written on the twentieth anniversary of Pope Paul VI's *Populorum progressio* and *Centesimus annus* on the hundredth anniversary of *Rerum novarum*. In general, John Paul II continues in the tradition of Catholic social teaching, while recognizing the new issues and problems that have come to the fore. All recognize a basic continuity within these documents, and there is no need to prove it, but there is also some significant discontinuity.

John Paul II has tried to put his own interpretation on the tradition, and he definitely adopts a methodological approach that differs from the 1971 letter of Paul VI, *Octogesima adveniens*. John Paul II has emphasized the continuity of the documents of Catholic social teaching, used the term "Catholic social teaching" to describe these documents, and consciously moved away from the more inductive and historically conscious methodology of *Octogesima adveniens*.

His last two social encyclicals, *Sollicitudo* and *Centesimus annus*, bear witness to his different interpretation of Catholic social teaching. The theological discussion at the time of their writing helps to explain his approach. In the late 1970s, the well-known French Dominican, Marie-Dominique Chenu, published in French and Italian a fascinating book titled *The "Social Doctrine of the Church" as Ideology*.[17] In this book, Chenu uses the term "social doctrine of the church" to refer to the social teaching proposed by Leo XIII and continuing with subsequent popes that he calls an ideology. On the basis of prefabricated and abstract concepts, claimed to be the eternal and natural law, the popes authoritatively proposed the plan and actions that should be followed in the world. Beginning with Vatican II, according to Chenu, a new approach began to emerge in the documents, which came from the bottom up, based on the concrete experience of the people of God with the help of the Holy Spirit trying to live out their Christian lives in their own historical and cultural circumstances. The definitive change from the older "Catholic social teaching" came with the 1971 apostolic letter *Octogesima adveniens* of Paul VI. All agree that the letter opposed a deductive, unchanging methodology based on a classicist understanding in favor of an inductive approach based on historical consciousness and beginning with the particular and the local. Paul VI begins by recognizing the great diversity in our world with regard to regions, sociological systems, and cultures:

> In the face of such widely varying situations it is difficult for us to utter a unified message and to put forward a solution which has uni-

versal validity. Such is not our ambition nor is it our mission. It is up to the Christian communities to analyze with objectivity the situation which is proper to their own country, to shed on it the light of the Gospel's unalterable words, and to draw principles of reflection, norms of judgment and directives for action from the social teaching of the Church.[18]

As further proof of his thesis, Chenu points out that the earlier documents until *Mater et magistra* in 1961 often refer to the social doctrine of the church, but the term does not appear in *Pacem in terris* (1963) and was purposely excluded from *Gaudium et spes*.[19]

Without even mentioning the Chenu thesis, John Paul II goes out of his way to refute it in his last two social encyclicals. First, *Sollicitudo* explicitly claims that Catholic social teaching is not "an *ideology* but rather the *accurate formulation* of the results of a careful reflection on the complex realities of human existence in society and in the international order, in the light of faith and of the Church's Tradition" (41.7). Anyone familiar with the Chenu thesis knows what the pope is referring to here.

Second, John Paul II resurrects and emphasizes the concept of the social teaching of the church. In this context, there is a translation problem. English can use either "doctrine" or "teaching" to translate the Latin *doctrina*. Also, other words can be translated as "doctrine" or "teaching." For example, "social teaching" appears four times in the English translation of *Sollicitudo*. Three times it translates *doctrina*, but once (9) "teaching" is the translation of *magisterium*. *Sollicitudo* uses the term "social doctrine" seven times, and it always translates *doctrina*. I will continue to use the concept of Catholic social teaching because it is the one generally used in English today, but in some ways "Catholic social doctrine" is more appropriate.

Sollicitudo makes very clear that "as her *instrument* for reaching this goal [ministry in the world] the Church uses her *social doctrine* . . . —the 'set of principles for reflection, criteria for judgment, and directives for action.'" (41) Five times in the two paragraphs in the final main section of the encyclical titled "Some Particular Guidelines," *Sollicitudo* refers to the social teaching of the church (41–42). But the social teaching of the church plays a prominent role right from the very beginning of the encyclical. One of its two objectives is "to reaffirm the continuity of the social doctrine as well as its constant renewal. In effect, continuity and renewal are a proof of the perennial value of the teaching of the Church" (3). Here again, the content of the social teaching of the church is described in the same way as above: "principles of reflection," "criteria of judgment," and "directives for action."

Doctrina socialis appears about twenty times in the Latin text of *Centesimus annus*. Early on, *Centesimus annus* sees Catholic social teaching as "a genuine doctrine . . . a *corpus* which enables her to analyze social realities, to make judgments about them and to indicate directions to be taken for the just resolution of the problems involved" (5.4). "In effect, to teach and spread her social doctrine pertains to the Church's evangelizing mission and is an essential part of the Christian message" (5.5). There can be no doubt that John Paul II has resurrected and retrieved the term "Catholic social doctrine" to describe this body of teaching and to emphasize the continuity within this corpus.

This insistence on the corpus of Catholic social teaching emphasizes the continuity of Catholic social teaching. Its threefold elements, three times repeated in *Sollicitudo,* are principles, criteria, and directives that do not change but are applied in different historical and cultural circumstances (3.2, 8.4, 41.5). When speaking of commemorating the twentieth anniversary of *Populorum progressio, Sollicitudo* maintains that the teachings of *Populorum progressio* "retain all their force *as an appeal to conscience* today." *Sollicitudo* brings this teaching of the earlier encyclical "to bear, with its possible applications, upon the present historical moment, which is no less dramatic than that of twenty years ago" (4.1). *Sollicitudo* sees *Populorum progressio* "as *a document which applies the teachings of the Council*" (6.1). Yes, there are new historical developments and cultural changes, but the principles of Catholic social teaching perdure and can and should be applied to these new situations.

The very first paragraph of *Centesimus annus* commemorating the hundredth anniversary of *Rerum novarum* speaks of the subsequent documents as having "applied it to the circumstances of the day" (1.1). *Centesimus annus* itself attempts to show the "fruitfulness of the principles enunciated by Leo XIII" (3.5). Yes, the very title of *Rerum novarum* recognizes a new situation, and there is another new situation after 1989, but the principles remain. John Paul II's emphasis on continuity shows in other ways. *Centesimus annus* praises the prognosis of Leo XIII in 1891, who saw the negative consequences of socialism, as was borne out by the events of 1989 (12). But *Centesimus annus* goes even further. Leo XIII affirmed the right of workers to freely discharge their religious duties. "It would not be mistaken to see in this clear statement a springboard for the principle of the right to religious freedom, which was to become the subject of many solemn *International Declarations and Conventions*, as well as the Second Vatican Council's well-known *Declaration*" (9). But Leo XIII strongly opposed religious freedom as we know it today. John Paul II has gone too far here in his quest for continuity in Catholic social teaching.

There can be no doubt that John Paul II not only did not follow the methodology of *Octogesima adveniens* but also tried to reinterpret the meaning and approach of that document to justify his methodology of applying universally agreed upon concepts, principles, and criteria to changing circumstances. *Octogesima adveniens* did not begin with such agreed-upon concepts, principles, and criteria but rather began with the experience of the local Christian community striving "to discern the options and commitments which are called for in order to bring about the social, political, and economic changes seen in many cases to be urgently needed" (4). In that same paragraph, Paul VI explicitly admitted that it "is difficult for us to utter a unified message and to put forward a solution which has universal validity. Such is not our ambition nor is it our mission."

Recall how John Paul II describes the constant element in Catholic social teaching at the beginning of *Sollicitudo* and repeats the exact same phrases in quotation marks in two other places— "Principles of Reflection," "Criteria of Judgment," and "Directives for Action" (3.2, 8.4, 41.5). The footnote reference in all three cases indicates that these words are found originally in *Octogesima adveniens* 4. But Paul VI did not understand them in the same way that John Paul II does. Thus, John Paul II claims that *Octogesima adveniens* recognizes these constant and universal principles, criteria, and directives and implies that they have been, are, and should be the starting point of the approach to Catholic social teaching. But *Octogesima adveniens* did not take such an approach.

Thus, like any other commentator, John Paul II uses his sources (in this case, the documents of Vatican II and of Catholic social teaching) in accord with his own interpretation. Such an interpretation by definition is selective, and there exist other possible interpretations, some of which might be more authentic. Such is the lot of anyone interpreting and commenting upon older documents. Look at all the disagreement today about the meaning of various scriptural passages or about the articles of the U.S. Constitution. However, in some important places, John Paul II clearly distorts the meaning of the original documents in order to make his own points.

Theological Aspects in General

Gaudium et spes decried the split between faith and daily life (43). *Optatam totius*, the Vatican II Decree on the Training of Priests, called for special attention to be given to the development of moral theology, which should be nourished by scripture and show the nobility of the Christian vocation of the faithful to bring forth fruit in charity for the life of the world (16). Pope John Paul II has certainly been faithful to this call for change and renewal in moral theology. We have already discussed his heavy emphasis on scripture in moral theology even though there were some problems with it.

Pre–Vatican II moral theology was based almost exclusively on natural law and human reason. John Paul II moved away from this approach and proposed a more theological ethic without, however, denying a role for natural law and reason. His approach, in his own words, is both anthropocentric and theocentric. The church and moral teaching should link theocentricism and anthropocentricism together. Without citing any particular text of Vatican II but obviously based on *Gaudium et spes* 22, Pope Wojtyla claims that this joining together of the two is "one of the basic principles, perhaps the most important one, of the teaching of the last Council." Since my "primary task [is] the implementation of the doctrine of the great Council, we must act upon this principle" (*DM* 1.4).

The early three Trinitarian encyclicals of his pontificate definitely bring together anthropology and theology. The whole purpose of his first encyclical, *Redemptor hominis*, is its response to this call of Vatican II. He cites his favorite text from *Gaudium et spes* 22—"The truth is that only in the mystery of the Incarnate Word does the mystery of man take on light. . . . Christ, the new Adam, in the very revelation of the mystery of the Father and of his love, *fully reveals man to himself* and brings to light his most high calling" (*RH* 8.2). *Dives in misericordia* again on the basis of *Gaudium et spes* 22 insists "that man cannot be manifested in the full dignity of his nature without reference . . . to God. Man and man's lofty calling are revealed in Christ through the revelation of the mystery of the Father and his love" (1.2). In *Dominum et vivificantem*, the pope insists on the Spirit who gives life. Christ became human by the power of the Holy Spirit. That same Spirit continues to give life to all today. "Man's intimate relationship with God and the Holy Spirit also enables him to understand himself, his own humanity, in a new way" (59.1). "The Holy Spirit strengthening in each of us 'the inner man,' enables man ever more 'fully to find himself through a sincere gift of self.' These words of the Pastoral Constitution of the Council can be said to sum up *the whole of Christian* anthropology" (59.3). John Paul II goes on to point out that the Holy Spirit works beyond the boundaries of the visible church and "in a manner known only to God offers to every man the possibility of being associated with this Paschal Mystery" (53.3). Thus, there can be no doubt that John Paul II keeps both the theological and the anthropological together and develops a truly theological understanding of the human person in the light of the person's relationship to the three divine persons.

John Paul II's emphasis on the theological aspects of the moral life runs into a unique problem in the area that he calls Catholic social teaching. The earlier documents of Catholic social teaching used almost exclusively a natural law methodology based on human reason discovering moral truth by reflecting on human nature and what God has made. Such an approach by definition prescinds from the explicitly Christian (there is, however, a theological aspect to natural law) and can readily and easily appeal to all human beings. Ever since Pope John XXIII's *Pacem in terris* (1963), papal social encyclicals have explicitly addressed all people of goodwill and called for all people to work together for the common good of society. This raises a problem. How can you propose a teaching based on Christian faith and still address all people of goodwill who are called to work together for justice, peace, and authentic human development? *Sollicitudo rei socialis* carries on the tradition of appealing to all people of goodwill, but the document also has a separate section titled "A Theological Reading of Modern Problems" (35–45). The pope describes the obstacles to authentic development, such as the all-consuming desire for profit and the thirst for power, as the root structures of sin. Christians then are called to conversion and to transform these sinful social structures. Christians are called to practice the Christian virtue of solidarity, which is not just a vague feeling of compassion but rather "*a firm and persevering determination* to commit oneself to the *common good*; that is to say, to the good of all and of each individual, because we are *all* responsible *for all*" (38.6). But in this very context, John Paul II also hopes that men and women without explicit faith would be convinced that the obstacles to integral development are not only economic but rest on more profound attitudes. All should become fully aware of the need to change the spiritual attitudes that define each individual's relationship with self, with neighbor, with even the remotest human communities, and with nature itself in view of higher values such as the common good and the development of the individual and of all people (38.3). This part of *Sollicitudo* speaks directly to the Catholic community in Catholic and Christian language, but the pope believes that all others can see the truth of the attitudes and virtues presented here even if they do not use or accept the Christian terminology.

As should be expected in such documents, the encyclicals do not develop at length the reasons why all people of goodwill can agree with what the pope proposes for human action working for justice, peace, and authentic human development on the basis of Christian truths and principles. But the documents briefly indicate three reasons supporting this approach.

First, Christ is the perfect human being. Here John Paul II cites Vatican II, describing Christ as "himself the perfect man who has restored in the children of Adam that likeness to God which had been disfigured ever since the first sin. Human nature, by the very fact that it was assumed, not absorbed, in him, has been raised in us also to a dignity beyond compare" (*RH* 8.2). In Christ, we have a basis for the dignity and welfare of each human person, the solidarity of all humans together, and for the human rights of all (*RH* 13–17).

Second, Christ fulfills the "deepest aspirations of the human spirit" (*RH* 11.2). All human beings can search in Christ "for the full dimension of its humanity, or in other words for the full meaning of human life" (*RH* 11.2). "In Christ and through Christ man has acquired full awareness of his dignity, of the heights to which he is raised, of the surpassing worth of his own humanity, and of the meaning of his existence" (*RH* 11.3). *Centesimus annus* speaks of "the person of Christ himself as the existentially adequate response to the desire in every heart for goodness, truth, and life" (24.2).

Third, as pointed out in the previous chapter, the pope explicitly recognizes what a pre–Vatican II theology called the universal salvific will of God. In this regard, *Dominum et vivificantem* cites Vatican II, which "reminds us of the Holy Spirit's activity also '*outside the visible body of the Church*.' The Council speaks precisely of 'all people of good will in whose hearts grace works in an unseen way. . . . The Holy Spirit in a manner known only to God offers to every man the possibility of being associated with this Paschal Mystery'" (53.3).

From a practical perspective, John Paul II's emphasis on solidarity provides a good example of how one can appeal to the two audiences of Catholic Christians and all human beings at the same time. *Sollicitudo rei socialis* gives specific theological reasons to ground solidarity as a Christian virtue, but the term "solidarity" by its very nature appeals to all human beings. The pope does not use a specific Christian theological term, such as "agape" or the "Kingdom of God." As chapter 3 will show, John Paul II's anthropology rests on the two basic realities of human dignity and human solidarity. Once again, he uses theological reasons to support the meaning and importance of human dignity, but the term itself can readily appeal to all humankind.

Christology

The theological approach of John Paul II focuses above all on Christology and Christ as redeemer. Christ the Redeemer is the subject of John Paul II's first encyclical. The pope raises the question how he should carry out his own mission. The fundamental question is how should the church draw closer to the everlasting Father. "Our response must be: Our spirit is set in one direction, the only direction for our intellect, will, and heart is—toward Christ our Redeemer, toward Christ, the Redeemer of man" (7.1–2). Yes, as pointed out, Pope Wojtyla surely insists on a Trinitarian approach, but Christ is the revealer to us of the mercy and love of the Father and is our way to the Father (*DM* 1–2). Also, John Paul II's pneumatology is intimately connected to his Christology. While Jesus is the first Paraclete, the Holy Spirit is the second Paraclete who will continue "the work of *the Good News of salvation*. Concerning this continuation of his own work by the Holy Spirit, Jesus speaks more than once during the same farewell discourse" (*DV* 3.2). *Dominum et vivificantem* insists on a "causal" connection and not just a chronological connection between the work of Jesus and the Spirit. "The Holy Spirit will come insofar as Christ will depart through the Cross: he will come not only afterward, but *because* of the redemption accomplished by Christ, through the will and action of the Father" (8.2). "Grace, therefore, bears within itself both a Christological aspect and a pneumatological one" (*DV* 53.2).

Redemptoris missio insists that "Christ is the one mediator between God and mankind" (5.4). Jesus Christ is "at the center of God's plan of salvation" (6.2). But salvation in Christ is offered to all (10.1). John Paul II understands the mystery of Christ as the basis of the church's mission (*RH* 10). The pope emphasizes Christology, but a Christology understood in relationship to the Trinity.

The Meaning of Redemption

How should we understand redemption? John Paul II distinguishes between the divine dimension in the mystery of redemption and the human dimension. The divine dimension of redemption is a tremendous mystery of love. Jesus Christ becomes our reconciliation with the Father. The cross and death of Christ show that the God of creation is also the God of redemption, who is faithful to himself and faithful to his love for humankind and the world (*RH* 9.1–2). This love "is stronger than death; it is a love always ready to raise up and forgive, always ready to go to meet the prodigal son" (*RH* 9.2). John Paul II's description of the divine dimension of the mystery of Jesus thus sees the redemption primarily as an act of God's love shown especially in the cross and death of Jesus.

John Paul II in this description also gives some role in redemption to justice and satisfaction. "His is a love that does not draw back before anything that justice requires in him. Therefore 'for our sake (God) made him (the Son) to be sin who knew no sin'" (*RH* 9.2). One paragraph of *Redemptor hominis* twice refers to Jesus as satisfying the Father's love "which man in a way rejected by breaking the First Covenant" (9.1).This does not seem to be a full-blown endorsement of the Anselmian notion of redemption as the sacrifice of Jesus that alone was able to make atonement to the demands of justice of the Father, but there is at least a hint of the Anselmian approach here. Note that the heavy emphasis on love together with some support for mentioning justice and satisfaction puts the primary emphasis of redemption on the cross and death of Jesus as the great outpouring of love and not on the resurrection. John Paul II on many occasions speaks of the Paschal Mystery as the central reality of redemption with its emphasis on the death and resurrection of Jesus, but he often insists only on the cross and death of Jesus because he sees redemption in terms of God's love for us as manifested in Jesus. To my knowledge, he never refers to redemption only in terms of resurrection.

The human dimension of redemption as described in *Redemptor hominis* 10 develops the often-used phrase that "Christ fully reveals man to himself." The human person cannot live without love and can never encounter the fullness of love unless it is revealed to the person. The human person "must appropriate and assimilate the whole of the reality of the Incarnation and Redemption in order to find himself." The pope does not spell out in a systematic or fully developed way what this means, but he mentions briefly various aspects of this human dimension of redemption. The first response is adoration—thanks for the gift that has been given to us by the redemption. But the human dimension of redemption also instills in the human person a deep sense of wonder about the person herself or himself. "How precious must man be in the eyes of the Creator if he 'gained so great a Redeemer,' and if God 'gave his only Son' in order that man 'should not perish but have eternal life.'" In redemption, "man finds again the greatness, dignity, and value that belong to his humanity." Humankind, through redemption, learns the fundamental importance of love, both receiving it and giving it. "The redemption that took place through the Cross has definitively restored his dignity to man and given back meaning to his life in the world, a meaning that was lost to a considerable extent because of sin." "Man's deepest sphere is involved—we mean the sphere of human hearts, consciences, and events" (*RH* 10.1–3). "In Christ and through Christ man has acquired full awareness of his dignity, of the heights to which he is raised, of the surpassing worth of his own humanity, and of the meaning of his existence" (*RH* 11.3).

The moral life of the Christian involves living out the human dimension of the mystery of redemption. This is the vocation of the Christian. More than once, John Paul II refers to carrying out the threefold office of Jesus as priest, teacher, and king (*RH* 18–22). Above all, the Christian is called upon to carry on the kingly role of Jesus in one's own life. "The essential meaning of this 'kingship' and 'dominion' of man over the visible world, which the Creator himself gave man for his task, consists in the priority of ethics over technology, in the primacy of the person over things, and in the superiority of spirit over matter" (*RH* 16.1). "Our sharing in Christ's kingly mission . . . is clearly linked with every sphere of both Christian and human morality" (*RH* 21.1).

Christ the Redeemer as the Bearer of Truth

Three aspects of John Paul II's Christology deserve further comment. First, the encyclicals emphasize Christ as the bearer of truth. Yes, the encyclicals definitely emphasize Christ's love, but there is no doubt that the papal emphasis on truth differentiates John Paul II's approach to Christology from most others. The encyclical *Veritatis splendor* by its very title and nature emphasizes the centrality and importance of truth. "Called to salvation through faith in Jesus Christ 'the true light that enlightens everyone' (Jn 1:9), people become 'light in the Lord' and 'children of light' (Eph 5:8) and are made holy by 'obedience to the truth' (1 Pet 1:22)" (1.1). But because of "original sin, committed at the prompting of Satan, the one who is 'a liar and the father of lies' (Jn 8:44), man is constantly tempted to turn his gaze away from the living and true God in order to direct it toward idols (cf. 1 Thess 1:9), exchanging 'the truth about God for a lie' (Rom 1:28)" (1.1–2). *Veritatis splendor* then quotes John Paul II's favorite passage from Vatican II, *Gaudium et spes* 22: "In fact *it is only in the mystery of the Word Incarnate that light is shed on the mystery of man*" (22).

The pope emphasizes Christ as the revealer of truth. Yes, Jesus reveals the love and mercy of the Father. *Dives in misericordia* begins by noting, "It is 'God who is rich in mercy' whom Jesus Christ has revealed to us as Father: it is his very Son who in himself, has manifested him and made him known to us" (1.1). But the same opening paragraph of *Dives in misericordia* speaks of the truth revealed by Jesus Christ. "I devoted the encyclical *Redemptor hominis* to the truth about man, a truth that is revealed to us in its fullness and depth in Christ" (1.2). Christ the Redeemer reveals and makes present for us the love of God, but John Paul II often speaks of this in terms of the language of truth and even subordinates love to truth. "The Church wishes to serve this single end: that each person may be able to find Christ, in order that Christ may walk with each person the path of life, with the power of the truth about man and the world that is contained in the mystery of the Incarnation and the Redemption and with the power of the love that is radiated by that truth" (*RH* 13.1).

His encyclical on the Holy Spirit begins with the credal affirmation of the Spirit as the Lord and the giver of life. But, in keeping with the close connection between Christology and pneumatology, the encyclical stresses the Holy Spirit as the giver of truth. The beginning of the first chapter of this encyclical emphasizes the "spirit of truth." John's Gospel records the prayer of Jesus as he was about to leave this world that the Father "will give you another Counselor, to be with you forever, even the Spirit of truth. It is precisely this Spirit of truth whom Jesus calls the Paraclete" (3.1–2). "The Holy Spirit, then, will ensure that in the Church there will always continue *the same truth* which the Apostles heard from their Master" (4). One paragraph develops in a number of different ways the understanding of the Spirit who "will guide you into all truth" (6). "This 'guiding into all truth' is connected . . . with everything that Christ 'did and taught'" (6.3).

James M. Gustafson some years ago pointed out different ways in which Christian ethicists have used and understood Jesus Christ in developing moral theology. Some of the different ways of understanding Christ in the moral life include the following models: Christ, the Lord, who is Creator and Redeemer; Christ, the sanctifier; Christ, the justifier; Christ, the pattern; and Christ, the teacher.[20] Without doubt, the most adequate description of John Paul II's understanding of Christ with regard to the moral life is Christ the Redeemer, who teaches the truth about God and humankind.

This understanding of Christ is totally consistent with the emphasis on truth as developed in chapter 1. The documents themselves give no indication as to why John Paul II so emphasizes Christ the Redeemer as the giver and revealer of truth. The broader context sheds light on this emphasis. The pope's encyclicals and other documents come from the papal teaching office. His whole purpose here is to teach the truth. Consequently, he stresses Jesus as the revealer of the truth about God and about humankind. In addition, Pope Wojtyla, by training, study, and writing as a philosopher and ethicist, emphasized both the importance and the goal of seeking the truth to guide life.

Christology from Above, Anthropology, and Ecclesiology

A second aspect of John Paul II's Christology is his emphasis on a "Christology from above." Contemporary Christology includes two different approaches—"Christology from above" and "Christology from below." Christology from above begins with the Trinity and the preexisting Logos, through whom all things were made. God has revealed God's self in creation and in history, but because of human sinfulness God becomes present to us through the Incarnation and redemption of Christ, the Son of God, who came into our world to reconcile us to the Father and to one another. Conversely, Christology from below begins with the humanity of Jesus—his life and mission in the world—and then considers Jesus's Paschal Mystery and his being raised up by the Holy Spirit in glory as Lord and King at the right hand of the Father, thus bringing in his relationship with God and divinity.[21]

John Paul II adopts a Christology from above. Such an approach has been the traditional one in Christian and Catholic theology. Recall that the pope cites John more than any other evangelist. John well illustrates a Christology from above. The Word was with God and was God from the very beginning. But the Word became flesh and dwelt among us. The pope emphasizes the Incarnation and frequently links together the Incarnation and redemption. The two form the one mystery of God's great love for us human beings. John Paul II sees human love primarily as a sincere gift of self precisely because it is modeled on the love of Christ for us shown in the Incarnation and redemption. Christology from below, however, would tend to bring out aspects that differ somewhat from those found in a Christology from above. For example, a Christology from below emphasizes that Jesus advanced in wisdom, age, and grace before God and human beings. The human Jesus knew struggles, doubt, and from the beginning did not have a full human awareness of his own mission. Thus, a moral theology or ethic based on such a Christology stresses much more the notions of struggle, growth, and development. A social ethic from the perspective of a Christology from below sees Jesus above all as a victim of injustice who is in solidarity with all victims of injustice.[22]

There are different emphases and different dangers in the two Christologies. John Paul II's Christology from above emphasizes Christ as the perfect human and tends to downplay the real humanity of Jesus with his own struggles and even doubts. In social ethics, a Christology from below will stress conflict and struggle more than a Christology from above. As will be pointed out, John Paul II, after some time, accepted the notion of a preferential option for the poor, but one can see why this understanding came to the fore in a Christology from below.

A third aspect of John Paul II's Christology concerns the relationship of Christology with anthropology and also with ecclesiology. As has been mentioned, John Paul II faithfully tries to relate faith to daily life and stresses the close connection between Christology and anthropology. But there is a problem here, for at times he makes too close a connection between the two.

The whole thrust of *Redemptor hominis*, which is frequently mentioned in subsequent encyclicals, is that Jesus Christ the Redeemer reveals to us the truth about humankind. I discussed these texts in some detail in chapter 1. But as I pointed out, these assertions about Christ revealing the truth about humankind exist at the very minimum in some tensions with other emphases throughout the encyclicals on the role of human reason, natural law, and human sources of moral wisdom and knowledge giving us the truth about humankind. The three social encyclicals explicitly address all people of goodwill and use human reason and human sources of moral wisdom and knowledge to describe how human beings should act in this world. The 1998 encyclical *Fides et ratio* reaffirms the traditional Catholic support for reason and philosophy as sources of the truth. "With its enduring appeal to the search for truth, philosophy has the great responsibility of forming thought and culture" (6.3).

There can be no doubt that John Paul II recognizes human sources of truth other than revelation in Jesus Christ. But the more general and unqualified statements, especially in the earlier Trinitarian encyclicals about Christ revealing the truth about humankind, are somewhat misleading and one-sided. John Paul II apparently so wanted to emphasize a Christological approach that he tended to absorb anthropology into Christology. From a Lutheran perspective, Karl P. Donfried has pointed out this same problem. Donfried, dealing only with *Veritatis splendor*, salutes the heavy biblical emphasis in the first part of the encyclical, with its strong insistence on a Christologically based ethics, but he then laments that instead of a Christological ethic *Veritatis splendor* proposes "a theonomous naturalism, a philosophical ethic in the natural law tradition."[23] What Donfried says about *Veritatis splendor* is even more applicable to the earlier encyclicals dealing with matters of faith. The encyclicals stress a total Christological approach to anthropology, but the later encyclicals recognize important anthropological insights based on human reason and experience. The problem with the emphasis on Christ giving the truth about humankind with no other qualifications or additions can be described as an anthropology from above analogous to the Christology from above discussed earlier. Here, Christology tends to absorb anthropology. If you have Christian revelation, you have the full truth about humankind. But there are many other truths about human beings that we need to know, even for our Christian understanding of morality and how human beings are to live in this world. The Catholic theological tradition—with its emphasis on "both-and," as illustrated in the relationship of faith and reason—has consistently recognized both revelation and reason as sources of moral wisdom and knowledge about humankind. A more fundamentalist Christianity might insist that Jesus Christ is the only revealer to us of the truth about humankind, but such has never been the Catholic position; nor is it the position adopted in practice by John Paul II. But the pope should have been more nuanced in his emphasis on Christ revealing the truth about humankind.

The problem with Pope Wojtyla's understanding of truth discussed in chapter 1 is related to his tendency toward an anthropology from above. He begins with "truth from above," the truth of revelation, and he often appears to absorb all other truths under this category. But in reality, he recognizes many other types of truth with different levels of certitude. Too often, he tends to use the truth of revelation as synonymous with a univocal concept of truth.

A similar absorption of another theological discipline into Christology concerns ecclesiology. What might be called an ecclesiology from above stresses above all the relationship of Christ with the church that carries on the work of Christ in time and space through the power of the Holy Spirit. As was pointed out in a previous chapter, John Paul II adopts such an understanding of the church and consequently downplays the human element in the church. The church is never perfect but always a pilgrim church on a journey precisely because the church is the pilgrim people of God.

Eschatology

Eschatology, as it is understood today, refers to the relationship between the fullness of the reign of God proclaimed by Jesus and the present reality of the world in which we live. Eschatology has a significant influence on moral theology. Should we be optimistic or pessimistic about human possibilities in this world? Should Christians cooperate and work with others, or should Christians see the world and non-Christians as basically evil and have nothing to do with them?

Many commentators, including myself, have criticized *Gaudium et spes* for being too optimistic and for having what is often called a too realized eschatology—too much of the reign of God is present here and now. We are all likely to be influenced by the times in which we live. There is no doubt that the 1960s were optimistic times both in the world and in the church. In political life, the torch was passed to a new generation born in the twentieth century. Progress and development were experienced in many ways. But a few years later, urban riots and the war in Vietnam changed the mood in the United States and brought about a more sober and much less optimistic understanding of the world. The growing gap between rich and poor, the sufferings of so many people in the world, and the escalating violence in cities and the world have made us much more realistic than people were at the time of Vatican II. Optimistic theologies of the secular city and the death of God arose in the 1960s, but now we are more aware of our sinfulness and the enormity of the problems in the secular city. In the Catholic Church, the invigorating change taking place at Vatican II in the beginning of the 1960s opened the door for dreams of great progress toward church unity and a more justice-filled world. But the dreams never came to fruition.

How should we understand Pope Wojtyla's eschatology? In his classic study *Christ and Culture*, H. Richard Niebuhr is really dealing with the contemporary question of eschatology. He proposes five models for understanding the relationship between Christ and culture. The two extremes either identify Christ and culture (the Christ of culture) or totally oppose the two (Christ against culture). The three middle positions are Christ above culture, Christ and culture in paradox, and Christ the transformer of culture, which sees Christians called to try to change and transform the culture with a realization that the reign of God will never be fully present in this world. Christians are called to struggle to make themselves, their culture, and their world better, but they will always know problems, frustrations, difficulties, suffering, and the lack of ultimate success.[24]

For the most part, John Paul II adopts a realistic culture-transforming model, but his basis for it in the Catholic tradition differs somewhat from the approach of Niebuhr. In his first encyclical, the pope refers to the "difficult road of the indispensable transformation of the structures of economic life" (*RH* 16.7). *Dives in misericordia* maintains, "The situation of the world today not only displays transformations that give grounds for hope in *a better future for man on earth*, but also reveals a multitude of threats far surpassing those known until now" (2.4). Frequently in these documents, but especially in *Sollicitudo*, the pope mentions the need for authentic human development, but this is not a straightforward or automatic process (*SRS* 27–40). John Paul II often refers to the call to holiness and perfection, which involves "*the moral growth of man*, who has *been called to perfection*" (*VS* 17.1). Thus, the Christian is called to grow and to be transformed in response to God's grace.

John Paul II's eschatology rests on his recognition of the theological realities of creation, sin, Incarnation, and redemption as having already occurred, but the fullness of the reign of God will never be here in this world. *Redemptor hominis*, the first encyclical, very succinctly brings together all these aspects. Redemption is seen as a new creation. The book of Genesis testifies to the fundamental goodness of creation. God made all things and saw that they were good. This good has its source in the wisdom and love of God. But through Adam, sin entered into the world and made creation subject to futility, and a people affected by sin has been groaning in travail until now. In keeping with the Catholic tradition, John Paul II does not want to see sin as totally destroying the goodness of creation, but it has definitely affected it. Christ's Incarnation and redemption have reconciled human beings with God after the sin of Adam. Christ restored "that likeness to God which had been disfigured ever since the first sin" (*RH* 8–9). A similar statement is found in a subsequent paragraph of the encyclical: Christ "through the Cross has definitively restored his dignity to man and given back meaning to his life in the world, a meaning that was lost to a considerable extent because of sin" (10.2). We live in the era of "the Church of the new Advent, the Church that is continually preparing for the new coming of the Lord" (20.7). I referred to Wojtyla's approach as "realistic transformation" because he recognizes the continuing presence and power of sin that stands in the way of an always progressive linear development. He frequently insists on the daily experience of suffering in our lives (*FR* 26) but also its redemptive value (*RM* 78; *CA* 25.1).

Throughout the encyclicals, the pope frequently mentions the realities of creation, sin, Incarnation, and redemption. Recall that the most frequently used text in the Hebrew Bible in the encyclicals is the book of Genesis, which describes both creation and the fall. The pope also cites the Gospel of John more than any other Gospel, and this Gospel accentuates the mysteries of the Incarnation and the redemption. There are not as many explicit references to the fact that the fullness of the reign of God will only come in the next world, but that is certainly implied throughout his writings and is occasionally made very explicit (*EV* 2.1; *DM* 8.2). To have such an eschatology calls for attempts to transform self, culture, and the structures of society but with the realization that such changes will not be easy, will often suffer reverses, and will always fall quite short of full transformation. On the personal level, he insists on the conversion of the human heart, which *Dominum et vivificantem* understands as under the influence of the Holy Spirit, who "*makes man realize his own evil* and at the same time *directs him toward what is good*" (42.2).

The three social encyclicals by their very nature constitute a call to transform the existing political and economic structures to serve better the dignity and equality of all human beings. Recall that these encyclicals are specifically addressed also to all people of goodwill. Thus, the culture, the world, and other human beings are not evil and to be avoided or to be opposed but rather all are called to work together in this world for what *Sollicitudo* calls "the authentic development of man and society" (1.1). *Centesimus annus* maintains that

Catholic social teaching has spurred on many millions of people representing "a *great movement for the defense of the human person* and the safeguarding of human dignity. Amid changing historical circumstances, this movement has contributed to the building up of a more just society or at least to the curbing of injustice" (3.4). Note here a realism that recognizes that it is easier to achieve the negative goal of curbing injustice than it is to bring about more justice. The ending of *Sollicitudo rei socialis* explicitly spells out the eschatological understanding of the struggle for true liberation and authentic human development:

> The Church well knows that *no temporal achievement* is to be identified with the Kingdom of God, but that all such achievements simply *reflect* and in a sense *anticipate* the glory of the Kingdom, the Kingdom which we wait at the end of history, when the Lord will come again. But that expectation can never be an excuse for lack of concern for people in their concrete personal situations and their social, national and international life since the former is conditioned by the latter, especially today.
>
> However imperfect and temporary are all the things that can and ought to be done through the combined efforts of everyone and through divine grace, at a given moment of history, in order to make people's lives 'more human,' nothing will be *lost* or *will have been in vain.* (48.1–2)

In the eschatological perspective of a realistic transforming eschatology, John Paul II frequently points out the problems and obstacles that have to be overcome to achieve authentic human development in our world. From the theological perspective, "the principal obstacle to be overcome on the way to authentic liberation is *sin* and the *structures* produced by sin as it multiplies and spreads" (*SRS* 46.5).

In *Sollicitudo rei socialis*, John Paul II introduces into the encyclical tradition of Catholic social teaching a new concept—sinful structures or social sin. The concept of social sin or sinful structures has existed to some extent outside the Roman Catholic theological tradition, but it has come to the fore in contemporary Catholic and Protestant theology, especially through the contribution of liberation theology in South America.[25]

Liberation theology uses sinful structures and social sin to refer to the existing social, economic, and political structures and institutions that incorporate the interest of the powerful at the expense of the powerless and oppressed and stand in the way of true justice. Generally, most people, even the victims, are not conscious or aware of these structures and their very negative role. Liberation theology calls for a raising of consciousness to make people aware of these sinful structures in order to change them.[26]

The Catholic tradition has emphasized the personal dimension of sin or the free acts of persons that have negative effects on society and its institutions. But structural sin recognizes a two-way street. Personal sin affects society in a free and conscious way, but social sin in an unconscious and mostly unrecognized way strongly affects human beings.

The Latin American bishops accepted the reality of social sin in their Medellín (1968) and Puebla (1979) documents. In Mexico before the Puebla meeting, John Paul II for the first time referred to sinful structures.[27]

Sollicitudo (36.2) mentions John Paul II's previous discussion of structural sin in the 1984 apostolic exhortation *Reconciliatio et paenitentia*, which was written on the basis of and in response to the 1983 meeting of the Synod of Bishops. In *Reconciliatio et paenitentia*, the pope insists on sin as a free personal act, which is the proper meaning of sin. Social sin can be properly understood in three ways. First, every personal sin has social effects. Second, some sins directly affect the neighbor. Third, social sin in an analogical sense refers to relations between various human communities. Here the document illustrates such social sin first by class struggle (notice here the pope's appeal to what he perceives as a problem in liberation theology) and the confrontation between blocs of nations. *Sollicitudo* blames the two blocs of the East and the West for some of the problems of the developing world. *Reconciliatio et paenitentia* maintains it is wrong to contrast personal and social sin in a way that leads to the watering down and almost the abolition of personal sin with a recognition only of social guilt and responsibilities. Social sin comes from the accumulation and concentration of personal sins that cause, support, or exploit evil or fail to do anything to overcome evil because of laziness, secret complicity, or indifference.[28] Notice here the primary and heavy emphasis on personal sin as creating the sinful situation. Very little is said about the unconscious and unrecognized influence of sinful structures on persons.

Sollicitudo retains much of this emphasis on social sin as resulting from free personal sin. Structures of sin come from "individuals' actions and omissions" (36.4). Two powerful attitudes contributing to sinful situations are the all-consuming desire for profit and the thirst for power that is present in both individuals and in nations. Moral evil leads to structural sin (37). The pope emphasizes the role of personal and free sinful actions in creating sinful social structures, and the remedy is to change the spiritual attitudes that bring about social sin (38.3). Both *Evangelium vitae* (59.2) and *Ut unum sint* (34) briefly mention social sin.

However, there are some indications of the unconscious and unaware influence of sinful structures on individuals. *Sollicitudo* maintains "The sum total of the negative factors working against a true awareness of the universal *common good*, and the need to further it, gives the impression of creating, in persons and institutions, an obstacle which is difficult to overcome" (36.1). In this connection, Gregory Baum, whose analysis I have closely followed, points out that John Paul II is well aware of the effects of ideologies on the lives of persons and institutions.[29]

John Paul II thus introduces into hierarchical Catholic teaching the concept of structural sin. His primary emphasis on personal moral agency as contributing to social sin reflects the traditional Catholic emphasis on personal sin as well as his own opposition to aspects of liberation theology, especially to what he sees as its heavy dependence on Marxism and its acceptance of class struggle. In addition, his whole philosophical and theological approach of personalism emphasizes the primacy of the subject over the object, labor over capital, and the need for all to participate responsibly in economic and political institutions and structures. These aspects are discussed in greater detail in subsequent chapters. John Paul II, nonetheless, has introduced a new understanding of sin into hierarchical teaching, has recognized some unconscious influence of structures and institutions that we are often unaware of, and has indicated in a very significant way that working for social justice by overcoming social sin is a constitutive dimension of the Gospel and of the redemptive mission of the church.

From his first encyclical, *Redemptor hominis*, John Paul II has pointed out the threats and problems facing humankind. Ours is a time of great progress but also a time of threats to all people of goodwill. The human situation today is far removed from the objective demands of the moral order and of justice. Individualism, consumerism, materialism, the devastation of the environment, and a growing gap between the rich and the poor are prevalent in the world. The task we face is difficult but not an impossible one (*RH* 16).

Both *Sollicitudo* and *Centesimus annus* point out the continuing threats to humankind in the world today but also indicate some positive events. Decolonization occurred in the second half of the twentieth century; human rights have come to the fore, as seen, for example, in the work of the United Nations. The year 1989 witnessed the fall of communist regimes in Central and Eastern Europe; the 1980s also saw the fall of some dictatorial repressive regimes in Latin America, Africa, and Asia. The revolution in Eastern and Central Europe was brought about for the most part by nonviolent means, using only the weapons of justice and truth. But the crisis of Marxism does not rid the world of the situations of injustice and oppression that Marxism exploited and on which it fed. Individualism, consumerism, and materialism are still strong realities in the world. Political and economic justice are far from being achieved, but some true transformation can and should take place (*CA* 20–29).

John Paul II uses this understanding of eschatology with the elements of creation, sin, Incarnation, redemption, and the fullness of the Kingdom of God in the future to develop a spirituality of work in *Laborem exercens*. His purpose is *"to form a spirituality of work which will help all people to come closer, through work, to God, the Creator and Redeemer, to participate in his salvific plan for man and the world and to deepen their friendship with Christ"* (24.2). The doctrine of creation heavily influences our understanding of work. *"Man,* created in the image of God, *shares by his work in the activity of the Creator"* (25.2). God himself worked for six days and so should human beings. Work provides the substance of life for workers and their families, and also benefits society by unfolding the Creator's work. Works produced by human talent and energy are not in opposition to God's power but are signs of it. By human dominion over creation, the human person shares in the creative work of God (26.1–5).

Human work has also been affected by sin: "All *work*, whether manual or intellectual, is inevitably linked with toil . . . the curse that sin brought with it." This toil of work even constitutes "*an announcement of death*" (27.1). But Christ the redeemer has also affected human work through the Paschal Mystery of his suffering and death. "By enduring the toil of work in union with Christ crucified for us, man in a way collaborates with the Son of God for the redemption of humanity . . . by carrying the Cross in his turn every day in the activity that he is called upon to perform" (27.3). Throughout the encyclicals, John Paul II frequently recognizes the suffering of people in this world and relates human suffering to the paschal mystery of Jesus (*RM* 78; *CA* 25.1; *EV* 67.3). The future fullness of the reign of God at the end of time also influences our work. "The expectation of a new earth must not weaken but rather stimulate our concern for the cultivation of this one" (27.6). Thus, John Paul II uses his eschatological understanding to develop a spirituality of work that *Laborem exercens* six times calls "the Gospel of work."

But the eschatology of *Evangelium vitae* stands in stark contrast to the eschatology found in the other writings. *Evangelium vitae* deals with "the struggle between the 'culture of life' and the 'culture of death'" (21.1). Such an approach basically coheres with the Christ-against-culture approach of Niebuhr. *Evangelium vitae* refers to the culture of death as a "veritable structure of sin." In a certain sense, the culture of death involves "*a war of the powerful against the weak*" and a "*conspiracy against life*" (12). This encyclical describes the darkness of Good Friday as "the symbol of a great cosmic disturbance and a massive conflict between the forces of good and the forces of evil, between life and death. Today we too find ourselves in the midst of a dramatic conflict between the 'culture of death' and the 'culture of life'" (50.2).

Such a culture of life versus culture of death approach sees the world in terms of opposition between the forces of good and the forces of evil, between light and darkness. This approach denies the fact that the goodness of creation, although affected by sin, continues to exist throughout the world, the basic aspiration for the true and the good in the hearts of all, and that God offers all people the gift of his love and salvation. Likewise, it cannot logically call for Christians to work together with all people of goodwill for the common good and authentic human development. This oppositional approach strongly disagrees with the realistic transforming model accepted in the other writings of John Paul II. The transforming approach recognizes that there is evil and sin in the world that at times we must strongly oppose, but it also sees human culture as not totally sinful and evil. There are positive aspects as well as negative aspects to human culture today.

In fairness, *Evangelium vitae* itself tries occasionally to soften the opposition between the culture of life and the culture of death and to some extent recognizes the problem of accepting such an oppositional understanding of Christ and culture. "It would therefore be to give a one-sided picture, which could lead to sterile discouragement, if the condemnation of the threats to life were not accompanied by the presentation of the *positive signs* at work in humanity's present situation" (26.1). All this culture of death cannot "stifle the voice of the Lord echoing in the conscience of every individual: it is always from this intimate sanctuary of the conscience that a new journey of love, openness and service to human life can begin" (24.2). Thus, John Paul II himself tries to nuance somewhat the dramatic struggle and war between the culture of death and the culture of life, but the main thrust of the encyclical remains the opposition between the culture of life and the culture of death.

Why does Pope Wojtyla develop this dramatic struggle between the culture of death and the culture of life in the encyclical *Evangelium vitae* when he does not use it in his other writings and because such an approach contradicts the eschatology proposed elsewhere? Obviously, the subject matter of *Evangelium vitae* has a role to play here. In this encyclical, John Paul II defends the Catholic positions on life with special emphasis on abortion and euthanasia. He knows that the Catholic position on these issues is strongly opposed by many in society. By seeing this opposition in terms of a culture of death versus a culture of life, he can give an even stronger support for his own position. But in the process, his opposition to these practices leads him to adopt an eschatology and a Christ-against-culture approach that goes against the positions he takes elsewhere. A final theological issue connected with eschatology concerns the existence and role of human sources of moral wisdom and knowledge that Christians share with all others. Chapter 1 includes a discussion of this issue under the rubric of the theological aspect of natural law. As noted there and developed earlier in this chapter, some tension exists within the encyclicals themselves on recognizing human reason reflecting on human nature as a source of moral wisdom and knowledge. The encyclicals dealing with matters of faith so emphasize Christ as giving the truth about humankind that they do not emphasize and seemingly do not recognize a common morality based on the human reason that all share. But the encyclicals dealing with moral theology, faith, and reason, and the three social encyclicals, all clearly recognize a common morality.

The Catholic tradition has based its theological defense of natural law on the doctrine of creation. God has given us human reason which, by reflecting on what God has made, can arrive at moral truths. Some in the classical Protestant tradition reject natural law either by insisting on a *sola scriptura* (scripture alone) approach or by seeing sin as basically affecting human reason and creation. How can a sinful human reason reflecting on a fallen creation come to moral truth or the law of God?[30] By insisting on the basic goodness of creation and human reason, the Catholic tradition has rejected those two arguments against natural law.

John Paul II is not writing a theological treatise on natural law, so one should not expect a full-blown discussion of the theological foundations for natural law. But the pope briefly but clearly indicates his theological rationale for natural law. The primary basis for natural law is the doctrine of creation. "Only God can answer the question about the good, because he is the Good. But God has already given an answer to this question: he did so *by creating man and ordering him* with wisdom and love to his final end, through the law which is inscribed in his heart (cf. Rom 2:15), the 'natural law.' The latter 'is nothing other than the light of understanding infused in us by God, whereby we understand what must be done and what must be avoided. God gave this light and this law to man at creation'" (*VS* 12.1).

By nature and creation, the human person is a seeker of truth (*FR* 28). There exists through God's creation "the human orientation toward truth" (*FR* 5.2). "The natural law is written and engraved in the heart of each and every man" (*VS* 44.1; cf. *EV* 29.3). The human being has a natural inclination to the good (*VS* 47).

But Pope Wojtyla also recognizes the reality of the fall and human sinfulness while rejecting the understanding that sin totally destroys reason's role in coming to moral truth. Sin has affected reason but not destroyed its capacity for truth. The pope describes reason after sin as "diminished" (*FR* 22.2), "impaired" (*FR* 22.3), and as "wounded and weakened by sin" (*FR* 51.1). Thus, sin weakens but does not destroy the God-given capacity of human beings to arrive at truth.

Redemption in Christ Jesus, however, overcomes the wounding and weakening of human reason's capacity for the truth brought about by sin. "The coming of Christ was the saving event which redeemed reason from its weakness, setting it free from the shackles in which it had imprisoned itself" (*FR* 22.3). *Veritatis splendor* calls attention to "the need, given the present state of fallen nature, for divine revelation as an effective means for knowing moral truths, even of the natural order" (36.3). John Paul II repeats the well-known formula of reason enlightened by faith. "Man is able to recognize good and evil thanks to that discernment of good from evil which he himself carries out by his *reason, in particular by his reason enlightened by divine revelation and by faith*" (*VS* 44.2). John Paul II's discussion of natural law consistently follows his eschatology beginning with the goodness of creation, the damage created by sin, and the restoration and redemption in Christ Jesus.

The encyclicals dealing explicitly with human reason and natural law thus develop a consistent theological rationale in defense of natural law, despite some Christological and eschatological approaches in other encyclicals that downplay and even seem to deny human reason as a source of true moral wisdom and knowledge. In sum, then, this chapter has analyzed and criticized the theological aspects of John Paul II's moral theology, especially his use of the sources of scripture, tradition, and reason, as well as his Christology and eschatology.

Notes

1. For a helpful study of John Paul II's use of scripture, see Terrence Prendergast, "'A Vision of Wholeness': A Reflection on the Use of Scripture in a Cross-Section of Papal Writings," in the *Thought of John Paul II: A Collection of Essays and Studies*, ed. John M. McDermott (Rome: Editrice Pontificia Università Gregoriana, 1993), 69–91.

2. Jeffrey S. Siker, *Scripture and Ethics: Twentieth-Century Portraits* (New York: Oxford University Press, 1997).

3. Prendergast, "Vision of Wholeness," 84; David H. Kelsay, *The Use of Scripture in Recent Theology* (Philadelphia: Fortress Press, 1975), 167–78.

4. See, for example, Thomas W. Ogletree, *The Use of the Bible in Christian Ethics: A Constructive Essay* (Philadelphia: Fortress Press, 1983); Sandra M. Schneiders, *The Revelatory Text: Interpreting the New Testament as Sacred Scripture* (San Francisco: HarperCollins, 1991); J. I. H. McDonald, *Biblical Interpretation in Christian Ethics* (Cambridge: Cambridge University Press, 1994); and Carol J. Dempsey and William P. Loewe, eds., *Theology and Sacred Scripture*, College Theology Society Annual Volume 47 (Maryknoll, N.Y.: Orbis, 2002).

5. Raymond E. Brown and Sandra M. Schneiders, "Hermeneutics," in *The New Jerome Biblical Commentary*, ed. Raymond E. Brown, Joseph A. Fitzmyer, and Roland E. Murphy (Englewood Cliffs, N.J.: Prentice Hall, 1990), 1158–61.

6. William C. Spohn, *What Are They Saying about Scripture and Ethics?* rev. ed. (New York: Paulist Press, 1995), 11–13.

7. J. Michael Miller, "Introduction to the Papal Encyclicals," in *The Encyclicals of John Paul II*, ed. J. Michael Miller (Huntington, Ind.: Our Sunday Visitor, 2001), 28.

8. Miller, "Introduction to the Papal Encyclicals," 28.

9. For critical essays on *Veritatis splendor*'s use of scripture, see William C. Spohn, "Morality on the Way of Discipleship: The Use of Scripture in *Veritatis Splendor*," in *Veritatis Splendor: American Responses*, ed. Michael E. Allsopp and John J. O'Keefe (Kansas City: Sheed & Ward, 1995), 83–105; and Karl P. Donfried, "The Use of Scripture in *Veritatis Splendor*," in *Ecumenical Ventures in Ethics: Protestants Engage John Paul II's Moral Encyclicals*, ed. Reinhard Hütter and Theodore Dieter (Grand Rapids, Mich.: William B. Eerdmans, 1998), 38–59. I have used some of their points in my analysis here.

10. Pope John Paul II, *Mulieris dignitatem*, 23–27, in *The Theology of the Body: Human Love in the Divine Plan* (Boston: Pauline Books, 1997), 478–83.

11. Pope John Paul II, "General Audience of August 11, 1982," in *Theology of the Body*, 309–11.

12. Miller, *Encyclicals of John Paul II*, 31.

13. For a negative view of John Paul II's implementation of Vatican II, see Hans Küng and Leonard Swidler, eds., *The Church in Anguish: Has the Vatican Betrayed Vatican II?* (San Francisco: Harper & Row, 1987).

14. Miller, *Encyclicals of John Paul II*, 305.

15. Léonie Caldecott, "Sincere Gift: The Pope's 'New Feminism,'" *Communio* 23 (1996): 64–81.

16. Mary Elsbernd, "The Reinterpretation of *Gaudium et Spes* in *Veritatis Splendor*," *Horizons* 29 (2002): 225–39.

17. Marie-Dominique Chenu, *La "doctrine sociale" de l'Église comme idéologie* (Paris: Cerf, 1979).

18. Pope Paul VI, *Octogesima adveniens*, n. 4, in *Catholic Social Thought: The Documentary Heritage*, ed. David J. O'Brien and Thomas A. Shannon (Maryknoll, N.Y.: Orbis, 1992), 266.

19. Chenu, *La doctrine sociale*, 87–96.

20. James F. Gustafson, *Christ and the Moral Life* (New York: Harper & Row, 1968).

21. Raymond E. Brown, *An Introduction to New Testament Christology* (New York: Paulist Press, 1994).

22. See, for example, Matthew L. Lamb, *Solidarity with Victims: Toward a Theology of Social Transformation* (New York: Crossroad, 1982).

23. Donfried, "Use of Scripture," 46.

24. H. Richard Niebuhr, *Christ and Culture,* 50th anniversary ed. (San Francisco: HarperCollins, 2002).

25. Kenneth R. Himes, "Social Sin and the Role of the Individual," *Annual of the Society of Christian Ethics* (1986): 183–218.

26. Gregory Baum, "Structures of Sin," in *The Logic of Solidarity: Commentaries on Pope John Paul II's Encyclical "On Social Concern,"* ed. Gregory Baum and Robert Ellsberg (Maryknoll, N.Y.: Orbis, 1989), 113–14.

27. Margaret Pfeil, "Doctrinal Implications of Magisterial Use of the Language of Social Sin," *Louvain Studies* 27 (2002): 136–38.

28. Pope John Paul II, *"Reconciliatio et Paenitentia,"* in *Post-Synodal Apostolic Exhortations of John Paul II*, ed. J. Michael Miller (Huntington, Ind.: Our Sunday Visitor, 1998), n. 16, pp. 283–87.

29. Baum, "Structures of Sin," 115–16.

30. Helmut Thielicke, *Theological Ethics*, vol. 1, *Foundations*, ed. and tr. William H. Lazareth (Philadelphia: Fortress Press, 1966), 383–445.

CHAPTER

3

ETHICAL
FOUNDATIONS AND
METHOD

THIS CHAPTER considers the ethical aspects of the methodology of
moral theology that depend on both specifically theological sources
and human sources available to all. It discusses anthropology, the
model and method of moral theology, and natural law.

Anthropology

Moral theology is based on anthropology, for it considers how the
human person should act. As a philosophical ethicist, John Paul II
has made the human person the center of his ethics, as is illustrated
in his book *The Acting Person*.[1] Much has been written on the philosophical anthropology of the pope.[2] Most commentators would
agree with Gerald A. McCool in describing the pope's philosophical
anthropology as a "personalist metaphysics of the moral agent."[3] In
the course of the pope's development as an ethicist, he moved from
a metaphysics of universal nature to a metaphysics of the conscious
concrete person.[4] There is no doubt that he emphasizes the subjectivity of the person but not to the denial of objectivity. Subjectivity
is the person's awareness of one's own subsistent being. The free
human person always stands under the obligation to the truth.[5]

John Paul II's papal writings obviously are influenced by his philosophical approach, but they are of a different genre. Papal moral teachings as such do not delve deeply into the philosophical background. Yet the pope insists time and again that anthropology is the basis for all moral reflection and teaching. *Veritatis splendor*, for example, six times refers to "the truth about man" as the criterion for judging human morality (31.3, 40, 48.3, 83.1, 86.1, 112.2). In addition, John Paul II sees his social teaching as based on anthropology "The main thread, and in a certain sense, the guiding principle of Pope Leo's Encyclical, and of all the Church's social doctrine, is a *correct view of the human person* and of his unique value" (*CA* 11.3). *Centesimus annus* later makes the point that the human person is "the principle which inspires the Church's social doctrine" (53.2).

Chapter 1 of this book showed how John Paul II brings together theology and anthropology in the light of the human person's relationship with the three divine persons of the Trinity. Christ fully reveals the meaning of the human. In addition, eschatology points out that this human person is created good by God, affected by human sin, redeemed through the Incarnation and redemption of Christ, and destined for eternal life. But in keeping with the Catholic tradition, John Paul II also recognizes the role of human reason, human experiences, and the human sciences in contributing to our understanding of anthropology. This section shows how, in light of these sources, he develops the understanding of the human person as the basis for his moral teaching.

The Incomparable and Unique Dignity of the Person

The basic anthropological assertion of John Paul II is the incomparable and unique dignity and value of the individual, concrete human person. John Paul II uses his scriptural and Vatican II sources to make his point about the unique value of the human person. On a number of occasions, he calls attention to the text from *Gaudium et spes* of Vatican II about the unique dignity of the human person. "One chapter of the Constitution *Gaudium et spes* amounts to a virtual compendium of the biblical anthropology from which philosophy too can draw inspiration. The chapter deals with the value of the human person created in the image of God, explains the dignity and superiority of the human being over the rest of creation, and declares the transcendent capacity of human reason" (*FR* 60.1).

Genesis testifies to the fact that the human person was created in the image and likeness of God. For John Paul II, that is the ultimate basis for human dignity. "To create means to call into existence from nothing: therefore, to create means *to give* existence" (*DV* 34). Thus, the human person exists because of God's love. The human person is the only creature created for itself, because the whole of the created world is given to humankind (*DV* 34). The human being has been given dominion over the earth and all creation with the command to fill the earth and subdue it. "Man is the image of God partly through the mandate received from his Creator to subdue, to dominate the earth. In carrying out this mandate, man, every human being, reflects the very action of the Creator of the universe" (*LE* 4.2). According to *Laborem exercens*, being the image of God means the human being "is a person, that is to say, a subjective being capable of acting in a planned and rational way, capable of deciding about himself, and with a tendency to self-realization" (6.2). *Dominum et vivificantem* points out that being the image and likeness of God "means not only rationality and freedom as constitutive properties of human nature, but also, from the very beginning, the capacity of having *a personal relationship* with God, as 'I' and 'you,' and therefore *the capacity of having a covenant*, which will take place in God's salvific communication with man" (34).

John Paul II often cites his favorite passage, *Gaudium et spes* 22, to show how the Incarnation adds to the unique dignity of human beings. "Only in the mystery of the Incarnate Word does the mystery of man take on light. . . . Christ, the new Adam . . . *fully reveals man to himself* and brings to light his most high calling. . . . Human nature by the very fact that it was assumed, not absorbed, in him, has been raised in us also to a dignity beyond compare. For by his Incarnation, he, the Son of God, *in a certain way united himself with each man*" (*RH* 82).

In addition to creation and Incarnation, redemption also grounds the basic dignity of the human person. "Man cannot live without love. He remains a being that is incomprehensible for himself, his life is senseless, if love is not revealed to him, if he does not encounter love, if he does not experience it and make it his own, if he does not participate intimately in it." But it is precisely the redemption of Christ that shows that love for human beings. Redemption also strengthens human dignity and value in another way. "How precious must man be in the eyes of the Creator if he 'gained so great a Redeemer'" (*RH* 10.1). John Paul II then concludes, "The Redemption that took place through the Cross has definitively restored his dignity to man and given back meaning to his life in the world, a meaning that was lost to a considerable extent because of sin" (*RH* 10.2). "In reality, the name for that deep amazement at man's worth and dignity is the Gospel, that is to say: the Good News" (*RH* 10.2). Thus, for John Paul II, creation, Incarnation, and redemption ground the incomparable and unique value and dignity of the human person—the most basic anthropological assertion. The defense and promotion of human dignity thus becomes the primary criterion for the development of John Paul II's moral teaching.

The incomparable dignity and value of the human person have significant consequences for moral teaching. This dignity forms the basis for much of the personal and social ethics that John Paul II develops. The individual person and the whole human community must respect, promote, and enhance human dignity. This dignity is the basis for the call for authentic human development of each and all human beings and their liberation from all oppression (*RM* 58). Human dignity requires that the person can never be reduced to a mere means (*VS* 48.3). As a result, things must always be subordinate to the person (*RH* 16.1; *LE* 13.3–5). In this context, *Laborem exercens* insists on the priority of the subjective aspect of work (the worker) over the objective aspect of work (what is produced) (*LE* 6–7). The same encyclical logically then insists on the priority of labor over capital (12). The incomparable dignity of the human person forms the basis for human rights (*CA* 11.3). The unconditional respect due to personal dignity of every person must be protected by absolute norms that do not admit of exception (*VS* 90.1). Thus, the incomparable dignity of the human person grounds much of the moral teaching of John Paul II.

The loving gift of God is the basis of the incomparable dignity and value of the human person. Human dignity does not depend, then, on what the human person does, makes, or accomplishes. Consequently, all human persons—poor or rich, young or old, healthy or sick—have the same equal dignity. No human person has more value than any other person. Notice how such an understanding challenges the thinking and practice so prevalent today.

The pope's personalism strongly opposes other forms of personalism, such as individualism, subjectivism, and pure humanistic personalism. He sees the human person in relationship with God, with all other human persons, with nature, and with self.

Relationship with God

The relationship with God is evident from all that has been said. One can properly understand the human person only in the light of the theological realities of creation, sin, Incarnation, redemption, and the future life of the reign of God. Recall the constant emphasis that Jesus Christ reveals the truth about the human person. Theology and anthropology are intimately related. *Dominum et vivificantem* summarizes the point very well, "*The Triune God* who 'exists' in himself as a transcendent reality of interpersonal gift, *giving himself in the Holy Spirit as gift to man, transforms the human world from within*, from inside hearts and minds. Along this path the world, made to share in the divine gift, becomes—as the Council teaches—'ever more human, ever more profoundly human'" (59.2).

God has made human beings with a thirst and a drive that will only be satisfied if human beings go beyond themselves and find their ultimate truth and happiness in the love of God. The human person alone among all of creation is capable of knowing and loving the Creator. Our human life is much more than mere existence in kind. We human beings have a drive toward the fullness of life. The Yahwist account of creation in Genesis speaks of a divine breath breathed into the human person so that the human being might live. This breath of God explains the perennial dissatisfaction that human beings always experience here on Earth. Made in the image of God, we humans are naturally drawn to God. Every human person, in heeding the deepest yearnings of the heart, makes one's own the words of St. Augustine: "You have made us for yourself, O Lord, and our hearts are restless until they rest in you" (*EV* 34.5–35.2).

For John Paul II, the transcendent aspect of the human person is the most important reality. "If one does not acknowledge transcendent truth, then the power of force takes over, and each person tends to make full use of the means at his disposal in order to impose his own interests or his own opinion, with no regard for the rights of others" (*CA* 44.2).

The most significant human values are found on the level of the spiritual and transcendent dimension of the human person. Without doubt, John Paul II gives priority to truth and transcendent truth, as is illustrated throughout his writings. Likewise, he gives great importance to love. John Paul II understands love primarily as "the sincere gift of self." This is actually a quotation from *Gaudium et spes* 24. The human person's "greatness, and therefore his vocation, consists in *the sincere gift of self*" (*EV* 25.4). For John Paul II, "the full meaning of freedom" is "the gift of self in *service to God and one's brethren*" (*VS* 87.2). Notice how such a concept of freedom differs from freedom understood simply as the choice to do X or Y. Freedom must always be seen in relation to the transcendent and spiritual realities of truth and love. This gift of self, a free act of love, is called for in daily life (*EV* 76.2, 86.2), in marriage (*CA* 39.1), in the family (*EV* 88.2, 92.4), and in religious life (*RH* 21.4). "Indeed, it is through the free gift of self that one truly finds oneself" (*CA* 41.3).

Morality for John Paul II, especially in *Sollicitudo rei socialis*, involves the authentic and integral development of the human person (31.5, 32.1). He chose the concept of development precisely because in *Sollicitudo* he was commemorating the twentieth anniversary of Pope Paul VI's *Populorum progressio*, which made development its basic theme. Development is often used in an economic sense, but John Paul II wants to use it in a moral sense. Moral development is based on the metaphysics of the person. In *Sollicitudo rei socialis* and elsewhere, John Paul II quotes both *Gaudium et spes* of Vatican II and *Populorum progressio* to insist on the difference between "having" and "being" (*SRS* 28.4; *LE* 26.6; *RM* 58.2; *CA* 36.4; *EV* 23.1, 98.1). Human beings are not static creatures. Genesis presents the human being as a creature, an image of God, subject to God's law with the task of developing in the light of these realities (30.2, 3). Moral development is based on "man's being and his true vocation" (28.7). The reality and vocation of the human person seen in one's totality includes the bodily but also the spiritual nature of the human person, the interior dimension that is "the *specific nature* of man who has been created by God in his image and likeness" (29.1–2). Development does not consist in the "dominion over and *indiscriminate* possession of created things . . . but rather in *subordinating* the possession, dominion and use . . . to the *transcendent reality* of the human being" (29.4).

From a narrow economic perspective, the problem in our world today is twofold—either underdevelopment or superdevelopment— too few or too many material goods. Superdevelopment involves the twofold problems of materialism and consumerism (*SRS* 28.1–2). John Paul II has frequently spoken out against the materialism and consumerism found in the richer countries of the globe. From the moral perspective, "The evil does not consist in 'having' as such, but in possessing without regard for the *quality* and the *ordered hierarchy* of the goods one has. *Quality and hierarchy* arise from the subordination of goods and their availability to man's 'being' and his true vocation" (*SRS* 28.7).

Relationship with Others

In addition to being in relationship with God, the human person is, from the very first moment, intimately related to others. *Redemptor hominis* describes the human person "in the full truth of his existence, of his personal being and also of his community and social being—in the sphere of his own family, in the sphere of society and very diverse contexts, in the sphere of his own nation or people . . . and in the sphere of the whole of mankind" (*RH* 14.1). Chapter 5 will discuss the human person's relationship with others in sexuality, marriage, and family. This section discusses the person's relationship with others in society in general.

A constant theme of Karol Wojtyla, the philosopher, was his insistence on the communitarian nature of the person. In a book of his older essays on this subject, which was published in English in 1993, he said, "The human being is not a person, on the one hand, and a member of society on the other. The human being as a person is simultaneously a member of society."[6]

This section focuses on an important concept based on communitarian personalism that John Paul II made central in Catholic social teaching: the virtue of solidarity. *Sollicitudo rei socialis* uses the word "solidarity" twenty-seven times and develops the concept, especially in paragraphs 38 to 40. The subsequent encyclicals, *Centesimus annus* and *Evangelium vitae*, also put heavy emphasis on solidarity.[7]

John Paul II refers to solidarity as a duty (*SRS* 9), a principle (*CA* 10.3), and a virtue (*SRS* 38, 40); but the heavy emphasis is on solidarity as a virtue. The pope develops solidarity primarily as a Christian virtue, but he also sees it as a fundamental call for all humanity (*SRS* 38–40). Solidarity is the virtue that responds to the growing awareness of greater interdependence among individuals and nations today. Solidarity, the virtue, is not just "vague compassion or shallow distress at the misfortunes of so many people," but rather "*a firm and persevering determination* to commit oneself to the *common good*; that is to say to the good of all and of each individual, because we are *all* really responsible for *all*" (*SRS* 38.6). Solidarity has implications for every national society and also for international society. Solidarity in a national society calls for recognition of the human dignity of all by opposing anything that makes a human person into a means, such as exploitation, oppression, or annihilation, and by a special concern for the poor and the weak (*SRS* 39.1). On the international level, solidarity recognizes that the goods of creation and what human industry produces must serve the needs of all human beings (*SRS* 39.3–7). For John Paul II, "solidarity . . . is the *path to peace and at the same time to development*" (*SRS* 39.8). The virtue of solidarity is based on and supportive of the pope's anthropology of personal communitarianism.

The person's social and communitarian nature serves as the basis for the social teaching of John Paul II that will be developed at greater length in a subsequent chapter. *Sollicitudo rei socialis* disagrees with both liberal capitalism and Marxist collectivism. "Each of the two ideologies, on the basis of two very different visions of man and of his freedom and social role, has proposed and still promotes, on the economic level, antithetical forms of the organization of labor and of the structure of ownership" (*SRS* 20.5). This anthropological understanding that sees capitalism and Marxist collectivism as opposite extremes is frequently found in Catholic social teaching. Marxist collectivism so stresses society that it fails to recognize the person, whereas liberal capitalism so stresses the individual person that it forgets about society and the person's relationship with others and with society. Communitarian personalism, thus, is a middle position between these two extremes.

John Paul II, from an anthropological perspective, also sees the two ideologies as closely related because they suffer from the same problem of materialism. In Marxism and dialectical materialism, "man is not first and foremost the subject of work and the efficient cause of the production process, but continues to be understood and treated in dependence on what is material, as a kind of 'resultant' of the economic or production relations prevailing at a given period" (*LE* 13.4). But the same problem of materialism was present in primitive capitalism in the eighteenth and nineteenth centuries and still exists today. The worker was treated simply as a means. Against the reduction of the worker to a cog in the manufacturing process stands "the definite *conviction of the primacy* of the person over things, and of human *labor over capital*" (*LE* 13.5).[8]

Relationship with Nature

In addition to the relationships of the human person with God and with other human beings, John Paul II also recognizes the relationship of the person with nature, the environment, and the realm of creation. The pope gives much less attention to this relationship of the person with nature and the environment than he does to the other two relationships. But this is to be expected, because the relationship with the environment and creation comes into play almost solely in the one area of ecology. The other two relationships have a much more profound effect on anthropology and relate to many other aspects of human existence.

His very first encyclical, *Redemptor hominis*, makes three very brief references to this relationship and the question of ecology in the context of the threats and problems that arise in our modern world. The pollution of the natural environment is a sign of the "world 'groaning in travail'" (8.1). One symptom of the moral disorder in our world today and of the abuse of freedom is the accelerating spoiling of "material and energy resources, and compromising the geophysical environment" (16.4). Human beings use their freedom and power, not as intelligent masters and guardians of the earth, but as heedless exploiters and destroyers of the earth (15.3).

But as is his wont, he also recognizes a positive aspect in our world. "Among today's *positive signs* we must also mention a greater realization of the limits of available resources, and of the need to respect the integrity and cycles of nature. . . . Today this is called *ecological concern*" (*SRS* 26.7).

But a deeper problem exists in the pope's approach. Environmentalists often see the philosophical emphasis on personalism as opposed to any environmental concern because of its emphasis on the dominion of the human person over the earth. Such an understanding of the person subordinates all nonhuman creation to human beings. All of nature and creation thus become simply a means for the human person and the human person's own good.[9] Thus it seems that John Paul II's personalism, by emphasizing the dominion of human beings over all of creation, is in theoretical opposition to the ecological concern he proposes.

But the pope wants to hold on to both his personalism and his ecological concerns. In fact, he maintains, "At the root of the senseless destruction of the material environment lies an anthropological error, which unfortunately is widespread in our day. . . . Man thinks he can make arbitrary use of the earth, subjecting it without restraint to his will, as though the earth did not have its own requisites and a prior God-given purpose, which man can indeed develop but must not betray" (*CA* 37.1). John Paul II here invokes two themes that constantly appear in his approach. The first, as already mentioned in chapter 1, is the understanding of freedom and its relationship with truth (*CA* 37.2). One has to have a proper understanding of human freedom. "The dominion granted to man by the Creator is not an absolute power, nor can one speak of a freedom to 'use and misuse' or to dispose of things as one pleases" (*SRS* 34.5). Thus freedom is always subject to the truth. The second point is the recognition that God has given to all beings their own nature and human beings must "take into account *the nature of each being* and of its *mutual connection* in an ordered system, which is precisely the 'cosmos'" (*SRS* 34.2).

Does the pope succeed in holding onto both his personalism and his ecological concern? To a degree, yes. But many environmentalists would still want to see less emphasis on the dominion of human beings and more on the intrinsic good of creation that has a value in itself apart from its relationship with human beings.

Relationship with Self

The human person must also be true to self. The "truth about man" is the fundamental cornerstone of all morality for John Paul II. God created the human being in God's own image and likeness and breathes into the human being a divine breath. "*The ability to attain truth and freedom are human prerogatives* inasmuch as man is created in the image of his Creator. . . . The life which God bestows upon man . . . is a drive toward the fullness of life; *it is the seed of an existence which transcends the very limits of time.* . . . (*EV* 34.5). "Because he is made by God and bears within himself an indelible imprint of God, man is naturally drawn to God" (35.2). The encyclical then goes on to quote the famous words of Augustine from the *Confessions*: "You have made us for yourself, O Lord, and our hearts are restless until they rest in you" (35.2).

John Paul II also cites this passage from Augustine in his first encyclical, *Redemptor hominis*. "In this creative restlessness beats and pulsates what is most deeply human—the search for truth, the insatiable need for the good, hunger for freedom, nostalgia for the beautiful, and the voice of conscience" (18.3). The human being must be true to oneself, but his true fulfillment only comes about as the gift of God's love in Christ Jesus. Christ reveals to us the truth about the human being. Life in Christ "is the final fulfillment of man's vocation. It is in a way the fulfillment of the 'destiny' that God has prepared for him from eternity" (*RH* 18.2).

Pope Wojtyla's emphasis on development also shows the important anthropological relationship to the self. True development is based on "the specific nature of man. . . . It is a bodily and a spiritual nature" (*SRS* 29.2). *Sollicitudo rei socialis* agrees with Pope Paul VI's emphasis on the importance of "being" over "having." "To 'have' objects and goods does not in itself perfect the human subject, unless it contributes to the maturing and enrichment of that subject's 'being,' that is to say unless it contributes to the realization of the human vocation as such" (28.4). The evil does not consist in having goods, "but in possessing without regard for the *quality* and the *ordered hierarchy* of the goods one has. *Quality and hierarchy* arise from the subordination of goods and their availability to man's 'being' and his true vocation" (28.7). John Paul II, in keeping with the Catholic tradition, thus recognizes a proper role for self-love and self-fulfillment.

A subsequent section of this chapter will discuss and disagree somewhat with John Paul II's use of natural law. But the use of natural law shows again the anthropological importance of the relationship with self and its fundamental role in morality.

Thus the incomparable dignity and worth of the person forms the basis for the moral teaching of John Paul II. The person, however, is not an isolated individual but exists in and through relationships with God, with all other persons, with all of creation, and with self.

Ethical Model

Moral theologians often speak of the theory or model used for understanding the moral life. As second-order discourse, moral theology analyzes the way in which people understand the moral life. Two classic approaches are called the teleological and the deontological. The deontological model sees the moral life in terms of duties, laws, and obligations. The teleological model sees the moral life in terms of goals and ends. Something is good if it brings me to my good goal. A third model, which I call a relationality–responsibility model, sees the moral life in terms of our multiple relationships with God, neighbor, world, and self and our responsibility in the midst of these relationships. Many other authors speak of these different approaches as normative ethical theories determining the ultimate source of moral obligation. I prefer the broader term "model." In my judgment, the relationality–responsibility model best corresponds to the Christian theological and philosophical anthropology of the human person.[10]

Catholic moral theology has been somewhat schizophrenic about its choice of model. Without doubt, the manuals of moral theology that were in vogue from the seventeenth century until the Second Vatican Council followed a legal model with law as the objective norm of morality. The popular catechetical approach used the Ten Commandments as the basis for moral teaching and thus was deontological in its approach. However, the theory of Thomas Aquinas (d. 1274), the most significant figure in the Catholic theological tradition, was not deontological but teleological.[11] Aquinas is a teleologist. He starts his discussion on the moral life with the ultimate end of human beings. Human acts are thus to be based on their relationship with the ultimate end.[12] Yes, Aquinas uses natural law, but he discusses it only in question 94 of his *Prima secundae*, in which he developed his moral theory. Even his understanding of natural law, despite the term "law," is teleological. Natural law for Aquinas is human reason directing us to our end in accord with our nature. However, Aquinas's teleology is an intrinsic teleology, as specifically differentiated from an extrinsic teleology, such as utilitarianism or strict consequentialism, that determines morality solely on the basis of the consequences of the act. Aquinas does not reduce morality only to consequences. Acts contributing to the end must be in accord with our nature, which has its own built-in finalities that must be observed, such as the finality of rational beings to live together in communities.[13]

Official Catholic, papal, and hierarchical teaching before John Paul II was also somewhat schizophrenic about the models of the moral life. Without doubt, the deontological or legal model is used in questions of personal and sexual morality. But Catholic social teaching does not follow a legal model with any consistency, even though at times a legal mode is used. John Paul II continues in this line of papal and hierarchical teaching. In personal morality, he strongly follows a legal model based on natural law, as illustrated in the encyclical *Veritatis splendor*, which will be discussed below in greater detail.

John Paul II's emphasis on the legal model in *Veritatis splendor* comes from two sources. From a practical perspective, he has insisted on the existence of negative moral precepts condemning certain acts as always and everywhere wrong (*VS* 13.3, 52, 67.2, 90.2, 99.1). From a more theoretical perspective, he sees the major problem today as coming from a concept of freedom that allows the person to do whatever one wants. In many ways, I agree with his analysis here. Morality for many people today means that I must be free to do my thing and you must be free to do your thing. To counteract this notion of freedom, John Paul II insists on the centrality of truth and of law. Genuine freedom recognizes *"the dependence of freedom on truth"* (*VS* 34.2). The emphasis on the obligation to the truth supports a deontological model. In a similar way, John Paul II strongly opposes a notion that sees freedom and law in conflict. The autonomy and freedom of the human person cannot mean that freedom and reason create values and moral norms. Genuine human moral autonomy involves the acceptance of the moral law and of God's command. By submitting to the law, freedom submits to the truth (*VS* 40).

However, as a Thomist, John Paul II, even in personal moral questions, sometimes employs a teleological model. For example, he insists, " The rational ordering of the human act to the good in its truth and the voluntary pursuit of that good, known by reason, constitute morality" (*VS* 72.2). "The moral life has an essential *'teleological' character*, since it consists in the deliberate ordering of human acts to God, the supreme good and ultimate end (*telos*) of man" (73.2). But he still puts the heaviest emphasis on the legal model. "The *morality of acts* is defined by the relationship of man's freedom with the authentic good. This good is established, as the eternal law, by divine wisdom which orders every being toward its end: this eternal law is known both by man's natural reason (hence it is 'natural law'), and—in an integral and perfect way—by God's supernatural revelation (hence it is called divine law)" (72.1). The story of the rich young man illustrates the same reality. The basic question is teleological—"What good must I do to have eternal life?" "Jesus, in his reply, confirms the young man's conviction: the performance of good acts, commanded by the One who 'alone is good,' constitutes the indispensable condition of and path to eternal blessedness" (72.1). John Paul II recognizes the teleological model but insists that acts toward the end are determined by the eternal, divine, and natural laws.

Veritatis splendor recognizes the universal call of all Christians to holiness (16–18). The call–response theme is characteristic of a relationality–responsibility model. The disciple must "be a follower of Christ . . . holding fast to the very person of Jesus" (19.3). John Paul II, however, tries to see this call to perfection and holiness in the light of a legal model. The call to holiness is based on the command to love one another as God has loved us and involves a free and loving obedience to the will of the Father (20.1, 19.3).

The three social encyclicals appeal to all three models. There are indications of a legal model as the most basic in his social encyclicals. John Paul II sees the central element in Catholic social teaching as principles of reflection, criteria of judgment, and directives for action that are then applied in changing historical and cultural circumstances (*SRS* 3.2). A teleological model comes through in the emphases on authentic and integral human development. Likewise, his insistence, in keeping with the Catholic tradition, on the common good as the end or purpose of society invokes the more traditional Thomistic teleological model.

But there seem to be strong indications of a relationality–responsibility model as primary. This chapter has already shown that John Paul II's anthropology in general is best understood in relational terms. The emphasis on interdependence throughout the social encyclicals and the frequent mention of our relationship with God, neighbor, self, and the world of nature (e.g., *SRS* 38.3) involve not only anthropology but the basic understanding of morality in the social encyclicals. These encyclicals stress the creative role of human beings in working for a more just human society and the need for all to participate in political and economic life. The dominion that human brings have over creation emphasizes human responsibility.

Without doubt, the greater complexity in social ethics makes it harder to use a strict legal model because so much of the reality involved cannot be encompassed by laws and norms. It is easier to use a legal model in personal ethics, for there is much less complexity here and the matter itself is more focused. Note that the Ten Commandments deal primarily with personal morality or one-to-one relationships but not with the complex issues facing society as a whole.

In my judgment, the relationality–responsibility model should be used for all moral theology, both personal and social. This does not mean there is no place for legal considerations and even absolute laws and norms, but the relationality–responsibility model should be primary. Thus, even in social morality, there is an important place for human rights that are absolute and universal. The need and significance of some laws and norms in personal morality are illustrated by the continuing significance and role of the Ten Commandments. The legal model cannot, however, be primary even in personal morality because it cannot deal adequately with the concrete realities of each individual called in a unique way to respond to the gift of God and the needs of others in our complex world. No legal model helps a person decide whom to marry and how to respond to the sufferings and injustices of human existence. Creativity, not conformity to a prearranged plan, should characterize the life of the individual Christian striving to be a faithful disciple of Jesus.

In conclusion, John Paul II uses different models in different contexts. The legal model comes to the fore in issues of personal and sexual morality, but the relationality–responsibility model predominates in the social encyclicals despite strong emphasis on principles and directives. John Paul II thus continues the tension in contemporary Catholic hierarchical teaching between the approaches to personal and social ethics.

From the General to the Particular

Without doubt, John Paul II's ethical method moves from the general to the specific, from the universal to the particular. His approach tends to be deductive. The deductive begins with a general truth or principle and then deduces conclusions from that truth based on logical analysis. The syllogism, so frequently used in the Catholic tradition, well illustrates such an approach. It begins with the principle or truth that all human beings are mortal. But Mary is a human being; therefore, Mary is mortal. The inductive method begins with the particular, the individual, and the concrete and works toward the general and the universal. The manuals of Catholic moral theology before Vatican II embraced a deductive methodology.

Clearly related to the deductive/inductive difference is the difference between classicism and historical consciousness. Classicism tends to see reality in terms of the static, the immutable, the eternal, and the unchanging. Historical consciousness gives a greater recognition to historicity, change, the particular, and the diverse. In the Catholic tradition, historical consciousness tries to hold onto both continuity and discontinuity, and it does not deny the possibility of general statements of universal validity and some general norms. Historical consciousness in this understanding differs from both sheer existentialism and many forms of postmodernism. Sheer existentialism sees only discontinuity and no continuity in human history. More significant today is postmodernism, which so emphasizes the individual, the particular, and the diverse that it sees no possibility of coming to the general and the universal.

Historical consciousness also affects the subject—the person who knows and decides. We all bring with ourselves the experience that has shaped our persons. People look through different lenses as they seek truth and try to do good. In addition, our own finitude and sinfulness color our knowing and acting. Classicism tends to assume the existence of a universal human reason that all have. This perspective does not stress experience, finitude, and sin as affecting how we know and act.

Without doubt, John Paul II's papal encyclicals, both those dealing with personal morality and those dealing with social morality, tend toward the deductive and classicist approaches. Here, I give two illustrations of how the social encyclicals move from the general to the specific in a somewhat deductive and classicist way.

First, the method of *Laborem exercens*. This encyclical is a moving and appealing meditation on work and its meaning for all humankind throughout the world today. In describing the reality of work, John Paul II employs his own phenomenological analysis to come to an understanding of work that is *"the essential key* to the whole social question" (3.2). His understanding of work also comes from the "Christian basis of truth that can be called ageless" (3.1). He proposes an understanding of work directed to all different kinds of workers. "Each and every individual, to the proper extent and in an incalculable number of ways, takes part in this great process whereby man 'subdues the earth' through his work" (4.4). John Paul II's personalism comes through in his emphasis on the subjective aspect of work. This approach thus begins with the general understanding of work but applies it in developing some very significant particular aspects that have an important effect on concrete reality, such as the primacy of labor over capital, and even the need for structural changes, such as the indirect employer (17–18).

The second illustration of this approach beginning with the general and involving a more deductive and classicist approach comes from John Paul II's very conscious attempt to refute Marie-Dominique Chenu's interpretation of Catholic social teaching. According to Chenu, *Octogesima adveniens* employed a newer approach based on an inductive methodology rather than the deductive method of the older documents of Catholic social teaching.[14]

Chapter 2 covered this reaction of John Paul II in great detail. Recall that the pope explicitly denied that Catholic social teaching is an ideology and stressed that Catholic social teaching involves "principles for reflection, criteria for judgment, and directives for action," which are then applied to changing historical issues and circumstances. Such a method thus goes from the general principle to the particular conclusion.

John Paul II's ethical method of going from the general to the particular is not surprising. His two philosophical roots in Thomism and phenomenology tend to move in this direction. In addition, he is writing as the bishop of Rome to all Catholics and even to all people of goodwill.

It is possible, however, to write for a general and even universal audience by building from the particular to the general and the universal. Papal teaching on social justice could—and, in my judgment, should—be developed by also going from the particular to the general. John Paul II never cites the many documents that have come from local and regional Catholic churches throughout the world. Papal social teaching could and should learn from what the local churches are saying and doing. Likewise, the process of writing such papal documents could and should involve broad consultation with local churches. As it is now, these documents are drafted by a small, unknown group around the pope and then proposed as authoritative teaching for all. A much better process would call for a draft to be sent to all local churches for discussion and input. Only then would a final official document be issued. Such an approach is also in keeping with a Catholic ecclesiology, which recognizes the role of local churches and the collegiality of all bishops together with the pope in their solicitude for the universal church. But John Paul II's papacy has stressed instead the centralization of the church in Rome and downplayed the role of local churches and the collegiality of all bishops.[15] Thus, John Paul II's philosophical background and his understanding of the church influence his ethical methodology in moving from the general to the specific.

Natural Law

The best illustration of John Paul II's use of a more deductive and classicist ethical method is found in *Veritatis splendor*'s use of natural law to defend hierarchical teaching on intrinsically evil acts and the existence of negative absolute norms, especially in the area of sexuality. *Veritatis splendor* differs from all the other encyclicals in terms of those to whom it is addressed and the way in which the pope develops the topic. It is addressed only to "all the bishops of the Catholic Church." The encyclical has "the aim of treating 'more fully and more deeply the issues regarding the very foundations of moral theology,' foundations that are being undermined by certain present day tendencies" (5.1). We are *"facing what is certainly a genuine crisis"* (5.2). Here John Paul II deals in depth, from a theological perspective, with questions of moral theology that would not be that well known or understood by the ordinary person or even the ordinary

Catholic. In this setting, and with the express intention of defending the Catholic teaching and method against even some Catholic theologians who are calling for changes, the pope develops in some depth the theory of natural law.

Veritatis splendor discusses natural law at length in the context of the broader relationship between law and freedom (35–53). The law–freedom relationship is closely related to the truth–freedom relationship that is so central in John Paul II's approach. Freedom must always conform itself to the truth. Truth is the primary concern and the ultimate reality for religious and moral life. The pope begins his discussion of freedom and law by arguing on the basis of God's command in Genesis not to eat of the fruit of the tree "that *the power to decide what is good and what is evil does not belong to man but to God alone*" (35.2). There can be no conflict between freedom and God's law, because humans do not determine what is morally good and evil. Many today wrongly see a conflict between law and freedom and even assert the absolute sovereignty of the human person. But human reason does not make something right or wrong, for judgments of right or wrong depend ultimately on divine wisdom. The human person is not morally autonomous. Yes, the human person is called to share in God's dominion over the world and in a certain sense over oneself. Thus, there is a true sense in which one can speak of a genuine moral autonomy for human beings, but this does not mean that the human person is ever free to disobey God's law or ever free to determine on one's own what is good or evil (38).

Veritatis splendor thus wants to hold onto both "man's self-determination" (41.1) and the fact that God determines what is good and evil. How is this possible? The encyclical rejects both autonomy (the human person determines what is good and evil) and heteronomy (the human person is ruled by some outside force that does not accept human self-determination). The encyclical, in line with the Catholic tradition, proposes "*theonomy* or *participated theonomy*, since man's free obedience to God's law effectively implies that human reason and human will participate in God's wisdom and providence" (41.2). The key word here is "participated" theonomy. Proper human self-determination participates in the wisdom and the providence of God. But how is this done? Natural law is the answer.

John Paul II's Understanding of Natural Law

Throughout this section of *Veritatis splendor*, the pope refers to natural law and develops his understanding on the basis of the teaching of Thomas Aquinas, according to which "participation of the eternal law in the rational creature is called natural law" (43.2). *Veritatis splendor* also cites Vatican II to the same effect—the "supreme rule of life is the divine law itself, the eternal, objective and universal law by which God out of his wisdom and love arranges, directs, and governs the whole world and the paths of the human community" (43.1). God has enabled human beings through human wisdom and reason to share in this law. The eternal law is the plan of God for the world. God gave us our human reason, which, reflecting on human nature and what God has made, can tell us how God wants us to act. God's law proposes what is for our own fulfillment and ultimate happiness. Consequently, there is no conflict between law and freedom and no conflict between God's wisdom and will and our true wisdom and will (43.2).

Veritatis splendor then goes on to claim that there is no conflict between nature and freedom and develops the pope's understanding of nature and the human body in questions of natural law (47–50). The occasion for the pope's discussion is the charge of physicalism, naturalism, or biologism that Catholic revisionist moral theologians have made against the natural law approach used by the hierarchical magisterium to defend its teaching, especially in the area of sexuality (47). Physicalism maintains that the hierarchical teaching, as illustrated in the case of artificial contraception, has identified the human moral act with the physical or the biological structure of the act. It is morally wrong to interfere with the physical act of sexual intercourse for married people. Revisionist Catholic moral theologians hold that for the good of the person or the good of the marital relationship, one can interfere with the physical structure of the sexual act in order to prevent procreation. "Faced with this theory, one has to consider carefully the correct relationship existing between freedom and human nature, and in particular *the place of the human body in questions of natural law*" (48.1). *Veritatis splendor* strongly insists on the basic compatibility between nature and freedom (46). With regard to the human body, the pope categorically rejects seeing the body simply as raw material to be shaped by freedom according to its own design. Physicalism contradicts "the truth about man and his freedom . . . [and] the *Church's teachings on the unity of the human person*, whose rational soul is *per se et essentialiter* the form of his body" (48.3). "*Body and soul are inseparable*: in the person, in the willing agent, and in the deliberate act, *they stand or fall together*" (49).

Pope John Paul II follows Thomistic natural law by insisting on the teleological understanding that human reason discovers the basic God-given inclinations of human nature to specific ends. The pope never explicitly develops the Thomistic concept of human nature with its threefold inclinations of what are common to all living things, to animals, and those that are proper to rational beings, but this section of the encyclical refers three times to inclinations in general.[16] According to the pope, these natural inclinations determine the moral assessment of individual acts. They are not merely physical or premoral goods (47, 48.2). In this context, *Veritatis splendor* at times seems to follow the new natural law theory of Germain Grisez, who maintains there are certain fundamental human goods that one can never directly go against (48.3, 79.2).[17]

"The true meaning of the natural law . . . refers to man's proper and primordial nature, the 'nature of the human person,' which is *the person himself in the unity of soul and body*, in the unity of his spiritual and biological inclinations. . . . Therefore this law cannot be thought of as simply a set of norms on the biological level; rather it must be defined as the rational order whereby man is called by the Creator to direct and regulate his life and actions and in particular to make use of his own body" (50.1).

Criticism of John Paul II's Approach to Natural Law

What about John Paul II's understanding of natural law? In my judgment, there are seven problems with his approach. The first is the concept of natural law as the participation of eternal law in the rational creature. Without doubt, this has been a characteristic and very important aspect of Catholic moral teaching, and I basically agree with it. But there is a danger here: that the characteristics of eternal law can be too readily and easily transferred to what one believes is natural law. In other words, the danger is that human reason can be seen as too readily and easily coming to the certitude of eternal law. The Catholic tradition itself has acknowledged the limitations of human reason in terms of both finitude and sinfulness. In his own way, John Paul II recognizes some limitations of human reason. He insists on the need for "divine revelation as an effective means for knowing moral truths, even those of the natural order" (36.3). For the same reason, he recognizes the need of the church and the magisterium as "authentically interpreting God's law in the light of the Gospel" (45.1). The pope does not go into the difficult issue of the nature of the assistance given to the church and the hierarchical magisterium to know the natural law. John Paul II thus recognizes some difficulty in human reason arriving at the demands of the eternal law. What one thinks is natural law might not truly be natural law that participates in the certitude and truth of eternal law.

A second problem concerns the meaning of "natural" and of "human nature." In the philosophical understanding of natural law theory, "nature" refers to the principle of operation in every living thing that directs its operations and actions. The nature of a dog determines how the dog looks and acts and the noises it makes. Dogs bark and do not meow like cats. The human being has a rational nature. *Veritatis splendor* uses the term "rational nature" in this sense—"the natural law . . . is inscribed in the rational nature of the person" (51.2).

But when discussing the "alleged conflict" between freedom and nature, *Veritatis splendor* uses "nature" in a different sense to refer to the laws of the material world (46.1). *Veritatis splendor* also refers to the "material and biological nature" of the human being (46.2). But human nature is not necessarily the same as the "material and biological nature" of the human being.

As mentioned above, *Veritatis splendor* often speaks of the inclinations in the human being, thus indicating an acceptance of the Thomistic understanding of human nature as involving the inclinations that we share with all living things, with animals, and those that are proper to us as rational human beings.[18] But notice that this involves a three-layered anthropology, with a bottom layer of what we share with all living things, a second layer of animality added on top of that, and a third layer of rationality on the top. In my judgment, this creates a problem for the Thomistic and papal anthropology. At times the rational can and should interfere with the level we share with all living things and with animals. This aspect will be developed more in subsequent considerations and is the ultimate reason why I judge the papal teaching to be guilty of physicalism—the identification of the physical or the biological act (e.g., the act of sexual intercourse) with the moral. Human reason, in accord with the papal teaching, can never interfere with the physical act of marital sexual intercourse.

A third and related problem concerns the teaching of *Veritatis splendor* on *"the place of the human body in questions of natural law"* (48.1). The pope opposes seeing the body as simply raw material that human freedom can shape in any way it pleases. He insists on the "unity of soul and body" and "the unity of his spiritual and biological inclinations" (50.1).

But Catholic papal teaching in the past has not made bodily integrity an absolute. Catholic hierarchical moral teaching recognizes that the body and the material are subordinated to the spiritual or higher dimensions in human existence. This is very much in keeping with the traditional Catholic hierarchical understanding of different levels of human existence. Pope Pius XII explained the reason for the traditional Catholic position that one has to use only ordinary and not extraordinary means to keep the person alive. "A more strict obligation would be too burdensome for most men and would render the attainment of the higher, more important good too difficult. Life, health, all temporal activities are in fact subordinated to spiritual ends."[19]

Pius XII also recognized the subordination of the body to spiritual and personal ends in his discussion of the principle of totality. He discussed the principle of totality in 1952. "Because he is a user and not a proprietor of his body, he does not have unlimited power to destroy or mutilate his body and its functions. Nevertheless, by virtue of the principle of totality, by virtue of his right to use the services of his organism as a whole, the patient can allow individual parts to be destroyed or mutilated when and to the extent necessary for the good of his being as a whole."[20] Pius XII here seems to limit totality to the good of the body as such, but in 1958 he went further: "But there must be added to the subordination of the individual organs to the organism and its end, the subordination of the organism itself to the spiritual end of the person."[21] Thus the body can be interfered with for higher ends. A rather prosaic example is the justification of cosmetic surgery. John Paul II has adopted too limited an understanding of the person's moral right to interfere with bodily functions.

PHYSICALISM

Fourth, the consideration of nature and the body sets the stage for a deeper discussion of the problem of physicalism as found in papal teaching, especially in the area of sexuality. The natural (understood to include inclinations that the human being shares with all living things and with animals) and the bodily are not absolutes that cannot be interfered with for the good of the person or for the good of the relationships in which the person is involved. Papal teaching insists that the sexual act of married couples must always be open to procreation and expressive of love union. One cannot interfere with the sexual act either to prevent procreation or even to encourage it. Thus the Catholic position condemns both artificial contraception and artificial insemination, even with the husband's semen. The "natural sexual act" must always be present. The basic teaching is found in the 1968 encyclical *Humanae vitae* of Pope Paul VI:

> In the task of transmitting life, therefore, they are not free to proceed completely at will, as if they could determine in a wholly autonomous way the honest path to follow; but they must conform their activity to the creative intention of God, expressed in the very nature of marriage and of its acts, and manifested by the constant teaching of the Church. . . . That teaching, often set forth by the Magisterium, is founded upon the inseparable connection willed by God and unable

to be broken by man on his own initiative, between the two meanings of the conjugal act: the unitive meaning and the procreative meaning. Indeed by its intimate structure, the conjugal act, while most closely uniting husband and wife, capacitates them for the generation of new lives, according to laws inscribed in the very being of man and the woman. By safeguarding both these essential aspects, the unitive and the procreative, the conjugal act preserves in its fullness the sense of true mutual love and its ordination toward man's most high calling to parenthood.[22]

The 1987 "Instruction on Respect for Human Life in Its Origins and on the Dignity of Procreation" of the Congregation for the Doctrine of the Faith insists that the nature of the conjugal act serves as the basis for the condemnation of both artificial contraception and of artificial insemination even with the husband's seed. "Contraception deliberately deprives the conjugal act of its openness to procreation and in this way brings about a voluntary dissociation of the ends of marriage. Homologous artificial fertilization, in seeking a procreation which is not the fruit of a specific act of conjugal union, objectively affects an analogous separation between the goods and the meanings of marriage."[23]

From my perspective, the faculty of human sexuality and human sexual acts must be seen in relation to the person and the person's marital relationship. For the good of the person or the relationship, one can interfere with the sexual faculty and its act. The physical conjugal act cannot and should not become a moral absolute. The encyclical *Humanae vitae* itself recognizes that it identifies the biological processes with moral norms. "In relation to the biological processes, responsible parenthood means the knowledge and respect of their functions; human intellect discovers, in the power of giving life, biological laws that are part of the human person" (10).

With his emphasis on personalism and some subjectivity, one might expect Pope Wojtyla to come to the same position, but he clearly does not. His metaphysics and anthropology still insist on the natural law approach that undergirded the Catholic Church's teachings in the area of human sexuality in the last century. This is part of his understanding of the truth about the human person. But it is true that he has proposed "personalistic reasons" to support the traditional teaching of the condemnation of artificial contraception for married couples. Artificial contraception goes against the reciprocal self-giving of husband and wife. It is a language that contradicts the total gift of self to the other, which is the ultimate meaning of marriage.[24] Thus while strongly defending the existing papal teaching on marriage and sexuality, John Paul II has developed more personalist arguments in trying to defend them. In chapter 5, I will discuss John Paul II's teaching on sexuality in depth.

In light of the ultimate criterion of the person and the person's relationships and in light of the subordination of the bodily and the material to spiritual ends, the charge of physicalism against some aspects of papal teaching makes sense. John Paul II's description of physicalism amounts to a caricature. Physicalism does not end up "treating the human body as a raw datum, devoid of any meaning and moral values until freedom has shaped it in accordance with its design" (*VS* 48.2). Nor does physicalism contradict the teachings of the church on the unity of the moral person. As was pointed out above, it is John Paul II who fails to recognize what Pius XII pointed out—that the bodily aspect of human existence is subordinate to personal and spiritual ends.

The problem of physicalism in my judgment is present in a number of areas in addition to questions of sexuality and marriage, for example, the concept of direct and indirect effect. But that discussion goes beyond the limits of this chapter.

FURTHER PROBLEMS

A fifth problem in the natural law theory proposed in *Veritatis splendor* is the failure to give enough importance to history and to recognize a more historically conscious approach. According to *Veritatis splendor*, we find moral truth about the human being written in human nature. The inclinations of nature are morally determinative. Moral truth is thus given in human nature and not in history. And because human nature remains basically the same, there is no real change or development. Moral reasoning begins with the first principles of natural law—good is to be done and evil is to be avoided

(59.2). The methodology is thus from the general to the specific and does not give that much attention to the signs of the times and the historical developments and diversity existing at the present time. *Veritatis splendor* explicitly acknowledges some development over time but not very much. "This truth of the moral law—like that of the 'deposit of faith'—unfolds down the centuries: the norms expressing the truth remain valid in their substance, but must be specified and determined '*eodem sensu eademque sententia*' in the light of historical circumstances by the Church's Magisterium" (53.3). In chapter 5, I will point out that not only *Veritatis splendor* and the social encyclicals but also the papal teaching on marriage and sexuality follow the same classicist methodology and fail to give enough importance to historical development.

The sixth problem with John Paul II's understanding of natural law is its failure to recognize that human reason is historically and culturally conditioned and limited. In addition, human sinfulness can and does affect human reason. We are all conscious that the strong and the powerful have used their human reason to justify and promote their own narrow interests.

Liberationist and feminist approaches in contemporary moral theology have pointed out the dangers and problems involved in what is purported to be universal reason but is really only the narrow perspective of the particular person or class. Such approaches are suspicious that what is proposed as universal human reason is often merely the projection of the powerful to protect their own interests. Thus, today many Catholic theologians begin not with the universal reason of all human beings but with the experience of the poor, the marginalized, and those on the fringe. But these Catholic theologians still recognize some universality and common ground.[25]

In the broader philosophical and theological discussions today, deconstructionists and particularists deny the possibility of any common morality and shared human values in light of the diversity existing in our world. Contemporary Catholic thinkers coming out of a tradition that has emphasized a more universal perspective on ethics tend to insist on the possibility of arriving at some common approaches to human values and human flourishing across cultural, linguistic, ethnic, gender, social, and economic boundaries. But such contemporary Catholic approaches, in the words of Lisa Sowle Cahill, call for "a much more pluralistic and decentralized philosophical, theological, and ecclesial situation."[26]

Contemporary debates about epistemology and universality lie beyond the scope of this book. But, at the very minimum, John Paul II's understanding of natural law fails to recognize how social location and even human sinfulness affect human reason, human knowing, and human acting.

Pope Wojtyla's eschatology logically recognizes the limitations of human reason and the fact that sin can also affect reason and human decision making. By emphasizing the goodness of creation and the fact that human sinfulness does not totally destroy creation or the goodness of human reason, the pope sets out the theological justification for accepting natural law—human reason reflecting on human nature and creation can arrive at some moral wisdom and knowledge. But creation means that we are all finite and limited and so is our reason finite and limited. None of us is ever able to see the total picture—we only have a partial and limited perspective. How often have all of us had the experience of looking back later and lamenting, if only we had known then what we know now, we would have acted differently. Likewise, human sinfulness can and does affect all of us in our decision making. With the pope, I agree that there could possibly be on occasion a just and legitimate use of military force. But the problem is that every nation that has gone to war has always claimed that it was justified in doing so.

John Paul II explicitly recognizes the limitations of reason and the possible effect of human sinfulness on human reason and decision making. For that reason, he insists on the need of revelation as an effective means for knowing moral truths of the natural order (*VS* 36.3) and also the need for the teaching role of the church and the magisterium (*VS* 45.1). Yes, Catholic theology does recognize the special assistance of the Holy Spirit given to the hierarchical magisterium in its teaching role. The pope does not develop in any detail the nature of this assistance; nor is it necessary to do so here. No matter what the nature of this assistance of the Holy Spirit is, the reality remains—as was pointed out in chapter 1 and will be developed in a different way in chapter 5—that papal teaching in the

Catholic Church on specific moral issues has changed so that the church now accepts what was once condemned (usury, religious freedom, human rights, democracy) and condemns what was once accepted (slavery, persecution of heretics, the patriarchal family). Thus, at some time in its formulation, papal teaching has been wrong. Thus, history bears out that even the papal teaching office itself has experienced the limitations of reason and even to some extent the sinfulness that affect all human reason and human decision making.

The seventh problem comes from the relationship between faith and philosophy, which John Paul II discusses at great length in *Fides et ratio*, where he insists that "the Church has no philosophy of its own nor does she canonize one particular philosophy in preference to others" (49.1). But *Veritatis splendor* definitely seems to be canonizing and making its own the philosophical theory of natural law proposed by Thomas Aquinas.

From my perspective, faith and the church will have to use some philosophical ideas and approaches in developing moral teaching with regard to the understanding of anthropology and in dealing with specific moral issues. But one cannot claim absolute certitude for these approaches and understandings that by their very nature are quite removed from the core of faith. Anthropology by definition is a very complex reality, even though anthropological understandings are necessary for dealing with many specific moral issues. The natural law theory developed by John Paul II in *Veritatis splendor* insists on a specific understanding of the ethical meaning of God-given human inclinations. But moral judgments about the nature and role of these inclinations by their very nature cannot claim absolute certitude. Likewise, on the level of the solution of complex conflict situations by the principle of double effect, one cannot claim to exclude all possibility of error. In my opinion, *Veritatis splendor* claims too great a certitude for its understanding of the specifics of natural law theory. But it is necessary to point out that there are comparatively few issues that involve the role of God-given human inclinations and conflict situations solved by the principle of double effect.

A final comment on John Paul II's discussion of natural law concerns how few references there are to natural law outside the encyclical *Veritatis splendor*. One might try to explain this by pointing out that *Veritatis splendor* concentrates on the theoretical aspects of moral theology, whereas the other encyclicals do not concern themselves primarily with moral theory but just with moral teaching. This might be a partial explanation, but still the fact of very few references to natural law in the other encyclicals is quite surprising especially in the light of the heavy emphasis on natural law in *Veritatis splendor*.

Take the social encyclicals. As late as 1963, Pope John XXIII based his whole teaching in *Pacem in terris* on natural law. The laws governing the relationship between people and states are found "where the Father of all things wrote them, that is in the nature of man."[27] From a theological perspective, natural law claimed to be based only on human reason and thus was convincing to all people regardless of their religion. The one reference to natural law in *Redemptor hominis* refers to it as the purely human position based on human reason and experience and as not involving faith (*RH* 17.8). Before Vatican II, Catholic social teaching insisted on its natural law basis. But post–Vatican II theology objected to the sharp distinction between the supernatural and the natural. Faith and grace should affect all aspects of life. Perhaps this explains why the three social encyclicals never use the term "natural law," despite the heavy insistence on natural law in *Veritatis splendor*. Yet Catholic hierarchical teaching after Vatican II did not abandon natural law but instead tried to integrate it into a total Christian perspective.

The encyclical *Fides et ratio* was written after *Veritatis splendor*. Because it deals with the relationship between faith and reason, one would expect some discussion of natural law—especially in light of the great importance that *Veritatis splendor* gave to natural law. But *Fides et ratio* never mentions natural law. Granted that *Veritatis splendor* is unique in its emphasis on theory and granted that the individual encyclicals address particular problems in a given context; it is still very strange that many of the papal encyclicals never mention natural law, even in those areas where one would expect to find some mention of it.

Perhaps John Paul II himself has some ambivalence about natural law. His own work in ethics before becoming the bishop of Rome employed a personalistic approach. He did not invoke natural law all that much, although he strongly supported the conclusions arrived at by the reigning neoscholastic natural law theory and found in existing church teachings.[28] There still, however, remains the inconsistency within the body of encyclicals with the heavy emphasis on natural law in *Veritatis splendor* and the failure to develop or even at times mention natural law in the other encyclicals dealing with moral theology.

This chapter has analyzed and criticized the anthropological foundations and ethical method of John Paul II. The incomparable, unique, and equal dignity of all human beings is a most significant contribution made by John Paul II that has important ramifications in all areas of moral theology. His relational understanding of the human person is most helpful in recognizing the various dimensions of anthropology. The ambivalence about which model is primary is somewhat understandable in the light of the occasional nature of the encyclicals, but he gives too great a role to the legal model. I am more negative in my evaluation of his method of going from the general to the specific, and especially his understanding and development of natural law based on an anthropology that gives absolute moral value to God-given inclinations of human nature.

Notes

1. Karol Wojtyla, *The Acting Person*, tr. Andrzej Potocki (Boston: D. Reidel, 1979).

2. Among the many books in English on the subject, see Rocco Buttiglione, *Karol Wojtyla: The Thought of the Man Who Became Pope John Paul II* (Grand Rapids, Mich.: William B. Eerdmans, 1997); Kenneth L. Schmitz, *At the Center of the Human Drama: The Philosophical Anthropology of Karol Wojtyla* (Washington, D.C.: Catholic University of America Press, 1993); and George Hunston Williams, *The Mind of John Paul II: Origins of His Thought and Action* (New York: Seabury Press, 1981).

3. Gerald A. McCool, "The Theology of John Paul II," in *The Thought of John Paul II: A Collection of Essays and Studies*, ed. John M. McDermott (Rome: Editrice Pontificia Università Gregoriana, 1993), 29.

4. McCool, "Theology of John Paul II," 36.

5. Joseph Murphy, "Human Solidarity and the Church in the Thought of John Paul II," in *Thought of John Paul II*, ed. McDermott, 124–25.

6. Karol Wojtyla, *Person and Community: Selected Essays*, tr. Theresa Sandok (New York: Peter Lang, 1993), 146.

7. Kevin P. Doran, *Solidarity: A Synthesis of Personalism and Communitarianism in the Thought of Karol Wojtyla / Pope John Paul II* (New York: Peter Lang, 1996); Marie Vianney Bilgrien, *Solidarity: A Principle, an Attitude, a Duty? Or the Virtue for an Interdependent World?* (New York: Peter Lang, 1999).

8. George H. Williams, "Karol Wojtyla and Marxism," in *Catholicism and Politics in Communist Societies*, ed. Pedro Ramet (Durham, N.C.: Duke University Press, 1990), 361.

9. Daniel Cowdin, "John Paul II and Environmental Concerns: Problems and Possibilities," *The Living Light* 28 (1991): 44–52.

10. For my development of the ethical model, see Charles E. Curran, *The Catholic Moral Tradition Today: A Synthesis* (Washington, D.C.: Georgetown University Press, 1999), 60–86.

11. For an in-depth study of the ethics of Aquinas, see Stephen J. Pope, ed., *The Ethics of Aquinas* (Washington, D.C.: Georgetown University Press, 2002).

12. Thomas Aquinas, *Summa theologiae*, 4 vols. (Rome: Marietti, 1952), *Ia IIae*, q. 1–5.

13. Aquinas, *Ia IIae*, q. 94.

14. Marie-Dominique Chenu, *La "doctrine sociale" de l'Église comme idéologie* (Paris: Cerf, 1979).

15. The postsynodal apostolic exhortations are based on much input from the members of the international synods meeting in Rome. The pope writes the final document on the basis of their discussions. But, in my judgment, the synod should issue documents in its own name. At the present time, the synod serves only in an advisory capacity to the pope. International synods should be more than consultative and should propose teaching and policy together with the pope for the church universal. In preparing *Evangelium vitae*, John Paul II personally wrote every bishop asking for his input (*EV* 5.2), but one has the feeling the final document was not that much influenced by this consultation. A consultation should be much more structured and should involve public discussion among the various national and regional conferences of bishops.

16. Aquinas, *Ia IIae*, q. 94, a. 2.

17. For pro and con discussions of Grisez's work, see Robert P. George, ed., *Natural Law and Moral Inquiry: Ethics, Metaphysics, and Politics in the Work of Germain Grisez* (Washington, D.C.: Georgetown University Press, 1998); and Nigel Biggar and Rufus Black, eds., *The Revival of Natural Law: Philosophical, Theological, and Ethical Responses to the Finnis-Grisez School* (Aldershot, England: Ashgate, 2000).

18. Aquinas, *Ia IIae*, q. 94, a. 2.

19. Pope Pius XII, "The Prolongation of Life" (November 24, 1951) in *Medical Ethics: Sources of Catholic Teachings*, ed. Kevin D. O'Rourke and Philip Boyle (St. Louis: Catholic Health Association of the United States, 1989), 318–19.

20. Pope Pius XII, "Address to the First International Congress on the Histopathology of the Nervous System" (September 13, 1952), in *Medico-Moral Problems*, ed. Gerald Kelly (St. Louis: Catholic Health Association of the United States and Canada, 1958), 10.

21. Pope Pius XII, "Address to the International College of Neuro-Psychopharmacology" (September 9, 1958), in *Principles of Medical Ethics*, 2d edition, ed. John P. Kenny (Westminster, Md.: Newman, 1962), 153.

22. Pope Paul VI, *Humanae vitae (On the Regulation of Birth)* (Washington, D.C.: United States Catholic Conference, 1968), nn. 10–12, pp. 6–8.

23. Congregation for the Doctrine of the Faith, "Instruction on Respect for Human Life in Its Origin and on the Dignity of Procreation" (February 22, 1987), II, B, 4, in *Religion and Artificial Reproduction: An Inquiry into the Vatican "Instruction on Respect for Human Life in Its Origin and on the Dignity of Human Reproduction,"* ed. Thomas A. Shannon and Lisa Sowle Cahill (New York: Crossroad, 1988), 161.

24. Pope John Paul II, *Familiaris Consortio*, n. 32, in *Post-Synodal Apostolic Exhortations of John Paul II*, ed. J. Michael Miller (Huntington, Ind.: Our Sunday Visitor, 1998), 176–78.

25. See, for example, Lisa Sowle Cahill, "Feminist Ethics, Differences, and Common Ground: A Catholic Perspective," in *Feminist Ethics and the Catholic Moral Tradition: Readings in Moral Theology No. 9*, ed. Charles E. Curran, Margaret A. Farley, and Richard A. McCormick (New York: Paulist Press, 1996), 184–204.

26. Lisa Sowle Cahill, "Toward Global Ethics," *Theological Studies* 63 (2002): 330.

27. Pope John XXIII, *Pacem in terris*, n. 6, in *Catholic Social Thought: The Documentary Herritage*, ed. David J. O'Brien and Thomas A. Shannon (Maryknoll, N.Y.: Orbis, 1992), 132.

28. Karol Wojtyla (Pope John Paul II), *Love and Responsibility*, rev. ed. (London: Collins, 1981).

CONSCIENCE, HUMAN ACTS, AND HUMAN LIFE

THE LAST TWO CHAPTERS have dealt with methodological aspects of moral theology. In this chapter, I consider two major topics of fundamental moral theology—conscience and human acts—and then discuss human life issues in light of all that has gone before.

Conscience

John Paul II treats conscience in a number of places in his encyclicals but especially in *Veritatis splendor* 54–64. He develops his understanding of conscience in light of the Catholic tradition's approach to conscience but with some different emphases at times. *Veritatis splendor* understands conscience in accord with the Catholic tradition as "a *practical judgment*, a judgment which makes known what man must do or not do or which assesses an act already performed by him" (59.2). Here is the traditional Catholic understanding of the difference between antecedent conscience that judges an act about to be done and consequent conscience that judges an act already done.

According to the Catholic tradition, conscience is a complex reality. The judgment of conscience is true or erroneous, depending on whether the judgment is in accord with objective reality. Conscience is sincere or insincere, depending on its relationship with the person who is performing the act. In light of its complex nature, conscience should be both true and sincere. An erroneous conscience is either vincible (culpable) or invincible (nonculpable).[1] Such an understanding is obviously in the back of Pope John Paul II's mind as he develops his understanding of conscience.

John Paul II's approach to conscience is totally consistent with his overall perspectives. He is fearful that many people today outside the church and even some inside the church emphasize human freedom at the expense of truth. This is seen in the subjectivism and individualism so present in the modern world. The emphasis on freedom leads to a creative understanding of conscience and fails to recognize that conscience does not make truth but only discovers truth and must conform itself to the truth (54).

John Paul II gives more emphasis to consequent conscience than has been the case in the Catholic tradition.[2] The Protestant tradition, with its insistence on grace, emphasizes consequent conscience because the individual recognizes one's sinfulness and the need for God's grace and forgiveness.[3] John Paul II's emphasis on consequent conscience is in keeping with his own anthropology, which recognizes the presence of human sinfulness and the need for conversion. He develops this understanding of conscience, often called an Augustinian approach, primarily in the encyclical *Dominum et vivificantem*: "The Gospel's 'convincing concerning sin' under the influence of the Spirit of truth can be accomplished in man in no other way than *through the conscience*" (43.2). Conscience discovers the roots of sin in the person, including how culture and circumstances have contributed to the presence of sin. But the human person with the help of God's grace is not just ensnared by sin but also "is obliged to wrestle constantly if he is to cling to do what is good" (44.3). "*This laborious effort of conscience* also determines the paths of human conversion: turning one's back on sin in order to restore truth and love in man's very heart" (45.1). This *metanoia* or conversion is accomplished through the Holy Spirit, who is the Spirit of truth working toward salvific "convincing concerning sin" (44.3). The pope understands the famous sin against the Holy Spirit and blasphemy against the Holy Spirit as consisting "precisely in *the radical refusal to accept this forgiveness,* of which he is the ultimate giver and which presupposes the genuine conversion which he brings about in the conscience" (46.4).

Conscience resides in the heart and the very core of the human person where one is not only in dialogue with oneself but also with God. "Conscience is *the witness of God himself* whose voice and judgment penetrate the depths of man's soul, calling him . . . to obedience" (*VS* 58). As was mentioned above, the pope has emphasized the role of the Holy Spirit in consequent conscience. But the Holy Spirit also plays an important role in antecedent conscience. "And this is what takes place through the gift of the Holy Spirit, the Spirit of truth, of freedom, and of love: In him, we are able to interiorize the law, to receive it, and to live it as the motivating force of true personal freedom: 'the perfect law, the law of liberty' (Jas 1: 25)" (83.2).

There can be no doubt John Paul II develops his understanding of conscience in terms of a legal model. Even the references to the role of God and to the Holy Spirit cited above put the emphasis on law and obedience. The development of antecedent conscience in *Veritatis splendor* focuses exclusively on the legal model and understanding of conscience. *Veritatis splendor* begins its discussion of conscience by asserting, "The relationship between man's freedom and God's law is most deeply lived out in the 'heart' of the person, and his moral conscience" (54.1). Paul's Letter to the Romans "indicates *the biblical understanding of conscience*, especially *in its specific connection with the law*" (57.1). "Conscience is the application of the law to a particular case" (59.2). Conscience is "*the proximate norm of personal morality*," whereas the divine law is "*the universal and objective norm of morality*. The judgment of conscience does not establish the law; rather it bears witness to the authority of the natural law" (60).

The emphasis on a legal model in *Veritatis splendor* is to be expected because the whole thrust of the encyclical is to insist on universal and absolute moral norms. But John Paul II's penchant for the legal model goes much deeper than that. His fundamental and all-embracing emphasis on the role of truth in the moral life means that conscience must always be seen in terms of obedience to the truth. Likewise, his insistence on the compatibility of law and freedom and the subordination of freedom to the demands of the eternal law again indicates that for him conscience must be understood primarily in relation to law.

But a legal model of conscience is not adequate. Experience reminds us that the vast majority of our moral decisions are not made by reference to a law. The most important decisions in life—marriage partner, vocation, friends, coping with limitations, shortcomings, and sufferings of human existence—are not made in response to a law. Yes, there must always be some place for law and laws in human existence, but law should not be the primary model for understanding the moral life in general or conscience in particular. Elsewhere, I have developed a theory of conscience on the basis of a relationality–responsibility model.[4]

"In the judgments of our conscience the possibility of error is always present. Conscience *is not an infallible judge*; it can make mistakes" (62.3). *Veritatis splendor* here cites Romans 12:2 that Christians should not be conformed to this world (62.2). Such a warning fits with John Paul II's recognition of the struggle in human existence against the power of sin and evil.

Erroneous conscience is either invincible (not culpable) or vincible (culpable). Conscience is erroneously culpable when the person shows little concern for the true and the good and is blinded by sin (63.2). Invincible ignorance is "an ignorance of which the subject is not aware and which he is unable to overcome by himself" (62.3).

Invincible ignorance raises some questions for John Paul II precisely because of his emphasis on the primacy of truth. Objective truth grounds the true or correct conscience. The invincibly erroneous conscience is based on what is subjectively perceived (but erroneously) as true. We cannot "confuse a 'subjective' error about moral good with the 'objective' truth" (63.1). The evil done in invincible ignorance does not cease to be an evil even if it may not be imputed to the agent. However, the Catholic tradition in moral theology, as recognized in the eighteenth century by St. Alphonsus, goes further than John Paul II in this matter. Alphonsus says it is a common opinion of theologians (despite the fact that Thomas Aquinas did not hold it) that an act done in invincible ignorance is not only not imputable to the agent but also can be a good and meritorious act.[5] John Paul II, with his emphasis on the primacy of objective truth, does not want to accept the position of St. Alphonsus and the common position of theologians today.

In the light of the obstacles and difficulties that conscience faces, *Veritatis splendor* briefly mentions the need for the formation of conscience that tries to develop the connaturality between the person and the good. Within the human person, there is the desire to seek the true and the good, but this must be strengthened and developed. The formation of conscience calls for "continuous conversion to what is true and what is good," as Romans 12:2 exhorts. The theological virtues of faith, hope and charity, and prudence strengthen and develop this connaturality to the true and the good (64.1). Note here the emphasis on the role of the virtues in the true formation of conscience.

Veritatis splendor sees this connaturality in the service of a legal model of conscience, but I have tried to develop a theory of conscience based on this connaturality in terms of accepting the criterion of a good conscience as the peace and joy of conscience. Such a criterion of peace and joy has been proposed by many spiritual writers going back to the early centuries of the church in their discussion of the discernment of spirits. Yes, there is the danger of abusing the criterion, but authentic subjectivity and true objectivity coincide.[6] *Veritatis splendor*, however, earlier condemned the "criterion of sincerity, authenticity, and 'being at peace with oneself'" as moving away from the inescapable claims of truth (32.1). John Paul II elsewhere, however, implicitly recognizes a basis in Catholic theology for accepting the peace of conscience as the criterion of a true and correct conscience. *Fides et ratio* refers to "a truth which the Church has always treasured: in the far reaches of the human heart there is a seed of desire and nostalgia for God. The Liturgy of Good Friday . . . [prays]: 'Almighty and eternal God, you created mankind so that all might long to find you and have peace when you are found'" (24.2). This peace that comes from the person's finding the true and the good is the basis for my theory of conscience.

Conscience and the Magisterium

Conscience and the judgments of conscience are susceptible to problems and obstacles, but *Veritatis splendor* points out, "Christians have a great help for the formation of conscience *in the Church and her Magisterium*" (64.2). The encyclical then cites the Declaration on Religious Freedom of the Second Vatican Council: "Her charge is to announce and teach authentically that truth which is Christ, and at the same time with her authority to declare and confirm the principles of the moral order which derive from human nature itself." In keeping with his opposition to the false conflict between truth and freedom, the pope insists that the magisterium thus does not oppose the true freedom of conscience because it "does not bring to the Christian conscience truths which are extraneous to it; rather it brings to light the truths which it ought already to possess. . . . The Church puts herself always and only at the *service of conscience* . . . helping it not to swerve from the truth about the good of man, but rather, especially in more difficult questions, to obtain the truth with certainty and to abide in it" (64.2).

John Paul II reiterates this teaching in a number of places in his encyclicals. For example, "*When people ask the church the questions raised by their consciences,* when the faithful in the Church turn to their Bishops and Pastors, *the Church's reply contains the voice of Jesus Christ, the voice of the truth about good and evil.* In the words spoken by the Church there resounds, in people's inmost being, the voice of God who 'alone is good' (cf. Mt 19:17), who alone 'is love' (1 Jn 4:8, 16)" (*VS* 117.2; see also *VS* 25.2, 27.3–4). Thus, the magisterium gives certitude to the Christian conscience. Such an approach derives from the pope's emphasis that Christ has revealed "the truth about man" and has entrusted his teaching mission to the church that exercises it through the magisterium.

The status of the nature of papal teaching on specific moral issues (e.g., sterilization and artificial insemination) has received much discussion in the past forty years that cannot be repeated here. But Catholic moral theologians agree that the teaching of the hierarchical magisterium on some specific moral issues does not always arrive at certitude.[7] Three considerations support this thesis. First, papal moral teachings in the past have been changed in the course of time. Think of such issues as religious freedom, democracy, slavery, usury, the right to silence, capital punishment, the ends of marriage, and the role of women in family and society. The very fact that such changes have occurred despite papal teaching to the contrary indicates that such papal teachings cannot always claim certitude and at times have been wrong.[8] Second, all agree that *some* of the papal teaching on moral issues belongs to the category of noninfallible teaching. By definition, noninfallible means fallible—the teaching can be wrong. So all Catholics have to recognize that some of the papal teaching on moral issues does not give or guarantee certitude. Blanket statements that the magisterium's teaching on moral issues provides "certitude" or contains "the voice of Jesus Christ, the voice of the truth about good and evil" are neither accurate nor truthful.

Yes, there is some discussion within Catholicism about whether specific moral teachings—such as the condemnations of artificial contraception, homosexual genital relationships, and direct abortion—are infallible. John Paul II has given some fuel to such a position by inserting into the Code of Canon Law a second type of teaching between the infallible teaching of a divinely revealed truth and the noninfallible teaching to which the faithful owe religious assent of intellect and will. The new category inserted into canon law by the pope is definitive (i.e., infallible) teaching by the magisterium of a doctrine concerned with faith and morals that is not directly revealed but is necessarily connected with revelation. The faithful must firmly and definitively hold this teaching.[9] Although this is a new category in canon law, it has some relation to what older theologians at times call the secondary object of infallibility, that is, truths necessarily connected with revelation.

Those defending the infallibility of some specific moral teachings today generally do not argue from the extraordinary ex cathedra magisterium of the pope but rather from the ordinary universal magisterium that the pope and all the bishops down through the centuries have authoritatively taught something to be held definitively by the faithful.[10] Perhaps John Paul II gives support to such a position by the way he phrases the condemnations of euthanasia and direct abortion in *Evangelium vitae*: "Therefore, by the authority that Christ conferred upon Peter and his Successors, in communion with the Bishops—who on various occasions have condemned abortion and who in the aforementioned consultation, albeit dispersed throughout the world, have shown unanimous agreement concerning this doctrine—*I declare that direct abortion, that is, abortion willed as an end or as a means, always constitutes a grave moral disorder*, since it is the deliberate killing of an innocent human being. This doctrine is based upon the natural law and upon the written word of God, is transmitted by the Church's Tradition and taught by the ordinary and universal magisterium" (62.3).

This is not the place for a lengthy discussion about such infallibility. My own position is that the condemnation of artificial contraception, direct abortion, and other practices is not definitive or infallible teaching.[11] Infallible teachings of the universal ordinary magisterium of pope and bishops must have been taught by all of these as something to be held definitively and not merely as something to be held and followed. But, in these cases, this cannot be proven. The Code of Canon Law (Canon 749.3) maintains, "No doctrine is understood as defined infallibly unless this is manifestly evident."[12] Some theologians, such as Germain Grisez, maintain that the Code of Canon Law refers directly only to the case of the extraordinary papal magisterium in its claim that infallibility must be certain.[13] But the obvious intent is broader and inclusive of all possible infallible statements. Something cannot be presumed to be infallible. If there is doubt about the infallibility of a teaching, it is not infallible.[14]

The third reason supporting the fact that some specific moral teachings of the hierarchical magisterium are not absolutely certain and that Catholics might in theory and practice disagree with such teaching comes from the inability to arrive at certitude on complex moral issues. In the Catholic tradition, as mentioned in chapter 1, Thomas Aquinas recognized this reality. Speculative truth and moral truth differ. Speculative truth is always and everywhere true; a triangle always has 180 degrees. But moral truths, in the form of secondary principles of the natural law such as deposited goods should always be returned to the owner, are not always and everywhere true and obliging. In the midst of the complexity and specificity of human affairs, circumstances might arise in a few cases where you should not return a deposit. The same is true for promises that generally oblige but not always. On occasion it might be morally impossible to keep the promise.[15]

The examination of the papal teaching condemning direct abortion also shows that on this complex issue one cannot arrive at certitude. Notice the insistence on direct abortion. But it was only in the twentieth century that the hierarchical magisterium came to its present understanding of direct abortion.[16] All have to recognize that the difference between direct and indirect abortion is based on one particular philosophical system or method that is not intimately connected with revelation and that cannot really claim absolute certitude. Very significant in the question of abortion is the fact that to this day the hierarchical magisterium recognizes in theory the possibility of delayed animation, because of which there would not be truly individual human life present from the moment of conception. *Veritatis splendor* (60.2, 61.4) obliquely recognizes this theoretical debate about animation. However, in practice, the Catholic teaching holds that one has to act as if there is truly human life present from the moment of conception. But there is no theoretical certitude about the beginning of truly individual human life. Below, the section of this chapter on norms against unjust killing will develop these points in greater detail.

Thus, the teaching of the papal magisterium on complex moral issues is not always a certain truth. To be truly accurate even in the words of the Catholic tradition itself, the papal teaching should recognize at the very minimum that most, if not all, of its teaching on controverted specific moral issues is noninfallible, or, in other words, fallible.

Theological Dissent

A related question concerns dissent by theologians from papal moral teaching. In many ways, the question of conscience and hierarchical moral teaching just discussed also raises this issue of dissent. The pope and the Roman Curia, however, seem to limit the term "dissent" to theologians. The pope wrote *Veritatis splendor* because of *"the lack of harmony between the traditional response of the Church and certain theological positions* encountered even in seminaries and in faculties of theology *with regard to questions of the greatest importance* for the Church and for the life of faith of Christians, as well as for the life of society itself" (4.3). The church is *"facing what is certainly a genuine crisis"* (5.2). "It is no longer a matter of limited and occasional dissent, but of an overall and systematic calling into question of traditional moral doctrine" (4.2).

Veritatis splendor then goes on to discuss the role of theologians in the third chapter, paragraphs 109–13. Basically here the pope does two things—he calls moral theologians to accept and teach what the magisterium teaches, and he condemns dissent (but understood in a very narrow way). As for the first point, "Moral theologians are to set forth the Church's teaching and to give, in the exercise of their ministry, the example of a loyal assent, both internal and external, to the Magisterium's teaching in the areas of both dogma and morality" (110.2). "The Church's magisterium . . . has the task of 'discerning by means of judgments normative for the consciences of believers, those acts which in themselves conform to the demands of faith and foster their expression in life and those which, on the contrary, because intrinsically evil, are incompatible with such demands'" (110.1). Moral theologians work "in communion with the Magisterium" (109.2) and "in cooperation with the hierarchical Magisterium" (110.2). Recent church documents have also called for theologians to have a mandate from the hierarchy precisely because they have this relationship with the hierarchy.[17]

Although theologians are called to give assent to the teaching of the magisterium, *Veritatis splendor* recognizes "the possible limitations of the human arguments employed by the Magisterium" and calls moral theologians "to develop a deeper understanding of the reasons underlying its teachings and to expound the validity and obligatory nature of the precepts it proposes" (110.2). Note that the reasons might be limited, but this does not affect the obligatory character of the precepts proposed. Moral theologians will also "be deeply concerned to clarify ever more fully the biblical foundations, the ethical significance and the anthropological concerns which underlie the moral doctrine and vision of man set forth by the Church" (110.2). Basically, moral theologians serve the magisterium and must give internal and external assent to its moral teachings.

As a second step, *Veritatis splendor* goes on to strongly condemn dissent, but dissent understood in a very narrow sense—"in the form of carefully orchestrated protests and polemics carried on in the media" (113.2). I know no Catholic theologian who has disagreed with papal teaching who would accept that interpretation of what the theologian is trying to do.

All recognize that the Wojtyla papacy has firmly emphasized the truth of the magisterial teaching on morality and other areas and the need for theologians to accept and teach such positions. The 1983 Code of Canon Law,[18] the 1989 Profession of Faith and Oath of Fidelity promulgated by the Congregation for the Doctrine of the Faith,[19] and the Congregation's 1990 "Instruction on the Ecclesial Vocation of the Theologian (*Donum veritatis*)"[20] all emphasize the decisive role of the hierarchical magisterium and the submission required by theologians.

Veritatis splendor, in footnote 177, refers to *Donum veritatis* "in particular Nos. 32–39, devoted to the problem of dissent." This document, however, recognizes the possibility for something between the two extremes of full internal and external assent on the part of theologians to noninfallible church teaching on moral issues and the condemnation of dissent understood in a very pejorative way. *Donum veritatis* insists, "The willingness to submit loyally to the teaching of the magisterium on matters per se not irreformable must be the rule."[21] If, after serious study showing his openness to the teaching, the theologian cannot give internal assent, the theologian is obliged to remain open to a deeper consideration of the issue. The instruction gives three directives for the theologian in such a situation. First, the theologian has the duty to make known his problem to the magisterial authorities. Second, the theologian can suffer in prayer and silence with the sure hope that the truth will ultimately prevail. Third, dissent—understood as public opposition to the magisterium of the church and causing the church severe harm—can never be justified.[22] This is as far as the Vatican documents are willing to go on the issue of a theologian disagreeing with a noninfallible teaching of the hierarchical magisterium.

To delve into the reasons behind the papal and Vatican's reluctance to admit any lack of certitude or possibility of error in noninfallible teaching would take us too far afield. But the theoretical source of the problem with the papal and Curial position is clear. The Vatican position starts with the presupposition that the church and the magisterium, thanks to the activity of the Holy Spirit, have the truth. Consequently, no one else can disagree. But, as chapter 1 pointed out, the magisterium must learn before it teaches. Even in the area of faith, the magisterium learned from others the Trinitarian understanding of three persons in one God and the Christological understanding of two natures in Jesus. Theologians and others first proposed these understandings that were accepted in the early church only after lengthy and somewhat divisive debates. In the changing area of moral theology, most of the issues involving the noninfallible teaching of the magisterium have to be learned before they can be taught. Issues such as artificial contraception, sterilization, the need to use only ordinary means to preserve life, euthanasia, artificial insemination, genetic engineering, the nature and purpose of the state, the principles governing economic systems, and many other such issues are not found in the deposit of faith. The hierarchical magisterium has had to learn these moral truths before it taught them.

The proper formulation of the issue, then, is not the magisterium with its truth as opposed by the conscience of believers or the position of theologians. In accord with John Paul II's own approach, the primary reality remains moral truth. Both the magisterium and the consciences of believers and theologians are striving to know that truth. All Catholics recognize that the magisterium has the assistance of the Holy Spirit in coming to the truth, but the magisterium still must first learn the specific moral truths and cannot claim absolute certitude for them.

Human Acts

John Paul II recognizes that some human acts are more central and all-embracing than others. Certain choices "'shape' a person's entire moral life and . . . serve as bounds within which other particular everyday choices can be situated and allowed to develop" (65.1).

Though strongly disagreeing with some contemporary theories of fundamental option, the pope recognizes "the specific importance of a fundamental choice which qualifies the moral life, and engages freedom on a radical level before God" (66.1).

Fundamental Choice

Veritatis splendor describes the fundamental choice in biblical terms, such as faith active in love, covenant response, the following of Jesus, the response to the gift of the Kingdom of God or to the invitation of Jesus to follow him. This choice is the pearl of great price for which one sells all else (66; also see 16–24). Throughout the encyclicals, references abound to conversion and discipleship as the fundamental Christian response that then directs our other acts to carry out this commitment.

Veritatis splendor insists that "the Magisterium has the duty to state that some trends of theological thinking and certain philosophical affirmations are incompatible with revealed truth" (29.4). In keeping with this purpose, the encyclical strongly disagrees with the theory of fundamental option proposed by some contemporary Catholic moral theologians. Briefly, the fundamental-option theory distinguishes between fundamental freedom on the transcendent level of human existence in the life of the person and categorical freedom with regard to the particular choices that an individual makes to do this or that.[23] The pope objects to the fundamental-option theory precisely because of its separation of the fundamental option from the categorical choices that the individual makes. "To separate the fundamental option from concrete kinds of behavior means to contradict the substantial integrity or personal unity of the moral agent in his body and in his soul" (67.2).

There is no doubt that fundamental-option theorists distinguish the two kinds of freedom and see them operating on different levels of the person, but they do not totally separate them or contradict the substantial integrity or personal unity of the moral agent.[24] I have expressed my own disagreement with the fundamental-option theory because it downplays the relational and historical aspects of salvation, but this is a matter for debate within the parameters of

Catholic moral theology.[25] John Paul II even goes so far as to claim, "These tendencies are therefore contrary to the teaching of Scripture itself" (67.1). But it is hard to see how a philosophical explanation of the fundamental-option theory, which does not totally separate the fundamental option from particular choices, goes against the teaching of scripture.

Intrinsically Evil Acts

In addition, *Veritatis splendor* explicitly deals with the morality of particular acts and insists on the existence of intrinsically evil acts that are always and per se true and never admit of exceptions (74–83). Human acts must be ordered to God. What ensures that acts are ordered to God? Here the pope appeals to the traditionally accepted Catholic teaching on the three sources of morality, "*intention* of the acting subject, the *circumstances*—and in particular the consequences—of this action, [and] the *object* itself of his act" (74.1). "The primary and decisive element for moral judgment is the object of the human act, which establishes whether it is *capable of being ordered to the good and to the ultimate end which is God*" (79.2). If the object of the act is morally bad, neither the intention of the agent nor the circumstances, especially the consequences, can make the action good (81.2). This is what is meant by intrinsically evil acts.

Veritatis splendor asserts that *Gaudium et spes*, the Pastoral Constitution on the Church in the Modern World (27), gives examples of such intrinsically evil acts. "Whatever is hostile to life itself such as any kind of homicide, genocide, abortion, euthanasia, and voluntary suicide; whatever violates the integrity of the human person . . . whatever is offensive to human dignity" (80.1). But the text does not always prove what the pope wants it to prove. The first thing mentioned is homicide, but homicide is not an intrinsically evil act. Homicide is the killing of a human being and can at times be morally licit as killing in self-defense, killing an unjust aggressor, or killing an enemy soldier in a just war. But here the problem might be one of translation. The official Latin version uses the word *homocidium*, which could mean homicide or murder.[26] The official English translation of the encyclical uses the English word "homicide," but two unofficial translations of the original Vatican II document use the word "murder."[27] At the very minimum, the official translation of the encyclical in English does not prove what the pope wants it to prove. In addition, "abortion" is mentioned. But the Catholic tradition and the pope do not claim that all abortion is intrinsically evil. Direct abortion is always wrong, but indirect abortion can be justified.

Intrinsically evil acts by definition constitute universal and absolute norms that "oblige *semper et pro semper*, that is without any exception" (82.1). Earlier, *Veritatis splendor* recognizes the difference between positive and negative precepts of the natural law—a traditionally accepted understanding in the Catholic tradition. Positive commands do not oblige always and everywhere. For example, take the difference between the obligation to tell the truth and the obligation not to lie. One can never tell a lie, but one does not always have to tell the truth. One can say nothing. The reason behind the distinction is that positive obligations often conflict with other positive obligations; for example, the obligation to tell the truth can conflict with the positive obligation to keep a secret. The pope does not mention this example, and the reason why positive obligations do not oblige always and everywhere, but he certainly builds on this understanding. He insists that even though negative commands oblige always and everywhere, they are not more important than positive norms. The negative norms constitute the lower limit or boundary that no one can go below. But the person through positive obligations is called to go above and beyond this minimal limit (52).

John Paul II recognizes that some and perhaps even many Catholic theologians do not accept his position on intrinsically evil acts based on the object of the act that constitute universal and absolute negative norms. Certain ethical theories called "teleological" disagree with the above analysis because they have "*an inadequate understanding of the object of moral action*" (75.1). The two forms of this "teleologism"are consequentialism and proportionalism. The moral criterion for consequentialism is derived solely from a consideration of the foreseeable consequences of the action done. Proportionalism focuses on the proportion between the good and bad effects of the act. These approaches maintain that it is never possible to formulate an absolute prohibition of particular kinds of behavior that would always be wrong (75).

John Paul II insists that "in the question of the morality of human acts, and in particular the question of whether there exist intrinsically evil acts, we find ourselves faced with *the question of man himself*, of his *truth* and of the moral consequences flowing from that truth. By acknowledging and teaching the existence of intrinsic evil in given human acts, the Church remains faithful to the integral truth about man. . . . Consequently, she must reject the theories set forth above, which contradict this truth" (83.1).

The Evaluation of Intrinsically Evil Acts

The evaluation of the complex teaching of John Paul II in this matter calls for a number of steps. The first step is to identify just what is the problem and what are the differences between the pope's teaching and the position of those who have been called revisionists or dissenting Catholic theologians. We are dealing with the areas in which these Catholic moral theologians have dissented from the teaching of the hierarchical magisterium. The primary area of difference involves human sexuality in general and issues such as contraception, sterilization, masturbation, artificial insemination, homosexuality, and to some extent premarital sexuality, and also the issue of divorce and remarriage. There has also been disagreement about the solution of conflict situations based on the distinction between direct and indirect, as well as a lesser dissent over the issue of abortion itself and even to a lesser extent the issue of euthanasia. Direct and indirect effects, as well as abortion and euthanasia, will be considered below. But even in the area of sexuality, the so-called dissenting or revisionist theologians still accept the existence of universal and absolute norms, such as the condemnation of adultery and of rape.

In general, Catholic revisionist theologians point to the problem of physicalism with this teaching. Physicalism is the a priori identification of the human moral act with the physical or biological structure of the act. As was mentioned in the section on natural law, in the hierarchical teaching on sexuality, the physical act, which is described as the depositing of the husband's semen in the vagina of the wife, must always be present and cannot be interfered with. This act is the only reason that justifies the use of the sexual faculty. The purpose of the faculty of sexuality is the procreation and education of offspring and the love union of the spouses, so every act of the faculty must be both open to procreation and expressive of love union and occur within a marital commitment. Contraception is wrong because one interferes with the act of marital intercourse. Artificial insemination is wrong because one does not procreate by means of the act of marital intercourse. Homosexual acts are wrong because they are not open to procreation.

This section further develops the problems with physicalism. The charge of physicalism is based on the recognition that the moral aspect of the act is the fully human aspect that includes all the partial aspects of the human—such as the physical, the biological, the psychological, the sociological, the hygienic, and the eugenic. The moral is the fully human aspect that embraces all these different aspects of the human.

In this world, no human act is necessarily perfect from every individual aspect. Very often, in the name of the fully human one must sacrifice one particular aspect. For example, the attainment of human knowledge is an important human good, but in the acquiring of human knowledge one cannot go against other aspects of the human. We do not allow researchers or investigators to violate the privacy of the person in order to know more. Human subjects of medical experimentation must fully consent after having been informed about all that is involved. In the name of the human, we must often say no to a particular aspect, such as the technological. John Paul II himself has been very adamant about the need for truly human development that, to a certain extent, relativizes all other aspects of development, especially the economic aspect (*SRS* 27–34). The fully human can never be reduced to only one aspect of the human. At times, the human can be identified with the physical, but this must be shown to be the moral meaning and not just the physical meaning. Thus the only human life we know is the physical life that we have. The human being is dead when physical death occurs.

In general, Catholic moral theology has recognized the problem and has not identified the fully human with the physical aspect. Theologians have never said that all killing is wrong. Killing is a physical act that can be justified at times, such as in self-defense. We rightly maintain that murder (unjust killing) is always wrong. Many contemporary Catholic moral theologians distinguish between the "physical" act of false speech and the moral act of lying. Not all false speech is morally wrong. Here, the analogy with sexual ethics is very close. The manuals of moral theology generally do not make a distinction between false speech and lying. Lying is speech that goes against what is in my mind. They base their condemnation of lying on a faculty–act analysis. The God-given purpose of the faculty or power of speech is to put on my lips what is in my mind. Consequently, every act of the faculty of speech cannot go against what is in my mind.[28]

In the early twentieth century, however, some moral theologians proposed a different reason for the moral malice of lying.[29] What if the person asking you the question has no right to the truth? The World War II situation of the Gestapo asking people if they were hiding Jews in their home serves as an excellent example. The newer approach recognizes that the faculty or power can never be viewed in itself but only in its relationship with the person and the person's relationship with other persons. The ultimate malice of lying does not consist in going against the God-given purpose of the faculty of speech (the perverted faculty argument) but in violating my neighbor's right to truth. If the other does not have the right to truth, what I say is false speech, but it is not the moral act of lying. Yes, there are dangers of abuse here, but the new approach has received widespread support in Roman Catholic moral theology.

A fascinating development concerning the morality of lying occurred in the *Catechism of the Catholic Church*. The 1994 edition of the *Catechism* understands a lie as "to speak or act against the truth in order to lead into error someone who has the right to know the truth."[30] Thus the *Catechism* accepted the newer approach to lying. When the definitive Latin edition of the *Catechism* appeared in 1997, Joseph Cardinal Ratzinger, the prefect of the Congregation for the Doctrine of the Faith, issued a short list of changes or corrections to what was found in the 1994 edition. Among the corrections is the following: The description of lying should read: "To lie is to speak or act against the truth in order to lead someone into error."[31] The malice of lying here does not consist in the violation of the neighbor's right to truth. Ratzinger well knew that many Catholic theologians today use the analogy of lying to argue against the faculty–act analysis with regard to human sexuality.[32]

In the question of contraception, revisionist theologians maintain that one can interfere with the marital act for the good of the person or the good of the marital relationship. Likewise, one can use artificial insemination (husband's seed) to enhance the possibility of having a child if this is for the good of the person or of the marriage. It is not necessary that procreation always occurs through the physical act of marital intercourse. In a similar way, a homosexual genital act is not determined by the nature of the sexual faculty and its act but by the good of the person and the person's committed relationship to another. Obviously, one would have to develop these arguments at much greater length to make them convincing, but the basic thrust is clear. One should not make moral judgments solely on the basis of the physical act or the teleology of the faculty–act relation apart from the person and the person's relationships.

What about the traditional Catholic teaching about the primacy of the object and the fact that neither the intention nor circumstances, especially consequences, can change the morality of an act whose object is bad? I have no problem with insisting on the primacy of the object, provided the object is the moral object of the act and not just a partial aspect or the physical aspect of the human moral object.[33] As pointed out above, the Catholic tradition has recognized the moral aspect of the object as distinguished from the mere physical aspect. For example, the Catholic tradition never said it was always wrong to forcibly strike another person in the face. This could be the good moral act of trying to revive an unconscious person. The moral object that is always wrong is to show disrespect to another person. But disrespect is clearly a moral term. Likewise, to take what another gained through lawful possession is not always and everywhere wrong. The Catholic tradition has consistently recognized that in extreme situations of human need all material goods are held in common. Thus, a person in extreme need, such as danger of dying, could take what another lawfully gained as one's own. The physical act of taking it would not be theft.[34]

What about the existence of intrinsically evil acts and absolute and universal norms? Again, the same rationale applies. There are intrinsically evil acts, but they are described in moral terms. All recognize that murder, injustice, and inhumane treatment are always and everywhere wrong. But these are moral objects. The problem often exists whether a particular act is an injustice or inhumane treatment. At one time, the Catholic tradition held that it was morally good and not unjust or inhumane to require a defendant to admit his or her guilt. Now the tradition accepts that the guilty defendant has a right to keep silent.[35] Recall the intrinsically evil acts that John Paul II sees in *Gaudium et spes* 27. But many of these refer to the moral object—"whatever violates the integrity of the human person . . . whatever is offensive to human dignity . . . degrading conditions of work which treat laborers as mere instruments of profit" (*VS* 80.1). Yes, there are universal and absolute norms that are always obliging based on the moral object of the act.

To his credit, John Paul II has recognized the importance of universal and absolute norms in the area of social ethics. In fact, there really can be no true morally good society unless there are some universal and absolute norms accepted by all. John Paul II has made human rights the centerpiece for his understanding of social morality. Fundamental human rights are true at all times, in all places, and in all cultures. The pope has recognized such civil and political rights as the right to religious freedom and freedom of association. But unlike some in the tradition of philosophical liberalism, he has also insisted on social and economic rights, such as the rights to food, clothing, shelter, and health care (*VS* 97–99; *CA* 47–52).

In the area of personal morality, there are other intrinsically evil acts that are always and everywhere wrong. Think of torture or rape. In these two cases, the integrity of the person is directly involved. I also hold that adultery is always wrong. Notice here the involvement of the mutual relationship of the married persons who have committed themselves to one another. It is precisely this personal and relational commitment that adultery violates.

There can be no doubt that *Veritatis splendor* caricatures the positions of the Catholic theologians who have dissented from the papal teaching on some intrinsically evil acts and absolute norms proposed by the papal magisterium. In reality, the dissenters do not deny the primacy of the object or the existence of intrinsically evil acts and of some absolute and universal moral norms. Nor do they maintain that the end or intention can justify a morally bad means.

Catholic revisionist moral theologians as a whole strongly agree with the pope in condemning subjectivism, relativism, and individualism. The pope is wrong in seeing these theologians who have dissented from some papal teachings as under "the more or less obvious influence of currents of thought which end by detaching human freedom from its essential and constitutive relationship to truth" (4.2). It is wrong to say with regard to revisionist Catholic moral theologians that "These tendencies are at one in lessening or even denying *the dependence of freedom on truth*" (34.2).

The difference between the pope and dissenting Catholic theologians centers on what is the moral truth in particular issues. Any objective observer of the controversies in the Catholic Church over moral theology would recognize that it is not a struggle between moral truth and those who oppose moral truth but a conflict over what is moral truth. The pope's erroneous description of the differences within Catholicism over moral teaching obviously comes from his too easily identifying what the church and the popes teach with the truth—the same truth about humanity that God has revealed to us in Christ Jesus.

Human Life Issues

This chapter serves as a bridge between the methodological aspects of the discussion and the specific content aspects. This section analyzes John Paul II's teaching on human life. The next chapter will discuss sexuality and marriage, and that is followed by a chapter on social teaching.

This analysis of the teaching on human life begins by summarizing the methodological approaches analyzed above and showing explicitly how John Paul II carries out these approaches in his discussion of human life. To avoid needless repetition, subsequent chapters will not explicitly discuss the methodological aspects grounding his sexual and social teachings.

The Methodology Employed in Defending Life

In the discussion of human life, *Evangelium vitae* stresses once again that truth is the most significant value while the culture of death comes from a false understanding of freedom that has severed its connection with truth. The "culture of death, taken as a whole, betrays a completely individualistic concept of freedom, which ends up by becoming the freedom of 'the strong' against the weak who have no choice but to submit" (19.3). "Freedom negates and destroys itself and becomes a factor leading to the destruction of others, when it no longer recognizes and respects *its essential link with the truth*" (19.5).

The teaching on human life issues, especially in the encyclical *Evangelium vitae*, well illustrates the sources that John Paul II uses in developing his thought. He relies heavily on scripture. The encyclical begins with the story of Cain and Abel, and there are frequent references to both the Hebrew Bible and the New Testament. The scriptural source is the most privileged source in the encyclical. John Paul II describes his own approach to chapter 2: "The Christian Message Concerning Life" as a meditation on the Gospel of Life (30.1). The frequent headings and subheadings in the text invariably contain a scriptural citation together with a short description of the matter to be treated in that section. As one might expect, the scripture citations are often proof texts used to affirm a particular point that is not all that clearly present in the original scriptural text. Thus, for example, "'*From man in regard to his fellow man I will demand an accounting' (Gen 9:5): reverence and love for every human life*" (39.1). Yet we all recognize that meditations on a scriptural text often use scripture in this way.

Evangelium vitae also relies to a great extent on tradition. In fact, tradition appears more often here than in the other encyclicals precisely because John Paul II is trying to show that the condemnations of direct killing, direct abortion, and euthanasia are also based on tradition (57.4, 62.3, 65.4). Thus, for example, chapter 3 of *Evangelium vitae* cites Gregory of Nyssa, John Damascene, the *Didache*, the letter of Pseudo-Barnabas, Augustine, Aquinas, and Alphonsus Liguori (fn. 38–45).

This encyclical, like all the other encyclicals, frequently cites previous hierarchical teaching and obviously always in agreement. Again, there are more citations to Vatican II than to any other source, but John Paul II uses other papal teachings more frequently in this encyclical than in any other, especially citations from Pope Pius XII on the questions of life, abortion, and euthanasia (fn. 66, 79, 80, 81). *Evangelium vitae* also appeals frequently to the *Catechism of the Catholic Church*, which had been published shortly before the encyclical.

What about human reason, and in particular natural law? As was pointed out in chapter 1, there is no significant development of the ethical role of either reason or natural law in *Evangelium vitae*. With regard to the role of reason in general, *Evangelium vitae* simply asserts a number of times that the teaching of the Gospel of Life based on scripture is "indeed written in the heart of every man and woman, has echoed in every conscience 'from the beginning' . . . in such a way that, despite the negative consequences of sin, *it can also be known in its essential traits by human reason*" (29.3). "The *Gospel of Life* is not for believers alone: *it is for everyone*" (101.2). "The commandment 'you shall not kill' . . . resounds in the moral conscience of everyone as an imperishable echo of the original covenant of God the Creator with mankind" (77.2; cf. 82.1). The references to natural law are similar—assertions that natural law proves the point but no development of the reasons why. Thus, for example, the condemnations of direct killing of the innocent, direct abortion, and euthanasia refer to the natural law basis for these considerations without developing in any depth specific natural law arguments (57.4, 62.3, 65.4).

From the viewpoint of theological method, the strong emphasis in *Evangelium vitae* is on God the Father in terms of the Creator and on Christ the Son of God and Redeemer. There are only three explicit references to the Holy Spirit (37.3, 45.1, 57.2). In keeping with John Paul II's consistent emphasis, the Christology is from above. The Christian message affirming life relies very heavily on the

Johannine writings, with their emphasis on a Christology from above. The papal meditation on the Christian message begins by citing the First Letter of John 1:2: "The life was made manifest, and we saw it" (29.1). This is "the eternal life which was with the Father and was made manifest to us" (30.1). Jesus is the way, the truth, and the life (Jn 14), the Son who from all eternity receives life from the Father (Jn 5:26). Whoever lives and believes in Him will never die (Jn 11:26) (29.2). The first nine scripture citations in this chapter on the Christian message concerning life all come from the Johannine writings (29–30).

As was mentioned above, the eschatology of *Evangelium vitae* differs from the usual eschatology found in John Paul II's writings. The format of the culture of death versus the culture of life certainly points to a Christ-against-culture model and does not give sufficient attention to the call of all people of goodwill to work for the common good that is so significant in the other encyclicals, especially the social ones. Why is *Evangelium vitae* so different in its eschatology? The subject matter helps to explain the eschatology. "Here though we shall concentrate particular attention on *another category of attacks* affecting life in its earliest and in its final stages, attacks which present *new characteristics with respect to the past and which raise questions of extraordinary seriousness*. . . . These attacks tend no longer to be considered as 'crimes'; paradoxically they assume the nature of 'rights'" (11.1). By focusing on the two issues of abortion and euthanasia where great changes occurred in the last few decades, the encyclical concentrates on the opposition between the Catholic teaching and what is now often proposed by many others.

As chapter 2 indicated, however, *Evangelium vitae* does not completely lack the basic transformationist motif found in the eschatology of John Paul II. Recall the occasional statements that reason itself and the human heart also bear witness to the Catholic position. After concentrating on the negative factors bringing about the culture of death for fourteen paragraphs (11–24), *Evangelium vitae* devotes two paragraphs (26–27) to the presentation of the positive signs at work in humanity's present situation. The pope explicitly recognizes that a consistent emphasis on the negative signs of a culture of death would lead to sterile discouragement about any hope of transformation or change in the present situation (26.1). But even after recognizing the positive aspects in the present situation, the encyclical still insists "that we are facing an enormous and dramatic clash between good and evil, death and life, the 'culture of death' and the 'culture of life'" (28.1). It seems that the pope has allowed his rhetoric and his concentration on two controversial issues to replace the eschatology that he has consistently developed elsewhere.

The anthropological bases for the discussion of human life are consistent with the anthropological insights found throughout the pope's writings. From a theological perspective, creation, fall, and redemption decisively affect our understanding of human life in this world. God created life and not death. Death came into the world through the devil, envy, and the sin of our first parents, and death entered the world in a violent way through Cain's killing of his brother Abel (7.1–2). A long section meditates on the story of Cain and Abel. But Jesus came to give us life and the fullness of life. The power of God's life in Christ Jesus ultimately constitutes the power that overcomes both sin and death (25).

As one would expect, the anthropology of *Evangelium vitae* insists on the *"incomparable value of every human person"* (2.3). The source of this dignity and equality ultimately comes from God's gracious gift. "The dignity of this life is linked not only to its beginning, to the fact that it comes from God, but also to its final end, to its destiny of fellowship with God in knowledge and love of him" (38.2). The living human person is the image of God. "Man has been given *a sublime dignity* based on the intimate bond which unites him to his Creator: in man there shines forth a reflection of God Himself" (34.2). The human person is at the summit of God's creative activity. Everything in creation is ordered to the human person and subject to the person (34.3).

John Paul II's anthropology that emphasizes the incomparable value and equal dignity of the human person also recognizes that all human persons are called to live in solidarity. John Paul II developed at length the concept of solidarity as a virtue in *Sollicitudo rei socialis* (38–40). Following on that encyclical, *Evangelium vitae* refers to solidarity more than fifteen times. The pope stresses "the values of the dignity of every individual and of solidarity between all people" (70.6). The followers of Jesus and all human beings are called to have a solidarity toward society's weakest members (8.5). The whole treatment of human life in *Evangelium vitae* occurs in the light of the conflict between the culture of death and the culture of life. Thus, the individual person is greatly affected by the culture in which one lives. *Evangelium vitae* expresses the hope that "the 'people of life' constantly grow in number and may a new culture of love and solidarity develop for the true good of the whole of human society" (101.7).

Evangelium vitae emphasizes a deductive and legal model of ethics because it strongly defends the absolute prohibitions of direct killing, direct abortion, and euthanasia. The important third chapter bears the title "You Shall Not Kill: God's Holy Law" (52.1). But John Paul II makes the point that this legal model is not legalistic in a pejorative sense. The law protects and promotes the value of life. "*The entire Law of the Lord* serves to protect life, because it reveals the truth in which life finds its full meaning" (48.2). "*God's commandment is never detached from his love*: it is always a gift meant for man's growth and joy. . . . In giving life to man, God *demands* that he love, respect, and promote life. *The gift thus becomes a commandment and the commandment is itself a gift*" (52.2).

Here, too, John Paul II points out that the commandment "Thou Shalt Not Kill" indicates the extreme limit that can never be crossed. "Implicitly, however, it encourages a positive attitude of absolute respect for life" (54.1). The fourth chapter of *Evangelium vitae* (78–101) develops in detail the need on the part of all to work for a new culture of human life. Here the encyclical insists on the importance of service, charity, and education, as well as the need for civil leaders, educators, healthcare personnel, and volunteers to work for the promotion of life. Special care must be given to the powerless, the needy, the elderly, and the newborn. It is in this context of living out the Gospel of Life "that heroic actions too are born" (86.2).

Absolute Norms against Unjust Killing

Chapter 3 of *Evangelium vitae* presents the official teaching on killing, abortion, euthanasia, and suicide that has been traditionally taught by the hierarchical magisterium especially in the twentieth century. These norms are proclaimed in a quite solemn way. The principle with regard to killing is: "*the direct and voluntary killing of an innocent human being is always gravely immoral*" (57.4). The commandment "Thou Shalt Not Kill" is not absolute because conflict situations can arise especially in the context of self-defense against an unjust aggressor. One has the right to defend oneself by rendering the aggressor incapable of continuing the harmful action even if sometimes it is necessary to take the life of the aggressor (55.1–2). The commandment "has absolute value when it refers to the *innocent person*" (57.1). The encyclical describes "direct and voluntary killing" by saying that the taking of innocent human life "can never be licit either as an end in itself or as a means to a good end" (57.5).

The precise principle or norm about abortion is: "*Direct abortion, that is, abortion willed as an end or as a means, always constitutes a grave moral disorder*, since it is the deliberate killing of an innocent human being" (62.3). In its condemnation of abortion as "the unspeakable crime" (58.1), *Evangelium vitae* stresses the teaching of tradition and especially later documents from the hierarchical magisterium. The unborn are absolutely innocent and also weak, defenseless, and totally entrusted to the care of others.

Scripture does not specifically and directly condemn direct abortion because it does not address the question. But such a conclusion logically follows from the great respect for the human being in the mother's womb found often in scripture in such texts as Psalm 139:1 and Jeremiah 1:4 (61.1–2).

The pope also responds to the objection that the result of conception, at least in the very beginning, cannot yet be considered a personal human life (60.1). In response, John Paul II makes his own the reasons proposed in the 1987 instruction of the Congregation for the Doctrine of the Faith titled *Donum vitae*. After conception, there is a new life different from that of the mother and the father. Modern genetics tells us that the future development of the human being is programmed in the fertilized ovum from the moment of conception (60.1). The pope also recognizes, if somewhat obliquely, that many in the Catholic tradition held in theory that animation took place only later (60.2, 61.4). But despite such philosophical differences, the Catholic tradition has always condemned abortion (61.4).

Here again the Catholic tradition has recognized conflict situations, but the pope does not allude to these. As in the question of killing, direct abortion is always wrong, but indirect abortion may be permitted. *Evangelium vitae* never explicitly recognizes that indirect abortion may be acceptable.

The Catholic teaching on the condemnation of direct abortion, however, is not as certain as John Paul II's rhetoric suggests. The question involves two issues—the status of the embryo-fetus after conception and the solution of conflict situations. First, with regard to the beginning of human life from the moment of conception, *Evangelium vitae* implicitly recognizes that in theory many Catholics have held a delayed-animation theory, even though still condemning abortion. Thus the existence of a truly individual or personal human life from the moment of conception is not certain, even in the Catholic tradition. But in practice, one has to act as if truly individual or personal human life is present. This theoretical uncertainty, however, may have further ramifications. Today not all Catholic theologians are convinced that there is indeed a truly individual or personal life from the very moment of conception.[36]

Second, the solution of conflict situations in papal teaching involves the concept of direct and indirect acts. The description of direct in *Evangelium vitae* points toward the traditional definition accepted in recent hierarchical teaching—a direct killing or abortion is an act that by the nature of the act or the intention of the agent aims at the evil either as an end or as a means.[37] The precise contemporary hierarchical teaching on direct abortion only came into existence in the twentieth century. As late as the 1890s, respected Catholic theologians held that removing the fetus from the womb was not a direct killing, even if the fetus was certain to die. It was only through a series of responses from the Holy Office in the end of the nineteenth century that the hierarchical magisterium came to its present teaching on what constitutes a direct abortion.[38] Today some Catholic theologians cannot accept the existing concept of direct when it comes to the conclusion that the fetus cannot be killed to save the life of the mother—a case that all admit is quite rare.

Note that here again the problem of physicalism occurs—the moral concept of directness is based on the physical structure or causality of the act. Catholic theologians who accept the theory of proportionalism maintain that direct killing understood as the physical causality of the act is not necessarily always morally wrong.[39] The "direct–indirect solution" to conflict situations is based on one philosophical approach (the twentieth-century neoscholastic) that is not accepted even by all Catholic theologians. Because the teaching that direct abortion is always wrong is not as certain as John Paul II implies, he definitely goes too far in quoting from Paul VI "that this tradition is unchanged and unchangeable" (62.3).

Evangelium vitae recognizes in a compassionate way that the decision by a woman to have an abortion is "often tragic and painful for the mother" because the decision is not necessarily based on selfish reasons or convenience. Women often are motivated to have an abortion to protect their own health or to protect the standard of living of their family. Yet however serious and tragic such reasons are, they can never justify the deliberate killing of an innocent human being (58.4). John Paul II directly addresses women who have had an abortion, which in many cases is a painful and shattering choice in light of the many factors influencing them. What happened was and will always remain wrong. But such women should not become discouraged and should become eloquent defenders of life (99.3). But notice the significant difference from the approach to suicide. "Suicide is always as morally objectionable as murder" (66.1). Even though difficult circumstances may influence a person to commit suicide, "thus lessening or removing subjective responsibility," suicide when viewed objectively is a gravely immoral act (66.1). In discussing abortion, the pope never mentions the possibility of "lessening or removing subjective responsibility."

Evangelium vitae also solemnly condemns euthanasia—"an action or omission which of itself and by intention causes death, with the purpose of eliminating all suffering" (65.1, 65.4). Even worse is involuntary euthanasia, which is truly murder (66.3). The condemnation of euthanasia in *Evangelium vitae* follows the format of the earlier condemnations of direct killing and direct abortion. All those condemnations presuppose the incomparable worth and equal dignity of each and every human being, which is the most fundamental value and principle. Contributing factors to the clamor for euthanasia today come from the loss of transcendence. Life is valued only to the extent that it brings pleasure and well-being and there is no recognition of suffering. Many also claim that the human person should be free to decide what to do about one's life and death (64.12). The condemnation of euthanasia is based "upon the written word of God" (65.4), but no specific scripture texts are mentioned in the section on euthanasia itself. Likewise, the condemnation is "based upon the natural law" (65.4), but again this teaching is just asserted without really attempting to prove it. In keeping with the Catholic theological tradition and in light of *Evangelium vitae*'s earlier condemnation of direct killing, one would have expected *Evangelium vitae* to condemn euthanasia as an instance of direct killing. But it does not explicitly do so (65.1).

In keeping with Catholic tradition and recent hierarchical teaching, the pope distinguishes euthanasia from forgoing disproportionate aggressive medical treatment and recognizes the legitimacy of using painkillers even if death is hastened (65.1–2). Perhaps because of the nature of the document, the pope never explains that these positions have been developed on the basis of the concept of direct and indirect killing. *Evangelium vitae* restricts the issue of not using disproportionate means to the situation "when death is clearly imminent and inevitable" (65.2). But the Catholic tradition recognizes the possibility of not using disproportionate or extraordinary means, even when death is not clearly imminent. One traditional example was that to live a longer life one does not have to move to a better climate if this causes disproportionate problems for oneself and one's family.[40]

Again, the teaching on euthanasia is not as certain as the pope implies. It is not based directly on sacred scripture or intimately connected with revelation. Condemnation rests on the definition of direct killing as an act that by the intention of the agent or the nature of the act aims at death either as a means or an end, as distinguished from indirect killing. An act that positively interferes to bring about death is a direct killing. An act that omits doing something to preserve life or that even positively takes away an "extraordinary means" such as a ventilator is an indirect killing and can be good if the means is truly extraordinary or disproportionate and the intention is not to kill.

Thus, the difference between euthanasia and indirect but permissible killing is not based directly on scripture or on the incomparable value of human life but on a philosophical understanding of the difference between the act of commission and the act of omission or even of actively withdrawing a disproportionate or extraordinary means.

In *Evangelium vitae*, John Paul II also repeats the Catholic condemnation of suicide; but, as pointed out above, recognizes that at times subjective culpability is lessened or even removed. There is no solemn condemnation of suicide or assisted suicide in *Evangelium vitae*. The brief rationale against suicide simply mentions without any development three natural law arguments often found in the Catholic tradition—the contradiction to the innate inclination to life, the rejection of a proper love of self, and a renunciation of one's obligations to other persons and society.

The specific teachings condemning direct killing, direct abortion, euthanasia, and suicide simply repeat what has been frequently proposed by the papal magisterium in the past. But the teaching on capital punishment is definitely new and different. The traditional Catholic position recognized the possibility of the death penalty on the grounds that the wrongdoer was not innocent, and it might be necessary for the state to take the wrongdoer's life in order to protect society.[41] The pope today recognizes that punishment exists to redress the violation of personal and social rights, to defend public order, to ensure people's safety, and to furnish rehabilitation for the criminal (56.1). To achieve these purposes, the extreme case of capital punishment can be justified only in cases of absolute necessity. "Today . . . such cases are very rare, if not practically nonexistent" (56.2). In theory, John Paul II points out, on the basis of God's protecting Cain from being killed, that "*not even a murderer loses his personal dignity*" (9.3). In practice, he lauds the sign of hope coming from the growing public opposition to the death penalty (27.3). This development in Catholic teaching obviously comes from a growing appreciation of the incomparable worth and dignity of the individual person.

This section has discussed the methodological bases and the substantive positions of John Paul II with regard to the meaning of human life as well as the specific issues of killing, abortion, and euthanasia. The methodology involved here is consistent with his other writings except in the area of eschatology. He develops strong scriptural arguments for the incomparable worth and equal dignity of all human persons—a position that resonates in the hearts of all people of goodwill. On the specific moral condemnations, there is less certitude than the pope is willing to admit. The earlier sections of the chapter analyzed and criticized John Paul II's understanding of conscience and human acts, two important topics in fundamental moral theology.

Notes

1. For a manualist approach to conscience, see Benedictus H. Merkelbach, *Summa theologiae moralis*, 10th ed. (Bruges: Desclée de Brouwer, 1959), 1, 186–99; I. Aertnys and C. Damen, *Theologia moralis*, 2 vols., ed. J. Visser, 17th ed. (Rome: Marietti, 1956), 1, 75–89; and Marcellinus Zalba, *Theologiae moralis summa*, 3 vols. (Madrid: Biblioteca de autores cristianos, 1952–58), 1, 239–63. For an English work on conscience as it has been understood in the Catholic tradition, see Philippe Delhaye, *The Christian Conscience* (New York: Desclée, 1968).

2. For example, Delhaye, *Christian Conscience*, mentions consequent conscience on only three pages—29, 158, 159.

3. C. A. Pierce, *Conscience in the New Testament* (London: SCM Press, 1955), 109.

4. Charles E. Curran, *The Catholic Moral Tradition Today: A Synthesis* (Washington, D.C.: Georgetown University Press, 1999), 172–96.

5. Louis Vereecke, *De Guillaume d'Ockham à Saint Alfonse de Liguori: Études d'histoire de la théologie morale moderne 1300–1787* (Rome: Collegium S. Alfonsi de Urbe, 1986), 553–60; Brian V. Johnstone, "Erroneous Conscience in *Veritatis Splendor* and the Theological Tradition," in *The Splendor of Accuracy: An Examination of the Assertions Made by Veritatis Splendor*, ed. Joseph A. Selling and Jan Jans (Grand Rapids, Mich.: William B. Eerdmans, 1995), 126–30.

6. Curran, *Catholic Moral Tradition Today*, 185–90.

7. For a recent survey of Catholic theologians on this subject, see Bernard Hoose, "Authority in the Church," *Theological Studies* 63 (2002): 107–22; also, Hoose, ed., *Authority in the Roman Catholic Church: Theory and Practice* (Burlington, Vt.: Ashgate, 2002).

8. Charles E. Curran, ed., *Change in Official Catholic Moral Teachings: Readings in Moral Theology No. 13* (New York: Paulist Press, 2003).

9. Pope John Paul II, *Ad tuendam fidem*, in *Origins* 28 (1998): 113–16.

10. See, for example, Germain Grisez, "The Ordinary Magisterium's Infallibility: A Reply to Some New Arguments," *Theological Studies* 55 (1994): 720–32; Lawrence J. Welch, "Replay to Richard Gaillardetz on the Ordinary Universal Magisterium and to Francis Sullivan," *Theological Studies* 64 (2003): 598–609.

11. Charles E. Curran, *Faithful Dissent* (Kansas City: Sheed & Ward, 1986).

12. John P. Beal, James A. Coriden, and Thomas J. Green, eds., *New Commentary on the Code of Canon Law* (New York: Paulist Press, 2000), 913–14.

13. Grisez, "Ordinary Magisterium's Infallibility," 731.

14. Francis Sullivan, "Reply to Germain Grisez," *Theological Studies* 55 (1994): 732–37; Richard Gaillardetz, "The Ordinary Universal Magisterium: Unresolved Questions," *Theological Studies* 63 (2002): 447–71. There has been much literature on this subject. A good summary of the discussions can be found in two different *"Quaestio Disputata,"* found in *Theological Studies* 55 (1994): 720–38, and *Theological Studies* 64 (2003): 598–615.

15. Thomas Aquinas, *Summa theologiae*, 4 vols. (Rome: Marietti, 1952), Ia IIae q. 94, a. 4.

16. John Connery, *Abortion: The Development of the Roman Catholic Perspective* (Chicago: Loyola University Press, 1997), 225–303.

17. Pope John Paul II, "Apostolic Constitution *Ex corde ecclesiae*," *Origins* 20 (1990): 265–76. For a discussion of the mandate and other issues in contemporary Catholic higher education, see Alice Gallin, *Negotiating Identity: Catholic Higher Education Since 1960* (Notre Dame, Ind.: University of Notre Dame Press, 2000).

18. Canons 747–55. For a commentary on these, see James A. Coriden, "The Teaching Function of the Church," in *New Commentary*, ed. Beal, Coriden, and Green, 911–19.

19. Congregation for the Doctrine of the Faith, "Profession of Faith and Oath of Fidelity," *Origins* 18 (1989): 661–63.

20. Congregation for the Doctrine of the Faith, "Instruction on the Ecclesial Vocation of the Theologian (*Donum veritatis*)," *Origins* 20 (1990): 117–26.

21. Congregation for the Doctrine of the Faith, "Instruction on the Ecclesial Vocation of the Theologian," n. 24, p. 122.

22. Congregation for the Doctrine of the Faith, "Instruction on the Ecclesial Vocation of the Theologian," nn. 30–32, pp. 123–24.

23. For a good explanation of fundamental option theory, see Timothy E. O'Connell, *Principles for a Catholic Morality*, rev. ed. (San Francisco: Harper-Collins, 1990), 51–102.

24. For a criticism of John Paul II's understanding of the fundamental option theory by the moral theologian most closely associated with the theory, see Josef

Fuchs, "Good Acts and Good Persons," in *Understanding Veritatis Splendor*, ed. John Wilkins (London: SPCK, 1994), 21–26.

25. Curran, *Catholic Moral Tradition Today*, 95–98.

26. *Veritatis splendor*, n. 80, *Acta Apostolica Sedis* 85 (1993): 1197.

27. Walter J. Abbott, ed. *The Documents of Vatican II* (New York: Guild, 1966), 226; Austin Flannery, ed., *Vatican Council II: The Conciliar Documents: The Basic Sixteen Documents: Constitutions, Decrees, Declarations* (Northport, N.Y.: Costello, 1996), 928.

28. Hieronymus Noldin et al., *Summa theologiae moralis*, vol. 2: *De praeceptis* (Oeniponte: F. Rauch, 1959), 553–60.

29. Julius A. Dorszynski, *Catholic Teaching about the Morality of Falsehood* (Washington, D.C.: Catholic University of America Press, 1949).

30. *Catechism of the Catholic Church* (Liguori, Mo.: Liguori, 1994), n. 2483, p. 595.

31. Joseph Cardinal Ratzinger, "Vatican List of Catechism Changes," *Origins* 27 (1997): 262.

32. In 1928, John A. Ryan, the foremost Catholic moral theologian in the United States in the first half of the twentieth century, disagreed with the intrinsic evil of artificial contraception based on the perverted faculty argument precisely because of the analogy with the newer approach to the morality of lying. However, Ryan still accepted the immorality of artificial contraception but did not condemn it as being intrinsically evil. See John A. Ryan, "The Immorality of Contraception," *American Ecclesiastical Review* 79 (1928): 408–11.

33. For a further development of the moral object of the act, see Jean Porter, "The Moral Act in *Veritatis splendor* and in Aquinas's *Summa theologiae*," in *Veritatis splendor: American Responses*, ed. Michael E. Allsopp and John J. O'Keefe (Kansas City: Sheed & Ward, 1995), 278–95.

34. Noldin, *Summa theologiae moralis*, 2, 384–86.

35. Patrick Granfield, "The Right to Silence: Magisterial Development," *Theological Studies* 27 (1966): 401–20.

36. For recent debates about the status of the embryo in the journal *Theological Studies*, see Thomas A. Shannon and Allan B. Wolter, "Reflections on the Moral Status of the Preembryo," *Theological Studies* 51 (1990): 603–26; Mark Johnson, "Reflections on Some Recent Catholic Claims for Delayed Hominization," *Theological Studies* 56 (1995): 743–63; Jean Porter, "Individuality, Personal Identity, and the Moral Status of the Preembryo: A Response to Mark Johnson," *Theological Studies* 56 (1995): 763–70; Thomas A. Shannon, "Delayed Hominization: A Response to Mark Johnson," *Theological Studies* 57 (1996): 731–34; and Mark Johnson and Thomas A. Shannon, "*Quaestio Disputata*: Delayed Hominization," *Theological Studies* 58 (1997): 708–17.

37. *The Catechism of the Catholic Church*, n. 2277, condemns euthanasia as direct killing understood as "an act or omission which, of itself or by intention, causes death in order to eliminate suffering."

38. For a detailed history of the theological discussion of the issues and the responses from the Vatican, see Connery, *Abortion*, 225–303. For an earlier study of direct and indirect abortion in light of craniotomy and ectopic pregnancy, see T. Lincoln Bouscaren, *The Ethics of Ectopic Operations*, 2d ed. (Milwaukee: Bruce, 1944).

39. The late Richard A. McCormick was the primary American proponent of proportionalism. For an overview of his position, see Paulinus Ikechukwu Odozor, *Richard A. McCormick and the Renewal of Moral Theology* (Notre Dame, Ind.: University of Notre Dame Press, 1995). For critical but favorable analysis of McCormick's position, see John Langan, "Direct and Indirect—Some Recent Exchanges between Paul Ramsey and Richard McCormick," *Religious Studies Review* 5 (1979): 95–101; James J. Walter, "The Foundation and Formulation of Norms," in *Moral Theology: Challenges for the Future: Essays in Honor of Richard A. McCormick*, ed. Charles E. Curran (New York: Paulist Press, 1990), 125–54; and Bernard Hoose, *Proportionalism: The American Debate and Its European Roots* (Washington, D.C.: Georgetown University Press, 1987). Germain Grisez is a strong opponent of proportionalism; for a succinct but accurate summary of his basic theory, see Germain Grisez and Russell Shaw, *Fulfillment in Christ: A Summary of Christian Moral Principles* (Notre Dame, Ind.: University of Notre Dame Press, 1991). For a negative evaluation of proportionalism, see Christopher Zaczor, *Proportionalism and the Natural Law Tradition* (Washington, D.C.: Catholic University of America Press, 2002).

40. Gerald Kelly, ed., *Medico-Moral Problems* (St. Louis: Catholic Health Association of the United States and Canada, 1958), 128–41.

41. James J. Megivern, *The Death Penalty: A Historical and Theological Survey* (New York: Paulist Press, 1997).

MARRIAGE, SEXUALITY, GENDER, AND FAMILY

JOHN PAUL II has written extensively on sexuality, marriage, and gender. The encyclical *Veritatis splendor* (1993) covers the whole field of moral theology and mentions sexuality and marriage in the process.[1] Other documents deal primarily and extensively with sexuality and marriage—the apostolic exhortation *Familiaris consortio* (1981),[2] the apostolic letter *Mulieris dignitatem* (1988),[3] the 1994 "Letter to Families,"[4] the 1995 "Letter to Women,"[5] and the "1995 World Day of Peace Message: Women—Teachers of Peace."[6] The most extensive discussion of sexuality and marriage comes from the talks given at the first general audiences of the pope held weekly from September 1979 to November 1984, which were published in English in one large volume, *The Theology of the Body: Human Love in the Divine Plan*.[7] Ordinarily a discussion of papal teaching does not focus on the short talks given at the pope's weekly audiences, but the introduction to this volume pointed out the significance of these talks as a source for John Paul II's teaching on marriage and sexuality.

John Paul II's discussion of sexuality and marriage faithfully follows his methodology and approach to moral theology as discussed above. The pope emphasizes that the primary reality is truth, and he seeks to teach the truth about marriage and sexuality. *Familiaris consortio* begins by pointing out that many today are "doubtful and almost unaware of the ultimate meaning and truth of conjugal and family life" (1.1). In this context, "Illuminated by the faith that gives her an understanding of all the truth concerning the great value of marriage and the family and their deepest meaning, the Church once again feels the pressing need to proclaim the Gospel, that is the 'good news' to all people without exception, in particular to all those who are called to marriage and are preparing for it, to all married couples and parents in the world" (3.1). The primary question for moral teaching in general and for marriage and sexuality in particular is the question of truth.

John Paul II's teaching on marriage and family uses different sources of moral wisdom and knowledge, but the previous teachings of the hierarchical magisterium hold a central place. *Mulieris dignitatem* begins by citing the recent official teachings that have dealt with the role of women—Pius XII, John XXIII, Vatican Council II, Paul VI, and the 1971 and 1987 Synods of Bishops (1). In his teaching on marriage and sexuality, as in all his teaching, he strongly supports and defends the specific moral norms associated with previous hierarchical teachings.

Theology and Meaning of the Body and Human Sexuality

Karol Wojtyla's training and profession was as an ethicist. His writings before becoming pope dealt primarily with issues of meaning and not primarily with casuistry. As pope, he has had to address many casuistic issues dealing with the moral norms of Catholic hierarchical teaching, but he still continues to probe the deeper question of meaning. His long series of general audience talks at the beginning of his pontificate well illustrates such an approach.

John Paul II develops the meaning and theology of the body and human sexuality in the light of his theological anthropology involving creation, the fall, and redemption of the body (*TB* 25–90). In the garden, in the state of original innocence before the fall ("In the beginning"), the human person experiences three aspects of humanity—original solitude, original unity or communion of persons, and original nakedness. Thanks to the gift of creation, in the very experience of his body, Adam perceives himself as different from all other creation, including the animals, because he has a unique relationship with God. The pope often refers to this as the "first covenant." Through this covenant given by God, Adam experiences his power of self-determination and self-choice, in which he recognizes himself as an image of God. But Adam also experiences that he is alone—he is missing someone to share love and life with him (*TB* 35–42).

The second aspect of creation is the original unity or the communion of persons in and through the body. God made woman—the equal and the partner of man. Human beings now appear as masculine and feminine. This sexual difference makes possible the communion of persons in and through their bodies, which reflects God's own Trinitarian life. This "nuptial meaning" of the body is shown in the sincere gift of one to the other. In this context, John Paul II often cites *Gaudium et spes* 24—"Man can fully discover his true self only in a sincere giving of himself" (*TB* 60–66). Here human persons find themselves an even more significant image of the triune God.

The aspect of original nakedness also contributes to the nuptial meaning of the body. This original nakedness signifies the absence of shame or interior division, which thus allows Adam and Eve to give themselves totally and completely to one another in the sincere gift of love. There is no holding back and no temptation to treat the other as object (*TB* 57–60).

The fall brought about a threefold break with regard to the human person—a break in the relationship of loving dependence on God, which Wojtyla refers to as a breaking of the covenant; the break in the relationship between man and woman; and a break or disunion in the human person brought about by concupiscence. In keeping with the Catholic understanding of the role of sin, the fall does not completely destroy what was present from the beginning but obscures or diminishes the image and likeness of God in the human being (*MD* 9).

The theology of the body puts special emphasis on concupiscence and lust that causes the division within the human person (spirit and body) and thereby affects the community of persons in their one-flesh unity. In this context, Genesis 3:7 is the primary text—"Then the eyes of both were open, and they knew that they were naked, and they sewed fig leafs together and made themselves aprons."

Genesis 3:10 adds another element. In response to the call of God after the fall in the garden, Adam replied, "I heard the sound of you in the garden, and I was afraid because I was naked, and I hid myself." Thus, the "man of original innocence" becomes the "man of lust." Lust manifests itself above all in the shame that human beings now experience after the fall. A disquiet exists within human beings. This is the second discovery of sex (*TB* 114–25).

Although John Paul II recognizes that original sin also affects the heart and the spirit (*TB* 122), the emphasis here is on the fact that the body is no longer subject to the spirit. Lust thus affects the relationship of man and woman and the nuptial meaning of the body. Gone is the joyous, spontaneous self-gift of one to the other. The pope mentions at various times three different but interconnected affects of the lust, concupiscence, and shame that affect the nuptial relationship of man and woman. The very fact that Adam and Eve hid themselves from one another behind their aprons shows a lack of trust. Notice how this hiding relates to the fact that they hid themselves from God previously because they knew they were naked (*TB* 121). Second, the husband "will rule over you" (Genesis 3:16). The domination of one over the other thus destroys the original equality (*TB* 122–24). Third, the heart is now a battlefield between love and lust. Concupiscence works against the self-control and interior freedom of the original communion of persons. Now the other is no longer a person but is reduced to an object of sexual gratification (*TB* 125–30). Such are the effects of sin on the nuptial meaning of the body and the sexual union of man and woman.

The pope bases the effect of redemption on the nuptial meaning of the body on a number of different scriptural texts in contradistinction to his concentration on Genesis in describing original innocence and the fall. Genesis, however, also points toward future redemption with its *proto-evangelium*—the woman (the new Eve) will crush the head of the serpent (*MD* 11). One series of talks from December 17, 1980, to May 6, 1981, bears the title: "St. Paul's Teaching on the Human Body" (*TB* 191–232). The human body is the temple of the Holy Spirit and member of Christ (1 Cor 6:15–20). 1 Thessalonians 4:4 calls for controlling the body in holiness and honor. Paul in Romans 8:23 refers explicitly to the redemption of the body. This redemption by God's grace overcomes the effect of the fall and makes possible once again the nuptial meaning of the body found in original innocence (*TB* 32–34).

The pope puts heavy emphasis on Matthew 5:27–28—if a man looks at a woman lustfully, he has already committed adultery in his heart. The meaning of adultery is thus transferred from the body to the heart (*TB* 142–44). Redemption thus overcomes the power of concupiscence and lust that sees the other merely as an object of sexual gratification. Concupiscence and lust depersonalize. The commandment forbidding adultery is carried out through purity of heart. Male and female through the redemption of the body now regain the nuptial meaning of the body because of which they can freely give themselves in the total self-gift of one to the other. The Sermon on the Mount calls us not to go back to original innocence but to rediscover—on the foundations of the perennial and indestructible meaning of what is human—the living form of redeemed humankind (*TB* 175). Through self-control, continence, and temperance, man and woman can now live out the nuptial meaning of the body. The power of redemption thus completes the power of creation (*TB* 147–80).

The Sacramentality of Marriage

John Paul II devoted a series of his general audience talks from July 28, 1982, to July 4, 1984, with some interruptions, to the sacramentality of marriage. In keeping with his methodology in these talks, he bases his approach on scripture and in particular on Ephesians 5:21–32. The very first talk begins with the citation of this long passage. This passage in general calls on spouses to love one another as Christ has loved the church. Because of this, a man leaves his mother and father to become one flesh with his wife. This is a great mystery in reference to Christ and the church. Note that the English word "mystery" here is a translation of the Latin word *sacramentum*. Thus the passage lends itself to be understood in a sacramental way. But, of course, to see the contemporary Catholic understanding of sacramentality in this passage, one has to read quite a bit into the biblical passage itself—which John Paul II is very willing to do (*TB* 304–6).

The passage also appeals to the pope for a number of other reasons. Ephesians here cites Genesis about a man leaving father and mother and becoming one flesh with his wife. Thus the passage refers back to the "beginning" to which the pope has paid so much attention in his previous talks. The passage puts heavy emphasis on the body, in keeping with his emphasis on the theology of the body. But in addition to referring to the human body in its masculinity and femininity, Ephesians speaks of the body in a metaphorical sense—the body of the church—and thus provides a basis for the sacramental understanding of the spousal relationship of husband and wife in light of the relationship of Christ with the church. In addition, the liturgy of the church sees this text in relation to the sacrament of marriage. Here the prayer of the church tells us something about the faith of the church (*TB* 304–6).

In chapter 2, it was pointed out how the pope interprets away the obvious meaning of the text "wives be subject to your husbands." The mutual relations of husband and wife flow from their common relationship with Christ. They are to be "subject to one another out of reverence for Christ." There is a mutual subjection of the spouses, one to the other, based on their relationship with Christ. Husbands are then told to love their wives, which "removes any fear that might have arisen (given the modern sensitivity) from the previous phrase: 'wives be subject to your husbands.'" Love excludes any subjection whereby the wife is a servant, slave, or object of domination by the husband. The communion of husband and wife is based on mutual love and mutual subjection (*TB* 310).

In addition, the pope does not deal with the analogy of Christ to the husband and the church to the wife. Christ is obviously the head of his body, the church. For many Christians, even some today, this means that the husband is the head of the wife and of the family. But the pope's own position is clear—there is a reciprocal and equal love relationship of husband and wife, with no one-sided domination by the husband.

In his discussion of marriage as a sacrament, John Paul II uses the term "sacrament" in both a broader and a more narrow or technical sense of one of the seven sacraments of the church. In the broader sense, a sacrament is a sign that effectively transmits in the visible world the invisible mystery hidden from eternity in God (*TB* 333–41). In this sense, creation and redemption are both sacraments. But marriage is the primordial sacrament signifying the loving relationship of God with his people and of Christ with the church. Marriage is the "primordial sacrament instituted from the beginning and linked with the sacrament of creation in its globality" (*TB* 339). Ephesians 1:3–4 tells us of the mystery hidden in God from all eternity. God chose us in Christ before the foundation of the world that we should be holy and blameless before him. "The reality of man's creation was already imbued by the perennial election of man in Christ." The one-flesh loving union of the first man and woman in Genesis in their holiness constitutes the sign of the mystery of God's covenant love hidden in God from eternity. The procreative powers of the first couple also continue the work of creation. Thus, marriage is the primordial sacrament of creation itself (*TB* 333–36).

But marriage is also the primordial sacrament of redemption. Although grace is lost after the fall, marriage never ceased to be in some sense a figure of the great mystery or sacrament of God's covenant love for his people. There is a continuity between creation and redemption. The sacrament of creation as the original gift of grace constituted human beings in the state of original innocence and justice. "The new gracing of man in the sacrament of redemption instead gives him above all the remission of sins." Grace abounds even more. Christ's redemptive love, according to Ephesians, is his special love for the church, of which marriage is the primordial sacrament (*TB* 337).

The sacrament of marriage in the narrower and stricter sense of one of the seven sacraments of the church, based on Ephesians, understands the relationship between husband and wife on the basis of the relationship between Christ and the church. This analogy operates in two directions. The relationship of Christ with the church tells us something about Christian marriage, whereas the spousal relationship tells us something about Christ's love for the church (*TB* 312–14). The Hebrew Bible prefigured this analogy, as found in the Prophets such as Isaiah, who rebukes Israel as an unfaithful spouse (*TB* 327–30). John Paul II also appeals to the Song of Songs, "found in the wake of that sacrament in which, through the language of the body, the visible sign of man and woman's participation in the covenant of grace and love offered by God to man is constituted" (*TB* 368). The Book of Tobit also tells us about the truth and power of marital love (*TB* 375–77).

The matrimonial consent of husband and wife shares in, signifies, and also tells something about the covenant of Christ with the church and of God with his people. "The analogy of spousal love indicates the radical character of grace." "The analogy of spousal love seems to emphasize especially the aspect of the gift of self on the part of God to man. . . . It is a total (or rather radical) and irrevocable gift" (*TB* 330–31).

Critical Appraisal

The pope has developed his understanding of marriage especially in the long series of general audience talks at the beginning of his pontificate. One cannot easily describe the genre of these talks. Although they have a homiletical tone at times, they are not homilies. Without doubt, the talks belong to the genre of teaching. Here the pope is proposing to the world his understanding of marriage and its meaning for Christians today. The talks occasionally cite philosophers and other secular thinkers; the talks also come complete with footnotes. But the theology of the body is not developed in a systematic and complete way. The very nature of short talks presented every week to a different audience militates against a totally systematic approach. Because the talks are not a complete and systematic presentation of the pope's teaching on marriage, many aspects remain somewhat unclear and certainly less developed than they would be in a truly systematic presentation.[8] I will consider four issues—the theology of the body in general, the spirit-body relationship, the meaning of love, and the role of sexual pleasure.

The Theology of the Body

The nuptial meaning of the body is the basic understanding developed by John Paul II in his approach to marriage and sexuality. The pope has definitely made a positive contribution that has never been found before in papal teaching. On the basis of a theology of the body, he develops his understanding of the meaning and spirituality of marriage. In the process, he uses both scripture and his own personalistic philosophy to develop the nuptial meaning of the body as a foundation for a better understanding of the spirituality of marriage.

The theology of the body as developed by John Paul II, however, cannot serve as a theology for all bodies. In other words, there are different theologies of the body. What the pope develops in terms of the nuptial meaning of the body really does not apply to people who are single or those who are widows or widowers. In a later discussion of virginity and celibacy, the pope does try to show how these realities also come under the influence of the nuptial meaning of the body. But there are many people for whom the nuptial meaning of the body as developed here is not appropriate.

Implicitly, John Paul II's theology of the body maintains that heterosexual marriage is the only context for human sexuality. This understanding obviously is based on the contemporary hierarchical Catholic teaching. The whole discussion of homosexuality lies beyond the scope of this book. But just as his nuptial theology of the body does not apply to all persons and all bodies, he also would have to prove that heterosexual marital sexuality is the only meaning for sexuality for all human beings. The theology of the body developed by John Paul II takes a very positive approach to the understanding of marriage, but the theology of the body and its accompanying understanding of sexuality do not necessarily apply to all human beings.

The Spirit–Body Relationship

There is no Manichean dualism in John Paul II's anthropology of human sexuality. The body and sexuality are not bad (*TB* 165–67). The very title of the book in English, *The Theology of the Body*, argues against any kind of total dualism between the spirit and body or matter. Yet in the world of human existence after sin, the pope frequently refers to lust and its effects on the human person especially in terms of the body.

In discussing lust, these talks frequently cite 1 John 2:15–16, which mentions the threefold aspect of lust—lust of the flesh, of the eyes, and of the pride of life (e.g., *TB* 116, 127, 165, 203). So lust also involves the spirit and not just the body. But there can be no doubt that John Paul II emphasizes the lust of the flesh. The passage from the Sermon on the Mount (looking lustfully at a woman) that he so often cites does not condemn the body or sexuality but "contains a call to overcome the three forms of lust, especially the lust of the flesh" (*TB* 165). In another context, the talks comment on 1 Cor 12:18–25, in which St. Paul refers to the less honorable parts or the unpresentable parts of the body. For John Paul II, Paul here calls for respect for the whole human body with no Manichean contempt for the body. But Paul is conscious of historical humanity after sin, and in using these terms for the sexual parts of the body testifies to the shame that has been present in human experience ever since the sin of Adam and Eve. This shame is the fruit of the three forms of lust, with particular reference to the lust of the flesh (*TB* 202–3). As a result of such an understanding, these texts frequently refer to "The Opposition in the Human Heart Between the Spirit and the Body," which is the title of the pope's July 30, 1980, address (*TB* 128). The problem with "the man of lust" after original sin is that the "body is not subordinated to the spirit as in the state of original innocence. It bears within it a constant center of resistance to the spirit" (*TB* 115).

In the light of such an understanding of the effect of lust and concupiscence for redeemed people, "the body is given as a task to the human spirit." This is the spirituality of the body (*TB* 215). For the redeemed person, the emphasis is on self-control. "It is precisely at the price of self-control that man reaches that deeper and more mature spontaneity with which his heart, mastering his instincts, rediscovers the spiritual beauty of the sign constituted by the human body in its masculinity and femininity" (*TB* 173). However, John Paul II is not entirely negative about passion. As the Book of Sirach points out, carnal concupiscence and passion suffocate the voice of conscience. Passion tends to satisfy the senses and the body, but such satisfaction brings no peace or true satisfaction. However, through the radical transformation of grace, passion can become a creative force (*TB* 145–46).

No one can deny the role of concupiscence and lust in human sexuality. Self-control and discipline are absolutely necessary. But John Paul II's incomplete discussion of concupiscence, lust, and self-control seems too one-sided. Yes, sin affects the body; but it also affects the spirit. Sin does not necessarily bring about an opposition between spirit and body or between the higher and the lower parts of the human person, as so often seems to be the case in the words used by John Paul II. The senses and passions are not simply forces that must be controlled and directed by reason. The senses and the passions, despite the influence of sin, still can point to and indicate the true and the good. Reason and spirit are not the only realities that can help us discern the true and the good. And like the senses and passions, they too can become disturbed by sin. Yes, there is need for self-control with regard to sexual passion, but sexual passion is basically a good that is often disturbed by sin. Its basic goodness should not be denied or forgotten. The impression given by *The Theology of the Body* is that passion and sexual pleasure are totally suspect and in need of control. The pope does not seem to acknowledge a fundamental goodness about sexuality, despite the ever-present danger of lust and concupiscence. There is just an occasional remark along more positive lines, but the heavy emphasis of the talks remains on the negative reality of sexual passion and the need for spirit and reason to control it.

The Meaning of Love

The lack of a systematic and complete theology of the body in the pope's talks also comes through in the sketchy understanding of human love. Though the subtitle of the English collection of these talks is "Human Love in the Divine Plan," there is no in-depth or systematic discussion of human love. The general approach is quite clear, but it usually presents just two extremes. Love involves a sincere gift of self to the other—"the personal and total self-giving" (*FC* 20.3). The opposite of love is treating the other as an object or as a means of sexual self-gratification. The contrast is between disinterested giving and selfish enjoyment (*TB* 130). A more complete picture should recognize that the gift of self also involves some human fulfillment and sexual enjoyment.

The primary understanding of marriage as a sign of the covenant love of God for human beings, of Yahweh for the people of the covenant, and of Christ for the church makes the love of giving self to the other the basic meaning of marital love. I pointed out in chapter 2 that the pope emphasizes the cross more than the resurrection of Jesus because of his emphasis on God's love for us as total gift. Theological literature refers to this love as "agape"—the total giving of self.[9]

Although John Paul II in his discussion of marriage gives primacy to agape love or the gift of self modeled on God's love—especially as seen in the Incarnation and death of Jesus—the other aspects of love as reciprocity and mutual communion and also some self-fulfillment are mentioned occasionally. Love as personal communion comes through, especially in the loving union of Adam and Eve that overcomes the problem of solitude. The body shares fully in the personal communion of love between husband and wife. Such a love makes Adam and Eve as husband and wife images of the love of the Trinity (*TB* 45–48).

The talks also refer to eros. Here the pope distinguishes between the common use of the term and the more philosophical use of eros going back to Plato. In common language today, the erotic signifies what comes from desire and serves to satisfy the lust of the flesh. This is precisely what Matthew 5:27–28 condemns and what the talks emphasize. But eros in the platonic sense has a positive role to play. Here eros is the interior force that attracts human beings to what is true, good, and beautiful. In the description of original innocence in the garden, the talks recognize that Adam longed for someone to share love and life with him. The attraction, and even the sexual attraction between man and woman, has a very positive aspect about it. The Song of Songs presents eros as the form of human love in which the energies of desire are at work. Agape love, as described by St. Paul in 1 Corinthians 13:4–8 (love is patient, kind, not jealous), purifies this eros love of the Song of Songs and brings it to completion (*TB* 168–71). Thus, in the talks, there are some indications that eros is not completely negative and even has a positive role to play.

At the very minimum, the full meaning of human love in marriage with all its dimensions is not developed in a systematic way in these talks. The emphasis is on agape love understood as self-gift. The talks recognize love as communion but fail to develop the mutuality and reciprocity aspects of marital love. In addition, the pope does not integrate love as communion with love as self-gift. John Paul II does not discuss at length the proper love of self in marriage. The focus is on love as self-gift without developing the point that some true self-fulfillment and happiness are achieved in and through this self-gift.

The emphasis on love as a sincere gift of self—the personal and total self-giving—together with a narrow focus on Genesis results in a somewhat romantic, narrow, and unreal understanding of marriage in its total life context. Married people have lives of their own and are involved in many other activities and pursuits. Too often in the past, understandings similar to John Paul II's approach have limited the life especially of married women to the sphere of the home with husband and children. Yes, the marriage commitment is of singular importance for married people, but individual married people have their own lives to live in the various spheres of human existence.

Sexual Pleasure

These talks for all practical purposes ignore the positive aspect of sexual pleasure. One would expect that talks dealing precisely with the body would recognize the role of sexual pleasure in marriage and insist that such pleasure is good. This failure to mention the role and goodness of sexual pleasure is somewhat connected with the previous discussions of lust and love. Lust primarily affects the flesh. All recognize that the drive for sexual pleasure often distorts what the pope calls "the nuptial meaning of the body." But sexual pleasure itself is a good that can and often is abused. The failure to develop the proper role of sexual pleasure seems to be associated with a fear of such pleasure and a tendency to see it primarily in a negative way. If the talks gave more importance to a proper self-love and true fulfillment, they would have furnished an appropriate context for the discussion of sexual pleasure.

Specific Norms

John Paul II, as is obvious, strongly supports and defends the existing hierarchical Catholic teachings on specific moral norms dealing with sexuality. With regard to marriage and sexuality, the two most significant and controversial norms are the prohibitions of divorce and of artificial contraception.

The Indissolubility of Marriage

Nowhere in his major papal writings does John Paul II develop the Catholic prohibition of divorce in a systematic and in-depth manner. Throughout his writings, however, he proposes four basic reasons for the indissolubility of Christian marriage and the prohibition of divorce.

The scriptural argument is primary and comes from Matthew 19. The very first audience talk on marriage in 1979 insists on the unity and indissolubility of marriage in the light of Matthew 19. Moses allowed you to divorce your wives because of the hardness of your heart, but from the beginning it was not so (*TB* 25–27). This scripture text reminds us of "God's original plan for mankind, a plan which man after sin has no longer been able to live up to" (*VS* 22.2). "Christ renews the first plan that the Creator inscribed in the hearts of man and woman" (*FC* 20).

The sacramental argument sees the marriage covenant as a sign or sacrament of the covenant love of God for the people in the Hebrew Bible and of Jesus for the church. But such covenant love of God and of Christ is an absolutely faithful love. "Just as the Lord Jesus is . . . the supreme realization of the unconditional faithfulness with which God loves his people, so Christian couples are called to participate truly in the irrevocable indissolubility that binds Christ to the Church, his Bride, loved by him to the end" (*FC* 20.4).

The theological argument for indissolubility insists on the role of the grace of God. "To imitate and live out the love of Christ is not possible for man by his own strength alone. *He becomes capable of this love only by virtue of a gift received.*" Jesus freely communicates to his disciples the grace he has received from his Father (*VS* 22.3).

A theological-ethical argument also grounds the prohibition of divorce. Christian marriage involves the commitment of the spouses to each other—"a total and irrevocable gift of self" (*TB* 330). Indissolubility is "rooted in the personal and total self-giving of the couple" (*FC* 20). Marital love, as the total gift of self, grounds the indissolubility of marriage.

Artificial Contraception

Pope John Paul II devoted a series of sixteen audience talks in the second half of 1984 to reflections on Pope Paul VI's 1968 encyclical *Humanae vitae*, which staunchly defends the condemnation of artificial contraception for spouses. This section very briefly summarizes the arguments proposed by the pope.

In keeping with his general approach to marriage and sexuality, John Paul II, in condemning artificial contraception, gives primary significance to truth and to the plan of God. In discussing the meaning of the marital act, "we are dealing with nothing other than reading the language of the body in truth as has been said many times in our previous biblical analyses" (*TB* 388). The pope insists "that the principle of conjugal morality, taught by the Church (Second Vatican Council, Paul VI), is the criterion of faithfulness to the divine plan" (*TB* 395). The pope directly appeals to the teaching of the hierarchical magisterium, especially the encyclical *Humanae vitae*. He sees his own exposition of *Humanae vitae* in terms of trying "to elaborate more completely the biblical and personalistic aspects of the doctrine contained in *Humanae vitae*." The questions raised by *Humanae vitae* "belong to that sphere of anthropology and theology that we have called the theology of the body" (*TB* 421).

Pope John Paul II insists with Pope Paul VI on the "inseparable connection, established by God, which man on his own initiative may not break, between the unitive significance and the procreative significance which are both inherent to the marriage act" (*TB* 386). John Paul II accepts the criterion proposed in Vatican II that sexual morality is "based on the nature of the human person and his or her acts." But here he develops especially his language of the body. The marriage act, in light of the theology of the body, shows the "value of 'total' self-giving. Thus the innate language that expresses the total reciprocal self-giving of husband and wife is overlaid, through contraception, by an objectively contradictory language, namely, that of not giving oneself totally to the other. This leads . . . to a falsification of the inner truth of conjugal love which is called upon to give itself in personal totality" (*FC* 32.4). The papal talks also insist that the church's teaching on the transmission of life calls for the development of discipline, continence, and self-control that ennoble human marital love (*TB* 399–415).

The many debates within Catholicism on the subject of divorce and artificial contraception lie beyond the boundaries of this volume. This section has merely tried to briefly describe John Paul II's approach to these issues in light of his understanding of marriage and sexuality discussed above. But two comments are in order.

With regard to the indissolubility of marriage, John Paul II stresses the total, radical, and irrevocable self-gift of the spouses to each other. But as pointed out above, he fails to give enough importance to love as communion or the mutuality and reciprocity aspects of love. Likewise, he does not develop the proper love of self. An understanding of love that recognizes the three aspects of self-gift, communion and mutuality, and a proper self-love can come to the conclusion that unfortunately, at times, marriages may break down.

With regard to artificial contraception, John Paul II takes a two-fold approach. The first and less-developed approach defends the natural law arguments condemning artificial contraception. The audience talks allude to these arguments, especially in citing *Humanae vitae*—without, however, developing the arguments in a systematic way. "'The Church teaches as absolutely required that in any use whatever of marriage there must be no impairment of its natural capacity to procreate human life' (*HV* 11)" (*TB* 386). In accord with *Humanae vitae* and previous hierarchical teaching, John Paul II accepts natural family planning and again cites *Humanae vitae* to differentiate natural family planning from artificial contraception. "The encyclical emphasizes especially that 'between the two cases there is an essential difference' (*HV* 16), and therefore a difference of an ethical nature: 'In the first case married couples rightly use a facility provided them by nature; in the other case, they obstruct the natural development of the generative process' (*HV* 16)" (*TB* 395). In chapter 3, there is a lengthy discussion and criticism of the natural law understanding behind the condemnation of artificial contraception. In keeping with his anthropology, John Paul II sees the natural law arguments against artificial contraception as the ontological and objective aspects of truth. The reasonable character of the condemnation of artificial contraception "does not only concern the truth of the ontological dimension, namely, that which corresponds to the fundamental structure of the marital act. It also concerns the same truth in the subjective and psychological dimension, that is to say, it concerns the correct understanding of the intimate structure of the marital act. It concerns the adequate rereading of the significances corresponding to this structure and of their inseparable connection" (*TB* 588–89). The subjective and psychological aspect of truth, which the pope stresses in his audience talks, develops the argument based on the language of the body as the total giving of the spouses to each other. But this approach puts too much emphasis on the meaning of each and every single sexual act.

No one act can ever perfectly express the total commitment of the spouses to each other. The pope's analysis demands too much meaning and symbolism from each and every single act. In addition, there are many sexual acts, such as embraces and kisses, that by the pope's understanding do not express total self-giving. The totality of the acts of the spouses in all their different dimensions shows their commitment to each other. But no one single act can always be said to require showing forth the symbolism of total gift. Notice here again the understanding of love as total self-giving.

Further Methodological Assessment

From a positive perspective, the moral teaching of John Paul II on marriage and sexuality avoids the danger often found in past hierarchical moral teaching and also in much of academic moral theology of dealing simply with specific issues, norms, and quandaries. The pope here is primarily interested in the meaning and understanding of marriage and sexuality. These talks also bring together moral theology and spiritual theology. Too often, in the past, even in the moral theology of the academy, the disciplinary boundaries of moral and spiritual theology have kept the two aspects separated in practice. The heavy emphasis on scripture brings in this important dimension, which in the past has often not been sufficiently used in Catholic moral teaching. In using scripture, the pope shows an awareness of some contemporary critical biblical scholarship. He distinguishes the two different creation accounts in Genesis in accord with the multiple-source theory of the first five books of the Bible. He begins his long discussion of the sacramentality of marriage based on Ephesians 5:21–32 with a recognition of the problems scholars discuss about the letter's authorship, date of composition, and intended audience (*TB* 306). But critical questions of method arise in a number of areas.

Scripture and Other Sources

First, with regard to scripture. Like all interpreters of scripture, the writings of John Paul II show the presuppositions that the person brings to an interpretation of scripture. I pointed out in chapter 2 that there is no such thing as the neutral, value-free interpreter of scripture. Without doubt, the pope is always going to see and interpret scripture as supporting existing Catholic teachings. Thus, for example, he uses many scriptural quotes to argue for the unity and indissolubility of marriage. In addition, as an academic he taught philosophical ethics and metaphysics. He obviously interprets scripture in the light of his own academic interest. He sees in the first account of creation "a powerful metaphysical content." The human being is defined here in a metaphysical way in terms of being and existence. He sees the good or value in light of this metaphysical approach. The first chapter of Genesis provides "a solid basis for a metaphysic and also for an anthropology and an ethic, according to which *ens et bonum convertuntur* [being and the good are convertible]" (*TB* 28–9). Most biblical commentators would not see such a metaphysic in the first chapter of Genesis. We all must be careful about the presuppositions we bring to our understanding of scripture, but it is evident how the pope's background influences his approach to scriptural interpretation.

The pope's discussion of two texts from scripture—Matthew 19 and 1 Corinthians 7—is curious. He gives a long and detailed analysis of Matthew 19 at the very beginning of these talks but never once refers to the famous exception clause (except for the case of *porneia*) with regard to divorce and the indissolubility of marriage. Especially because he is defending the condemnation of divorce in all circumstances, one would have expected him to deal with this issue. He does not refer as much to 1 Corinthians 7 as he does to Matthew 19, but here too he never mentions what later Catholic teaching calls the Pauline privilege. A person who becomes a baptized Christian is free to remarry if the previous non-Christian spouse refuses to peacefully live together.

The papal teaching on marriage and sexuality explicitly gives great attention to scripture and also to hierarchical teaching but fails to employ other sources of moral wisdom and knowledge that have consistently characterized the Catholic theological tradition. Tradition itself in the strict sense of the term has played a significant role in Catholic theology. Roman Catholic theology has insisted on the need for both scripture and tradition. In fact, in the past, Catholic theology gave the impression of seeing them as two totally separate realities. But the insistence on scripture and tradition today recognizes that scripture itself is historically and culturally conditioned and thus differs somewhat from present-day circumstances. The task of tradition is to understand, appropriate, and live the word and work of Jesus in the light of the present conditions of time and place.[10] One coming out of the Catholic tradition is also surprised by the lack of explicit development of natural law that continues to be the basis even for John Paul II's position on norms governing sexuality. Likewise, the talks give no role to contemporary experience. Contemporary Catholic moral theology recognizes a significant role for experience in moral theology, but such experience needs to be evaluated and cannot be reduced to what the majority of people think or do. The emphasis on the discernment of experience in Catholic tradition is not something that has arisen only recently. The *sensus fidelium* (the sense of the faithful) has consistently been recognized as a possible source of truth and wisdom.[11] Especially in the area of marriage and sexuality, the *sensus fidelium* has played a significant role.

The heavy and almost exclusive emphasis on scripture in these talks by the pope thus goes against the traditionally accepted Catholic understanding of the sources for moral wisdom and knowledge. But the somewhat homiletical nature of the talks might furnish a partial explanation of the emphasis on scripture and the failure to develop other traditional Catholic sources of moral wisdom and knowledge.

The Lack of Historical Consciousness

Another methodological shortcoming is the lack of historical development and historical consciousness in these papal talks, which was mentioned at the beginning of this chapter. In chapter 3, I criticized the static and classicist methodology emphasized by John Paul II. The meaning of Christian marriage is the same at all times and all places. At the very beginning of his talks, the pope sees in the two accounts of creation a metaphysical and a psychological definition of the human being. These definitions are true for all human beings. The "Elohist" or first account of creation, which comes from a later period than the second account of creation in Genesis, gives a metaphysical definition of the "human being in terms of being and existence" (*TB* 27–29). The "Yahwist" or second account of creation gives "the subjective definition of man." This psychological and subjective understanding of the human being stresses "man's self-knowledge." But this subjectivity corresponds to the objective reality of man created "in the image of God" (*TB* 29–31). The papal talks frequently refer to the divine plan of God for sexuality and marriage that was first revealed in the creation stories of Genesis—in the beginning. Again, the subtitle of the book containing these talks on the theology of the body is *Human Love in the Divine Plan*.

The pope somewhat frequently refers to historical human beings in these talks, but his historical perspective is theological—human beings before the fall, after the fall, and fallen and redeemed. He even explicitly recognizes his use of the historical in this theological sense (*TB* 131–32; see also 106, 119). He very occasionally recognizes historical and cultural conditioning but insists that the words of Christ, "in their essential content, refer to the man of every time and place" (*TB* 212). He does recognize changes that occurred in the Old Testament with regard to divorce and polygamy, but these changes are due to the theological reason of the fall. Redemption in Jesus has now restored the original meaning of marriage in its fullness and holds for all Christians down through the ages (*TB* 133–38). Thus, there is no recognition of historical development with regard to the meaning of marriage, nor is the subjectivity of persons different in different historical and cultural circumstances.

But historical studies have indicated very great changes and developments in the church's understanding of marriage. For example, for more than half its existence, the Catholic Church did not officially accept marriage as one of the seven sacraments. The problem arose because sacraments are to give grace to the recipients. But, with a negative view of sexuality even in marriage, many early theologians and canonists held that marital intercourse necessarily involves some sin. The early scholastics in the second millennium offered an ingenious solution to the problem. The grace given in marriage is not the positive grace of holiness but the medicinal grace that enables the spouses to temper lust within marriage. Implicitly, the Catholic Church only accepted marriage as the seventh sacrament at the Second Lateran Council in 1139, and the acceptance became explicit only with the Council of Verona in 1184.[12]

Marriage has been seen as an institution arranged by parents, a contract freely entered into by the couple, and as a covenant relationship. Some in the early church refused remarriage to widows. The roles of love, procreation, and sexual pleasure have changed greatly in the course of the unfolding Catholic understanding of marriage.[13]

In defense of the pope, one could point out that there are some constants in the understanding of marriage, such as the marital commitment of the spouses. Yes, there obviously is continuity with regard to our understanding of marriage over the centuries, but there is also great discontinuity that is not recognized in John Paul II's approach.

Historical studies have shown the development and even discontinuity that have occurred in the two norms strenuously defended by John Paul II with regard to marriage and sexuality—artificial contraception and the indissolubility of marriage. In discussing both cases, I rely on the historical work of John T. Noonan, a highly respected historian and jurist.

The condemnation of artificial contraception for spouses developed within a complex historical context.[14] Many factors influenced this teaching. General biblical values, especially the sanctity of marriage and the condemnation of unnatural sexual acts, were prominent. In the development of the church, it was necessary to find rational purpose and limits to sexuality. Societal factors, many of which have changed dramatically—such as the role of women, underpopulation or overpopulation, shorter or longer life spans, agrarian or industrial society—also had a role to play. The teaching itself was formulated and defended against various opponents. Thus, in the beginning, the teaching was aimed at Gnostics, Manichees, and later the Cathars, who were hostile to all procreation. Then, in the nineteenth and twentieth centuries, the teaching was defended against those who advocated artificial contraception, especially the Anglican Church in 1930. Within this context, the teaching on marriage itself changed and developed radically, with a much greater emphasis today on the role of love in marriage.

History shows that great development and change have occurred within Catholic teaching about marital intercourse. Catholic theologians once held as common positions that intercourse during menstruation is a mortal sin, intercourse during pregnancy is forbidden, and that there exists a natural position for intercourse. Great changes occurred with regard to the role of procreation in marriage. In the early church, the intention of procreation was necessary to justify marital intercourse. Later, the couple did not have to intend procreation. Sterile spouses could have marital intercourse. In the twentieth century, with the acceptance of rhythm and natural family planning, not only did the couple not have to intend procreation but they also could intentionally use the infertile periods in a woman's cycle to consciously avoid procreation.[15]

Noonan's book, *Power to Dissolve*, points out historically expanding types of marriages that, according to Catholic teaching and canon law, could be dissolved.[16] By the end of the twentieth century, five types of marriages were dissoluble in the eyes of the Catholic Church. The only indissoluble marriage is the consummated marriage between two baptized persons that is properly entered into. The five other types of marriages that are dissoluble are as follows: (1) A marriage that is virginal by vow, agreement, or intent, and is contracted by two baptized persons, is dissoluble by religious profession or papal dispensation. (2) A marriage that is sexual in intent, contracted by two baptized persons, and unconsummated by sexual intercourse is dissoluble by religious profession or papal dispensation. (3) A consummated marriage of two baptized persons, but with limited or negative procreative intent, can be declared invalid at the option of the courts. (4) A marriage impermanent by intention, custom, or assumption, even though contracted by two baptized persons, and consummated by sexual intercourse, can be declared invalid at the option of the courts. (5) A marriage that is sexual in intent, contracted by at least one baptized person, and consummated by sexual intercourse can be dissolved by the conversion and remarriage of the unbaptized partner in certain cases or by papal dispensation in all cases.[17]

Noonan succinctly tries to give some explanation for this change. St. Paul made an exception in absolute indissolubility with what is today called the Pauline privilege—if one of two married unbelievers converts and the other party does not but deserts the convert, the convert is free to remarry (1 Cor 7:10–16). This rule was then expanded under the extreme conditions of African slavery in South America. And the change that occurred then was further developed in modern religiously mixed societies when it became common for nonbaptized persons and Catholics to fall in love and want to be married. Noonan sees historical experience, canonical ingenuity, and the exaltation of papal power as playing a dominant part in these changes.[18] On the basis of this historical evidence, one cannot say that from the very beginning of creation God intended all marriages to be indissoluble.

Noonan has studied and pointed out the changes that have occurred in a number of different moral norms proposed by the church. He summarizes the changes on the issues of usury, the indissolubility of marriage, slavery, and the persecution of heretics in this fashion: "What was forbidden became lawful (the cases of usury and marriage); what was permissible became unlawful (the case of slavery); and what was required became forbidden (the persecution of heretics)."[19]

From a theological perspective, historical consciousness gives a significant role to experience. Noonan points out that experience obviously played a great role in these changes, but raw experience in and of itself does not suffice because it can be wrong. An experience suffered or perceived in light of human nature or in light of the Gospel can be judged good or bad. It is just such experience that Noonan sees behind the changes that have occurred in the issues mentioned above.[20]

John Paul II seldom appeals to the *sensus fidelium* because of his insistence on the plan of God from the very beginning. Noonan points out in the area of usury "that the experience and judgment of the laity had a value for moral teaching." In this context, he quotes the sixteenth-century theologian Navarrus (Martin Aspilcueta, d. 1586) pointing out the infinite number of decent Christians taking interest on loans. Navarrus could not accept an analysis that would damn the whole world.[21] All should recognize that the *sensus fidelium* is a complex reality that cannot be reduced to majority vote or public opinion polls. But it has been an important factor in developing Catholic moral teaching.

In his analysis of the change in the teaching on usury, Noonan points out that in a short space of time—thirty years at most—the papal bulls condemning usury were deprived of force to influence the behavior of people in the church. He concludes that such acts of papal authority—when isolated from theological support and contrary to the conviction of Christians familiar with the practices condemned—cannot prevail. They might have accurately reflected the assumptions and traditions of an earlier age, but they no longer correspond to present reality. Noonan sees the theologians in this case as having the last word because acts of papal authority are inert unless taught by theologians, because those who cared about the issue consulted them, because they taught the next generation, and because the older papal teaching itself was shaped by Christian experience and theological analysis.[22]

John Noonan, like any good Catholic scholar, is not a historical relativist. He insists, for example, that the Catholic condemnation of abortion has been an almost absolute value throughout history.[23] Noonan likewise does not accept raw experience and opinion polls as a basis for sound development within church teaching. He is working on a theory of moral development in the Catholic Church as a criterion for distinguishing legitimate from illegitimate change.[24]

Noonan's historical work also shows how laws themselves come into existence. He frequently points out that laws exist to protect and promote human values. But as other values enter into the picture or as the priority of values shifts, then new laws develop. Thus, he sees the condemnation of artificial contraception for spouses as defending and promoting five significant values. The condemnation serves as a wall to protect these values, but "the wall could be removed when it became a prison rather than a bulwark."[25] Such a historically conscious understanding recognizes that specific norms have a lesser certitude than values because they exist to promote and protect the different values involved. With a classicist and somewhat deductive approach, John Paul II gives too great a certitude to specific moral norms.

Virginity and Celibacy

As expected, John Paul II strenuously defends virginity and celibacy. Paragraph 16 of the apostolic exhortation *Familiaris consortio* succinctly states the traditional Catholic understanding, while a series of fourteen talks to the general audiences (March 10–July 21, 1982) develops his approach to virginity in a more complete way (*TB* 262–303). Catholicism has traditionally seen virginity as exemplified both in Jesus and in Mary.

The pope insists that although virginity is superior to marriage, the two are complementary: "If continence for the sake of the king-

dom of heaven undoubtedly signifies a renunciation, this renunciation is at the same time an affirmation" (*TB* 286). Continence
affirms "what is most lasting and most profoundly personal in the
vocation to marriage"—the radical and total sincere gift of self to the
other that in the dimension of temporality is bound to the nuptial
meaning of the body in its masculinity and femininity (*TB* 286–87).
There are two types of conjugal love expressed through the total gift
of self but expressed in two different ways in virginity and marriage.
The attitudes and values of the two states of virginity and marriage
"complete and in a certain sense interpenetrate each other." The
conjugal love of virginity should lead to spiritual paternity or maternity analogous to marital paternity and maternity (*TB* 277–78).

Virginity, too, is based on the theology of the body developed to
such a great degree in the discussion of marriage and sexuality. The
nuptial meaning of the body in its masculinity and femininity makes
possible "the personal realization of oneself 'through a sincere gift of
oneself'" (*GS* 24). Yes, the celibate renounces marriage but at the
same time confirms the nuptial meaning of the body as the total gift
to the other. This total gift to the other for the virgin involves the
gift of self for the sake of the Kingdom by one who is trying to please
the Lord. In virginity and celibacy, the whole interior meaning of
the nuptial meaning of the body is affirmed, but the corporeal aspect
is not (*TB* 285–87).

In some discontinuity with the discussion on marriage, the pope
here gives heavy emphasis to eschatology. The words of Christ in
Matthew 19 about those who make themselves eunuchs for the kingdom of heaven do not directly appeal to eschatology. However, the
"idea of virginity or of celibacy as an anticipation and eschatological
sign derives from the association of the words spoken here with
those which Jesus uttered on another occasion, in the conversation
with the Sadducees, when he proclaimed the future resurrection of
the body" (*TB* 264)—there will be no marriage in the kingdom of
heaven (Mt 22:23–30; Mk 12:25). Virginity or celibacy bears witness
to "the eschatological marriage of Christ with the Church" and "the
new world of the future resurrection" (*FC* 16.3). The pope thus gives
great importance to future eschatology as justifying virginity and
celibacy.

The pope's teaching on virginity closely follows the recent Catholic approach. Virginity or celibacy is a charism or a counsel, but not a command for all (*TB* 287–89). Virginity enables one to "give himself totally to Christ" (*TB* 284). In the words of 1 Corinthians 7:32–35, the unmarried is anxious about the affairs of the Lord and how to please the Lord, while the married is anxious about worldly affairs and about pleasing the spouse (*TB* 289–92).

The pope also insists on the traditional superiority of virginity to marriage because of "the wholly singular link which it has with the Kingdom of God" (*FC* 16). But here he adds a significant nuance to what has often appeared in the Catholic tradition. What has been known as the state of perfection is not based solely on virginity or continence but also on a life lived in accord with the evangelical counsels of poverty, chastity, and obedience in religious life. In addition, the person who lives in the world and is not a religious can reach a superior degree of perfection whose measure is charity than someone who is in religious life. The general audience talks strongly oppose dividing the Christian community into two camps—"those who are 'perfect' because of continence and those who are 'imperfect' or 'less perfect' because of the reality of married life" (*TB* 276). John Paul II has proposed a very nuanced understanding of the role of virginity and of religious life as a state of perfection superior to marriage.

With regard to the nuptial meaning of the body as the basis for both marriage and virginity, some problems arise. At the very minimum, the nuptial meaning of the body is not univocal. The role of the body in marriage and virginity is not the same. Thus, the pope himself recognizes a fluidity and pluralism with regard to the nuptial meaning of the body. It is not the same for all people at all times.

Of greater importance is the fact that the emphasis on virginity seems to downplay and perhaps even denigrate the role of the body itself in marriage. Virginity subordinates the body to the spiritual spousal love of the virgin for God. The body does not have a positive role in virginal love. This problem raises again some of the issues discussed above about the nuptial meaning of the body in marriage itself. John Paul II's discussion of marriage and sexuality fails to give enough importance to the role of the body in the loving relationship of the spouses as expressed in all forms of love—agape, communion or mutual love, and proper love of self. The papal teaching on marriage and sexuality fails to develop or even mention the role of sexual pleasure in marriage. The emphasis on virginity as superior coheres with the criticism above that the papal teaching on marriage does not give enough importance to love as mutual and reciprocal, to a proper love of self, to the role of the body in all aspects of marital love, and to a proper role for sexual pleasure.

John Paul II recognizes a possible problem here. How can the renunciation of the body made by the virgin affirm the very reality from which the virgin abstains in accord with the evangelical counsels? This can seem paradoxical, but many of the most eloquent and profound statements in the Gospel are paradoxical (*TB* 285). Yet the emphasis on paradox does not really solve the problem. Virginity certainly affirms the total and radical self gift of the married spouses to each other but does not affirm the role of the body in this relationship. Thus, the papal teaching tends to downplay the role of the body in married love itself.

With regard to the superiority of virginity over marriage, even the nuanced papal position has some problems. The pope accepts here the concept of a state of perfection. However, he proposes the criterion that could justify doing away with the very concept of the superiority of virginity over marriage. He recognizes that the perfection of the Christian life for all is charity that involves love of God and love of neighbor (*TB* 276). Vatican II recognized the universal call of all Christians to holiness and perfection. The primary vow for any Christian is the vow of baptism. Every other vow, such as the marriage vow or the vow of religious life or the vow of virginity, simply specifies the basic baptismal vow and indicates the means by which one is going to strive for holiness. There is another problem here that will surface again—the papal insistence on both the superiority of virginity and also the complementarity of virginal and marital love.

The Role and Dignity of Women

John Paul II's anthropology stresses the original unity of male and female. Masculinity and femininity play important roles in his anthropology. In keeping with the contemporary emphasis on the role of women as well as disputes within the Catholic Church about their role, the pope gives great attention to their role. His 1988 apostolic letter *Mulieris dignitatem* discusses the dignity and role of women in depth. In addition, he touches on these issues in many other documents—*Familiaris consortio* (1981), the 1988 postsynodal apostolic exhortation *"Christifideles laici,"*[26] and throughout *The Theology of the Body*. Two other documents that develop a somewhat different perspective on the role of women in the light of addressing issues confronting the modern world are the 1995 "Letter to Women" on the occasion of the Fourth World Conference on Women in Beijing and the "1995 World Day of Peace Message: Women—Teachers of Peace."

John Paul II's Approach

John Paul II insists on the equality and equal dignity of women and men (*FC* 22; *MD* 16). "There is an urgent need to achieve *real equality* in every area: equal pay for equal work, protection for working mothers, fairness in career advancements, equality of spouses with regard to family rights and the recognition of everything that is part of the rights and duties of a citizen in a democratic State" (*LW* 4). The pope strongly supports the equality of men and women in marriage and expressly opposes any subordination of the woman to the man. Recall his position that even Ephesians 5:22 does not support the subordination of the wife to the husband because love excludes every kind of subjection of the wife to the husband and makes the husband simultaneously subject to the wife (*TB* 310–11). In his insistence on the equality and dignity of women in both marriage and the broader social, cultural, and political world, John Paul II goes against what had been official Catholic teaching less than fifty years before.[27] No pope has ever so strongly defended and proclaimed the equality and dignity of women. In addition, John Paul II even supports "women's liberation." Yes, there have been mistakes, but the journey "has been substantially a positive one even if it is still unfinished" because of the many obstacles that stand in the way of women's dignity in many parts of the world today (*WTP* 4; *LW* 6).

The pope explicitly recognizes "the many discriminations of which women are the victims." Women have been marginalized in society and even in the church. Women especially are victimized by the tendency to treat human beings as objects or things and not as persons (*CL* 49, 2–3). We must *"examine the past with courage*, to assign responsibility where it is due in a review of the long history of humanity" and discrimination against women. Women have been excluded from equal educational opportunities, undereducated, ignored, and not appreciated for their intellectual accomplishments. Sadly, the science of history registers very little of women's accomplishments in history (*LW* 3). Women have often been the victims of violence against their own person and sexuality (*LW* 5). In keeping with his practice, the pope apologizes if objective blame has belonged to not just a few members of the church (*LW* 3). Note the pope's failure here and elsewhere to blame the church itself while acknowledging the failures of the members of the church. But surely the church is the people of God. In addition, the hierarchical leadership in the church has been responsible for some discrimination against and marginalization of women in history. What is the papal solution to this victimization of, discrimination against, and marginalization of women?

The anthropological foundations of masculinity and femininity found in the Word of God provide the answer to the problem (*CL* 50; *LW* 7). Thus the pope goes back to the ontological foundations of truth as proposed especially in the anthropology found in revelation. Here he alludes to all the aspects of theological anthropology developed in *The Theology of the Body*. Following his theological methodology, he argues that from the beginning there was no such discrimination or inequality. There was no victimization or marginalization of the woman in the Garden of Eden. However, the fall affected the loving communion between man and woman, and with it came the subordination, victimization, and marginalization of women. However, redemption in Christ has overcome the power of sin also in this regard (*CL* 50; *MD* 6–16).

The *Proto-Evangelium* in Genesis foretells the overcoming of the evil of sin through the victory of the woman (*MD* 11). Jesus Christ, born of Mary, brings about the redemption foretold in Genesis that renews the true dignity and vocation of women. One of the nine sections of *Mulieris dignitatem* deals with Jesus and his relationship with women, which shows forth the ethos of redemption (12–16). Jesus associated with many women, used them to illustrate his parables, treated the woman taken in adultery with great compassion and respect, and offered the Samaritan woman the gift of eternal life. In the Gospel narratives, women are the first witnesses to the resurrection. Mary Magdalene is rightly called "the Apostle of the Apostles" (*MD* 16). For two thousand years, the church has experienced the "genius of women" in the women martyrs, saints, mystics, and doctors of the church (*LW* 11; *MD* 27). The pope goes on to point out that biblical language attributes both "masculine" and "feminine" qualities to God. God is even referred to as a mother (*MD* 8).

The Problem of Complementarity

However, from my perspective, relying heavily on feminist insight, there are four problems with John Paul II's understanding of the vocation and role of women. First, he insists on the complementarity between man and woman. Such an understanding is central in his thought and occupies a prominent position in all his discussions of women. Two very significant reasons—one theoretical and the other more practical—ground this emphasis on the complementarity of male and female.

The theoretical reason comes from his anthropological understanding of marriage as the complementary union of male and female as revealed in the Genesis account of creation, especially the second account which "*helps us to understand even more profoundly* the fundamental *truth* which it contains *concerning man* created as man and woman in the image and likeness of God" (*MD* 6). The Catholic tradition illustrated in Thomas Aquinas understands the human person to be an image of God precisely because the human being like God has intellect, free will, and the power of self-determination.[28] John Paul II recognizes this traditional understanding of the human being as an image of God (*MD* 6), but he now insists that Adam and Eve, the original man and woman, are images of God as a "unity of the two." They are called "to live in a communion of love, and in this way to mirror in the world the communion of love that is in God, through which the Three Persons love each other in the intimate mystery of the one divine life" (*MD* 7). Their masculinity and femininity allow them to make the mutual sincere gift of self to one another (*MD* 7). About one-fifth of the apostolic letter *Mulieris dignitatem* deals with Genesis. The first series of talks to general audiences at the very beginning of the Wojtyla papacy bears the English title, "Original Unity of Man and Woman," and is devoted almost exclusively to a meditative reflection on Genesis. Thus, on theological, anthropological, and scriptural grounds, John Paul II insists on the complementarity of man and woman.

But a very important practical concern of the pope also plays a significant role in supporting complementarity. He has strongly opposed the ordination of women in the Roman Catholic Church by insisting that this is a matter of divine law and cannot be changed by anyone in the church. His emphasis on complementarity allows him to claim to accept the fundamental equality of man and woman and oppose discrimination and marginalization while still maintaining that women cannot be ordained priests. He first refutes the argument that women were not apostles because of the sociological inferiority of women at that time. In choosing only men as apostles, Jesus did not merely conform to the widespread mentality of his times. Rather, he acted in a completely free and sovereign manner just as he opposed the current mentality in his approach to women (*MD* 26).

Christ is the bridegroom who has given life to the church. The Eucharist is the sacrament of our redemption; it is the sacrament of the bridegroom and of the bride—Christ and the church. The priest who is the sacramental minister of the Eucharist is a man who acts in the person of Christ representing the bridegroom who gives himself to the church (*MD* 26). Yes, the church as a hierarchical institution is limited to males, but the hierarchical structure of the church exists in the service of the holiness of church members. "In the hierarchy of holiness, it is *precisely 'the woman,'* Mary of Nazareth, who is the figure of the church. She 'precedes' everyone on the path to holiness; in her person 'the church has already reached that perfection whereby she exists without spot or wrinkle' (cf. Eph 5:27). In this sense, one can say that the church is *both* 'Marian' and 'Apostolic-Petrine'" (*MD* 27). Thus, Peter, as male, is the icon of the bridegroom, while Mary, as female, is the icon of the holiness of the bride who represents the holiness of the church.[29]

This is not the place for a long discussion of women's ordination in the church, but many point out the weakness of the argument based on men as icons who alone can represent Christ the bridegroom.[30] Women, through baptism, share in the priestly, kingly, and prophetic role of Jesus. There seems to be no reason why they cannot also share in the ministerial priesthood of the church. If the metaphor of the church as bride includes both men and women, why cannot the metaphor of Christ as bridegroom include men and women? The pope thus claims to find in his insistence on complementarity a way to try to defend both the equality of women and the difference of roles within the church.

In a consistent and logical manner, the pope recognizes that complementarity requires feminine and masculine qualities and gifts. The true liberation of women must not involve a masculinization in which women appropriate to themselves male characteristics contrary to their feminine originality. Such an approach will only deform women and lose what constitutes women's essential richness (*MD* 10). There is a special kind of prophetism found in the woman. The woman in Genesis and the bride in the metaphor of Ephesians receive love in order to love in return. All human beings are first loved by God and then express love in return. But it is precisely the woman who manifests this truth to everyone. "This *'prophetic' character of women in their femininity* finds its highest expression in the Virgin Mother of God" (*MD* 29).

The pope does not develop at length or in depth what are these feminine qualities. *Christifideles laici* calls attention to two great tasks entrusted to women. First of all, the task of bringing full dignity to the conjugal life and to motherhood. She can help the man—husband and father—to overcome forms of absenteeism and better respond to his parental responsibilities. Second, women have the task of shoring up the moral dimension of culture (51.10–11).

I have further difficulties with the papal emphasis on and understanding of complementarity. Such an emphasis means that men and women who are not married are not complete and lack something about their humanity. But this obviously goes too far. The different qualities attributed to man and woman are often culturally derived and conditioned. The two tasks assigned to women by *Christifideles laici* definitely seem to be culturally conditioned. The man and the husband should also contribute to the full reality of family life and to the moral dimension of culture.

The Genesis story, the bridegroom–bride image, and the prophetic witness of women to receive love and then give love to others seem to emphasize the more passive and receiving role of women and downplay their active and initiating roles. These complementary roles assigned to women thus seem to make women subordinate. Traditionally, feminists have argued that complementarity always involves the subordination of women. Recall that John Paul II himself insists on the complementarity of virginity and marriage while still insisting on the superiority of virginity.

Further Problems

A second problem with the papal understanding of the dignity and vocation of women comes from some overemphasis on the maternal and family role of women. Men, in the pope's understanding, are not defined primarily by their roles as husbands and fathers. *Familiaris consortio* points out a wrong tradition that sees "women's role to be exclusively that of wife and mother without adequate access to public functions, which have generally been reserved for men." "On the other hand, the true advancement of women requires that clear recognition be given to the value of their maternal and family role, by comparison with all other public roles and all other professions" (23.2). The "1995 World Day of Peace Message" makes the same basic point (9).

There can be no doubt that *The Theology of the Body* and *Mulieris dignitatem* pay practically little or no attention to the role of women in the world and in the public sphere. The entire focus is on women as wives, mothers, and members of families. The genre of *Mulieris dignitatem* and the general audiences talks is, in the pope's own words, a form of meditation (*MD* 2). As was pointed out above, the primary source in these documents is biblical with little or no attention paid to other sources of moral wisdom and knowledge (*TB* 419). The scriptural texts speak of woman primarily in terms of the role of wives and mothers. Nothing is said about their role in the public sphere. Also, the heavy emphasis on Mary as the model for women and "*the highest expression of the 'feminine genius'*" supports the focus on women as mothers and virgins and not with a role in the public sphere (*LW* 10).

The 1995 "Letter to Women" on the occasion of the Beijing Conference and the 1995 Day of Peace message have a different flavor. They are not meditations as such. They address more the life of women in the world and give more emphasis to the public role of women than the more meditative genre of writings. However, even here the Genesis and Mary themes are prominent (*LW* 7–11). The "Letter to Women" gives proportionally more space to the public role of women but still the maternal and familial roles of women receive great importance. The letter begins with thanks to the following categories of women—mothers, wives, daughters, sisters, women who work, consecrated women, every woman (2). Thus the motherly and distinctively feminine roles of women receive disproportionate attention.

A third negative critique of the papal understanding of women involves the danger of putting women on a pedestal. Women are looked upon as morally superior. Recall the 1988 postsynodal apostolic exhortation developing the two specific roles for women as bringing full dignity to conjugal life and assuring the moral dimensions of culture (*CL* 51.10–11). *Mulieris dignitatem* recognizes that God entrusts every human being to each other and every other human being. "But this entrusting concerns women in a special way—precisely by reason of their femininity—and this in a particular way determines their vocation" (*MD* 30). The abstract and mystical tenor of the papal writings adds to the pedestalization by being so far removed from the realities and struggles of everyday life.

A fourth negative criticism concerns the danger of overemphasizing the role of self-gift and service in the life of women. The pope constantly insists that the perfection of human beings consists in their mutual sincere gift of self to each other (*MD* 7). There is no doubt that the pope calls for a mutual gift of both husband and wife. But he develops the role and vocation of women modeled on that of Mary, who put herself at God's service and also at the service of others: a service of love (*LW* 10). Recall the earlier comment that the pope fails to give enough importance to self-fulfillment and the proper love of self. This seemingly one-sided emphasis on gift and service has special consequences for women who too often in the past have been told their life is to be one of service to others without giving enough importance to their own proper self-love and fulfillment.

The Family

John Paul II discusses the family in a number of places. The three social encyclicals occasionally mention the family as do the general audience talks. But two documents discuss the family in depth and include the aspects mentioned elsewhere: the 1981 postsynodal apostolic exhortation *Familiaris consortio* and the 1994 "Letter to Families" written on the occasion of the United Nations' proclaiming 1994 as the International Year of the Family and the church's celebration of the Year of the Family.

These two documents obviously draw on the same themes and methodologies already discussed. Truth, anthropology, and metaphysics are important factors in these discussions of the family. The church's teaching on the family is "illuminated by the faith that gives her an understanding of all the truth concerning the great value of marriage and the family and their deepest meaning" (*FC* 3). Both documents emphasize the plan of God and "the truth of God's plan for marriage and the family" (*FC* 6, 17). The crisis of our world today is a profound crisis of truth that in the first place involves a crisis of concepts. "Do the words 'love,' 'freedom,' 'sincere gift,' and even 'person,' and 'rights of the person' really convey their essential meaning?" (*LF* 13). As a result of this crisis of truth, today we face many problems coming from a one-sided freedom resulting in utilitarianism and consumerism (*LF* 13; *FC* 6). These documents situate the family in society in the light of the Catholic teaching on the common good and the principle of subsidiarity (*FC* 44–48). In terms of theological methodology, both documents, but especially the 1994 Letter, follow the three-part anthropological approach of the beginning, the fall or sin, and redemption in Christ Jesus. Also the oppositional motif between the church and others occasionally appears. Indeed although there is on the one hand the civilization of love, "there continues to exist on the other hand *the possibility of a destructive 'anti-civilization,'* as so many present trends and situations confirm" (*LF* 13).

In these documents, the pope also applies to the family aspects he has developed in other contexts. *Redemptor hominis* insisted that "man is the way of the church" but so too the family is the way of the church (*LF* 1–2). "Just as the person is a subject, so too is the family" (*LF* 15).

A good part of the discussion of family repeats what has already been mentioned in the discussion of marriage and the role of husband and wife. The pope insists on the equality of the spouses but again emphasizes the complementarity of man and woman and the maternal role of the woman (*FC* 19–24).

Familiaris consortio develops the role of the family in terms of four tasks. First, "forming a community of persons" deals with many of the aspects discussed under marriage but also includes sections on the rights of children and the elderly in the family (18–27). The second task, "serving life," develops in some depth both the procreational and educational aspects of the family, affirming in the process the hierarchical teaching on artificial contraception (28–41). The third task of the family, "participating in the development of society," emphasizes the family as the first and vital cell of society. Procreation and education are not enough, for the family has important social and political roles including influencing the laws and institutions of society to defend the rights and duties of the family (44). But society also has the task of respecting and fostering the family in accord with the principle of subsidiarity. This section includes fourteen rights of the family (46) later developed by the Pontifical Council on the Family in the 1983 "Charter of the Rights of the Family." Most of these rights defend "the family against the intolerable usurpations of society and the State" (46). However, the rights do include the right to decent housing and the rights especially of the poor and the sick to obtain physical, social, political, and economic security (46). Families must also work for a new international order (48).

The fourth task of the family is "sharing in the life and mission of the church," which is developed in accord with sharing in the threefold role of Jesus as prophet, priest, and king. As prophetic, the family is a believing and evangelizing community. As a priestly community, the family is a community in dialogue with God, especially through the sacraments and prayer. As a kingly community, the family strives to live out the law of the Spirit (51; for a similar treatment, see *EV* 92–94).

In the two concentrated discussions of the family, John Paul II's favorite metaphor for the family is "the domestic church." According to J. Michael Miller, the word domestic church appears twelve times in *Familiaris consortio*.[31] In the beginning, the "Letter to Families" refers to the metaphor of the domestic church applied to the family as a meaningful term expressed from the very beginning of Christianity. Vatican II used this metaphor: "In our own times we have often referred to the phrase 'domestic church' . . . the sense of which we hope will always remain alive in people's minds" (*LF* 3). However, a problem exists with such a metaphor that has escaped the pope's attention. He recognizes that the church has a hierarchical structure and that women are excluded from it. For many people today, the understanding of the family as the domestic church is not a very appealing metaphor, despite its ancient use.

Familiaris consortio, even more so than the 1994 Letter, does not fit into the meditative genre of many of John Paul II's writings on marriage and the family. Perhaps this comes from its origins as a development of the 1980 discussion of the Synod of Bishops on the family. The very subject matter of the apostolic exhortation, "the role of the Christian family in the modern world," indicates more practical, pastoral, and contemporary approaches in the document itself. This document gives a lesser role to scripture and recognizes other sources of moral wisdom and knowledge. *Familiaris consortio* insists again on the eternal plan of God but also recognizes some historical development. Thus the somewhat abstract, mystical, primarily scriptural, and meditative aspects of John Paul II's other documents are muted in *Familiaris consortio*.

The first part of the document begins with the signs of the times—"Bright Spots and Shadows for the Family Today." The church can learn from history. "The call and demands of the Spirit resound in the very events of history, and so the Church can also be guided to a more profound understanding of the inexhaustible mystery of marriage and the family by the circumstances, the questions, and the anxieties and hopes of the young people, married couples, and parents of today" (4). Such an understanding calls for discernment by the church that also involves the laity—the *sensus fidelium* (5). This is one of the few times John Paul II refers to the *sensus fidelium*. In the struggle against sin, conversion, growth, and gradualness challenge the lives of families (9). *Familiaris consortio* also recognizes the need to inculturate the faith (9).

Familiaris consortio recognizes both positive and negative aspects in the contemporary developments facing families, for history reveals a conflict between the love of God and the love of self. But the document puts much greater emphasis on "the troubling signs"—the spread of divorce, the acceptance of purely civil marriage, rejection of the church's moral norms, and faithless celebrations of the sacrament of marriage (6). "Our age needs wisdom" (8). Yes, discernment is important but the pastors of the church have the role to authoritatively judge the contemporary experience (5). Yes, there is progress in the Christian life, but "the law of gradualness" does not mean the "gradualness of the law" (34). John Paul II ends the entire discussion of the signs of the times, historicity, the sense of the faithful, and inculturation in part 1 by noting, "So that the goal of this journey might be clear and consequently the way plainly indicated, the Synod was right to begin by considering in depth the original design of God for marriage and the family: it 'went back to the beginning,' in reference to the teaching of Christ" (10). Then immediately follows part 2—"The Plan of God for Marriage and the Family." Thus, the historical journey goes back to the original starting point.

In theory, *Familiaris consortio* gives more importance to historicity and historical-mindedness than any other document written by John Paul II on the subject of marriage and sexuality. But in reality, historical consciousness does not affect the basic teaching. The pope obviously realizes that many Catholics have used these appeals to call for some change in church teachings. He strongly opposes any change in the teaching and thus limits the emphasis on historicity, the sense of the faithful, growth, and inculturation. The methodological approach has practical consequences. *Familiaris consortio* remains somewhat general and abstract in relation to historical reality. In fairness, any document intended for a worldwide audience by its very nature is going to be somewhat abstract, but there seem to be deeper problems with this document. Yes, the pope does mention the special concerns of the poor and the needs of the developing world (6), but the real struggles of families today are still missing. In addition, the two-parent family is not only the ideal but is also the only type of family developed in the document.

The lack of historicity and historical consciousness in John Paul II's understanding of the family comes through in a surprising way in his insistence on the equality of husband and wife. He makes the startling claim that the author of Ephesians 5:22 called for this equality. In addition, he fails to point out explicitly that popes and the Catholic tradition until very recently consistently and strongly supported a patriarchal understanding of the family.[32] John Paul II is reluctant to admit discontinuity or change in Catholic teaching. This concludes the analysis and appraisal of John Paul II's understanding of marriage, sexuality, the dignity and role of women, and the nature and role of the family.

Notes

1. Pope John Paul II, *Veritatis splendor*, in *The Encyclicals of John Paul II*, ed. J. Michael Miller (Huntington, Ind.: Our Sunday Visitor, 2001), 584–661. Note that all Vatican documents can be found on the Vatican website, http://www.vatican.va.

2. Pope John Paul II, *Familiaris consortio*, in *The Post-Synodal Apostolic Exhortations of John Paul II*, ed. J. Michael Miller (Huntington, Ind.: Our Sunday Visitor, 1998), 148–233. Subsequent references in the text will be to *FC* followed by the paragraph number.

3. Pope John Paul II, *Mulieris dignitatem*, in John Paul II, *The Theology of the Body: Human Love in the Divine Plan* (Boston: Pauline Books, 1997), 443–92. Subsequent references in the text will be to *MD* followed by the paragraph number.

4. Pope John Paul II, "Letter to Families," *Origins* 23 (1994): 637–59. Subsequent references in the text will be to *LF* followed by the paragraph number.

5. Pope John Paul II, "Letter to Women," *Origins* 25 (1995): 137–43. Subsequent references in the text will be to *LW* followed by the paragraph number.

6. Pope John Paul II, "1995 World Day of Peace Message: Women—Teachers of Peace," *Origins* 24 (1994): 465–69. Subsequent references in the text will be to *WTP* followed by the paragraph number.

7. Pope John Paul II, *Theology of the Body*, 25–432.

8. For a positive appraisal of John Paul II's approach, see Janet E. Smith, *Humanae Vitae: A Generation Later* (Washington, D.C.: Catholic University of America Press, 1991), 230–65; for a negative appraisal, see Luke Timothy Johnson, "A Disembodied 'Theology of the Body': John Paul II on Love, Sex, and Pleasure," *Commonweal* 128, n. 2 (January 26, 2001): 11–17.

9. Bernard V. Brady, *Christian Love: How Christians through the Centuries Have Understood Love* (Washington, D.C.: Georgetown University Press, 2003).

10. Harold C. Skillrud, J. Francis Stafford, and Daniel F. Martensen, eds., *Scripture and Tradition: Lutherans and Catholics in Dialogue IX* (Minneapolis: Augsburg, 1995).

11. Richard R. Gaillardetz, *Teaching with Authority: A Theology of the Magisterium in the Church* (Collegeville, Minn.: Liturgical Press, 1997), 230–35.

12. Theodore Mackin, *The Marital Sacrament* (New York: Paulist Press, 1989), 274–324.

13. Mackin, *Marital Sacrament*.

14. John T. Noonan Jr., *Contraception: A History of Its Treatment by the Catholic Theologians and Canonists*, enlarged ed. (Cambridge, Mass.: Belknap Press of Harvard University Press, 1986).

15. Noonan, *Contraception*, 532.

16. John T. Noonan Jr., *Power to Dissolve: Lawyers and Marriages in the Courts of the Roman Curia* (Cambridge, Mass.: Belknap Press of Harvard University Press, 1972).

17. Noonan, *Power to Dissolve*, 403.

18. John T. Noonan Jr., "Development in Moral Doctrine," *Theological Studies* 54 (1993): 675.

19. Noonan, "Development in Moral Doctrine," 669.

20. Noonan, "Development in Moral Doctrine," 674.

21. John T. Noonan Jr., "The Amendment of Papal Teaching by Theologians," in *Contraception: Authority and Dissent*, ed. Charles E. Curran (New York: Herder & Herder, 1969), 74. For his original historical work on usury, see John T. Noonan Jr., *The Scholastic Analysis of Usury* (Cambridge, Mass.: Harvard University Press, 1957).

22. Noonan, "Amendment of Papal Teaching," 75.

23. John T. Noonan Jr., "An Almost Absolute Value in History," in *The Morality of Abortion: Legal and Historical Perspectives*, ed. John T. Noonan Jr. (Cambridge, Mass.: Harvard University Press, 1970), 1–59.

24. Noonan, "Development in Moral Doctrine," 662–67. For Noonan's brief description of the theory of development implicitly found in Vatican Council II, see John T. Noonan Jr., *The Lustre of Our Country: The American Experience of Religious Freedom* (Berkeley: University of California Press, 1998), 352–53.

25. Noonan, *Contraception*, 533.

26. Pope John Paul II, *Christifideles laici*, in *Post-Synodal Apostolic Exhortations*, ed. Miller, 362–462. Subsequent references in the text will be to *CL* followed by the paragraph number.

27. For how John Paul II changed previous papal teaching on the role of women, see Christine E. Gudorf, "Encountering the Other: The Modern Papacy on Women," *Social Compass* 36 (1989): 295–310.

28. Thomas Aquinas, *Summa theologiae*, 4 vols. (Rome: Marietti, 1952), Ia IIae, *Prologus*.

29. For the official papal document strongly opposing the ordination of women, see Pope John Paul II, *Ordinatio sacerdotalis*, *Origins* 24 (1994): 49–52.

30. See, for example, Christine E. Gudorf, "Probing the Politics of Difference: What's Wrong with an All-Male Priesthood?" *Journal of Religious Ethics* 27 (1999): 377–405.

31. Miller, *Post-Synodal Apostolic Exhortations*, 775.

32. Lisa Sowle Cahill, *Family: A Christian Social Perspective* (Minneapolis: Fortress Press, 2000), 86–95.

SOCIAL TEACHING

THIS CHAPTER concentrates on the three encyclical letters of John Paul II on social issues—*Laborem exercens* (1981), *Sollicitudo rei socialis* (1987), and *Centesimus annus* (1991)—because encyclical letters are the most authoritative documents in which the pope proposes social teaching. These three encyclicals belong to the genre of what John Paul II himself calls the social doctrine or social teaching of the church (*CA* 2.1). The social teaching of the church includes the authoritative documents on social issues begun by Leo XIII with *Rerum novarum* in 1891 and continued by subsequent popes, often on the anniversary of previous documents.[1] With three social encyclicals, John Paul II has contributed more to this body of Catholic social teaching than any of his predecessors. This genre addresses social issues facing the world at large and not just internal issues facing the Catholic Church and its members. John Paul II, following the custom begun by John XXIII in *Pacem in terris*, addresses these encyclicals not only to Catholics but to all people of goodwill. The nature of the issues touched upon and the audiences addressed in these documents affects how John Paul II develops his teaching.

Characteristics of John Paul II's Social Teaching

In these three encyclicals, the pope recognizes the need for all people to work together for the common good and to overcome the injustices in our world. *Sollicitudo rei socialis* (47.5) and *Centesimus annus* (60.4) end with urgent pleas for the cooperation of all to overcome these injustices. As a result, the primary emphasis is not always on Christ and redemption, as it is in his other encyclicals. The social encyclicals, however, often mention the specific Christian dimension, and an entire chapter of *Sollicitudo rei socialis* deals with "A Theological Reading of Modern Problems" (35–40). John Paul II in these encyclicals appeals to human reason, experience, culture, and dialogue, but the significant absence not only of a development of natural law but even of references to natural law was pointed out in chapter 3. This lack of even references to natural law in these encyclicals is somewhat puzzling in light of the heavy emphasis on natural law in the 1993 encyclical, *Veritatis splendor*, and in light of references to natural law in the earlier documents of Catholic social teaching.

In these documents, the opposition between the culture of life and the culture of death does not appear. In fact, there is an optimism that Christians in union with others can overcome the social injustices of our world. *Laborem exercens* recognizes that the Christian expectation of a new earth should not weaken but rather stimulate our concern for cultivating this earth. Here on this earth grows the body of a new human family, which even now gives some foreshadowing of the new age (27.6). *Sollicitudo rei socialis* recognizes the sad experience of recent years, but "the Church must strongly affirm the *possibility* of overcoming the obstacles which . . . stand in the way of development" (47.1). "The Church has *confidence also in man*, though she knows the evil of which he is capable" (47.2). *Centesimus annus* recognizes the need for all people of goodwill to work together for social justice (60). Here we have a somewhat optimistic picture of what all humankind can accomplish in this world.

In keeping with his basic presupposition, John Paul II sees the truth about the human person as the foundation for the teaching proposed in these documents and in all other papal teaching on social issues. John Paul II here again emphasizes the two aspects of anthropology or the truth about the human person developed in chapter 3—the incomparable dignity of the human person and the social nature or solidarity of the human person with all others.

First, the dignity of the human person. *Laborem exercens* in the very beginning justifies its teaching on human work as part of "her task always to call attention to the dignity and rights of those who work" (1.4). *Sollicitudo rei socialis* begins by asserting that the social concern of the church is "directed toward an authentic development of man and society which would respect and promote all the dimensions of the human person" (1.1). *Centesimus annus*, in its introduction, sees Catholic social teaching as spurring "*a great movement for the defense of the human person* and the safeguarding of human dignity" (3.4). The second important aspect of anthropology is human solidarity. The Catholic tradition has insisted that the human person is social by nature. As *Rerum novarum*, the first encyclical of Catholic social teaching, phrased it: "the natural propensity of man to live in society."[2] John Paul II continues and develops this understanding by his emphasis on solidarity especially in *Sollicitudo rei socialis*. Solidarity insists on the interdependence of all human beings, with the consequences that we are all really responsible for all (38.6). Solidarity is based on strong human and natural bonds but faith especially insists on the fatherhood of God and the brotherhood of all in Christ, thus providing a new model of the unity of the human race (40.3). Solidarity helps us to see "the other"—whether a person, people, or nation—as our "neighbor" to be made a sharer on a par with ourselves in the banquet of life to which all are equally called by God (39.5). Thus, the two aspects of anthropology, human dignity and human solidarity, form the basis for our care and concern for all God's people, especially those who are poor or victims of injustice.

Human dignity and human solidarity together play a very significant role in Catholic social teaching and in John Paul II's understanding of political and economic life and structures. The insistence on both these aspects opposes a one-sided individualism that fails to consider the social aspect of human beings and a one-sided collectivism that fails to appreciate the dignity of the individual human person. According to John Paul II, however, "The Church's social doctrine *is not* a 'third way' between *liberal capitalism* and *Marxist collectivism*, nor even a possible alternative to other solutions less radically opposed to one another: rather, it constitutes a *category of its own*" (*SRS* 41.7). In the light of an anthropology insisting on human dignity and human solidarity, Catholic social teaching involves a "set of principles for reflection, criteria for judgment, and directives for action" to evaluate and criticize contemporary realities (*SRS* 41.5).

John Paul II's social teaching fits into this body of Catholic social teaching going back to Leo XIII's *Rerum novarum* in 1891. Although

John Paul II stresses the continuity within this teaching, some significant development has occurred. Six aspects of John Paul II's social teaching insofar as they relate to this broader historical tradition merit further consideration.

First, John Paul II has continued to insist upon the insight of the 1971 Synod of Bishops: "Action on behalf of justice and participation in the transformation of the world fully appear to us as a constitutive dimension of the preaching of the Gospel, or, in other words, of the Church's mission for the redemption of the human race and its liberation from every oppressive situation."[3] The social teaching and social mission of the church is a constitutive dimension of the Gospel and of Christian faith. The pre–Vatican II approach saw social teaching and social mission as part of the humanizing role of the church but not part of its divinizing role. Social teaching and mission dealt with the realm of the natural and not the supernatural. Vatican II insisted on the need to overcome the split between faith and daily life. The reign of God and grace affect all that happens in our world.[4] John Paul II frequently emphasizes the evangelizing nature of the social teaching and social mission of the church—"To teach and to spread her social doctrine pertains to the Church's evangelizing mission and is an essential part of the Christian message, since this doctrine points out the direct consequences of that message in the life of society and situates daily work and struggles for justice in the context of bearing witness to Christ the Saviour" (*CA* 5.5, *SRS* 41.5–9). *Sollicitudo rei socialis* refers to the injustices in our world as "structures of sin." According to this perspective, these structures of sin affect "the will of the Triune God, his plan for humanity, his justice, and his mercy" (36.6).

Second, and clearly related to the first point discussed above, the post–Vatican II documents on Catholic social teaching moved away from an exclusive natural law foundation to a more scriptural, theological, and Christological approach. However, the two different audiences for social encyclicals of the members of the church and of all humankind limited to quite an extent the approach based on specifically theological aspects. But John Paul II developed more than his predecessors the theological bases and approach of the social teaching. The whole fifth part of *Laborem exercens* develops the elements for a spirituality of work. The pope sees human work in the light of creation, sin, and the cross and resurrection of Jesus (24–27). Recall that *Sollicitudo rei socialis* devotes the fifth part of the document to "A Theological Reading of Modern Problems" (35). Here the pope identifies the obstacles to development as sin and the structures of sin. Christians are called to convert and to live out the virtue of solidarity. Many of the church's saints show a marvelous witness of such solidarity and serve as examples in our present difficult situation (35–40). *Centesimus annus* closes with a sixth part on "Man is the Way of the Church" (53–62). Thus John Paul II has developed more than his predecessors the theological aspects of Catholic social teaching.

Third, John Paul II presents a somewhat enlarged picture of the ethical aspects of Catholic social teaching. Catholic social teaching deals with contemporary issues and the social problems facing the world. Occasionally the earlier documents, especially near their end, called for a change of heart as well as a change of structures.[5] But the emphasis was on particular problems and structures. John Paul II tries to integrate the change of heart and the virtues into a broader understanding of the approach to social issues. Recall his emphasis on the spirituality of work and the need for conversion mentioned above. In *Sollicitudo rei socialis*, the pope hopes that even those women and men without explicit faith who work for a more human life for fellow human beings "will become fully aware of the urgent need to *change* the *spiritual attitudes* which define each individual's relationship with self, with neighbor, with even the remotest human communities, and with nature itself; and all of this in view of higher values such as the *common good*" (38.3). Christians see such a change in terms of conversion. "It is above all a question of *interdependence . . .* accepted as a *moral category*. When interdependence becomes recognized in this way the correlative response as a moral and social attitude as a 'virtue,' is *solidarity*." (38.6) The pope then goes on to clarify the ramifications of such solidarity (38.6). John Paul II thus explicitly recognizes, and to some degree develops, the role of virtue and virtue ethics in Catholic social teaching.

Fourth, the documents of Catholic social teaching have shown significant development toward a greater appreciation of the person and the freedom and rights of the person. Some have called this a move to the subject.[6] In keeping with his long philosophical emphasis on the person as subject, John Paul II has further developed this growing emphasis in Catholic social teaching.

John Paul II's emphasis on the subject comes through especially in his teaching on work. *Laborem exercens* distinguishes between work in the objective sense—what is done—and work in the subjective sense—the person who does it. Once again, the pope appeals to the Genesis narrative. The human person is an image of God because the person is a conscious, free, and rational subject who is able to decide about the self. Genesis describes the person as one who "dominates," which refers more to the subjective dimension than to the objective dimension (5–6). Such an understanding "constitutes in itself the most eloquent 'Gospel of work' showing that the basis for determining the value of human work is not primarily the kind of work being done but the fact that the one who is doing it is a person" (6.5). The preeminence of the subjective meaning of work over the objective meaning grounds the fundamental rights of the worker, does away with the distinction of peoples according to classes, provides the basis for worker solidarity, and emphasizes the primacy of labor over capital (6–10). All have to recognize the radical nature of this understanding.

Fifth, although John Paul II accepted and fully developed the turn to the subject in Catholic social teaching, he rejected the historical consciousness and the more inductive approach exemplified especially in Paul VI's *Octogesima adveniens*. Chapter 2 developed this point in some depth.

Sixth, John Paul II stresses the continuity in the body of Catholic social teaching and downplays the discontinuity. Such an emphasis coheres with his more deductive method, his classicism, and his tendency to downplay change in Catholic teachings. Whereas scholars, especially in the past few decades, have emphasized the development and discontinuity in Catholic social teaching,[7] John Paul II emphasizes the continuity with regard to the "principles of reflection," "criteria of judgment," and "directives for action" (*SRS* 3.2). These unchanging principles, criteria, and directives are then applied to the changing historical contexts and circumstances. His 1991 encyclical celebrated the one hundredth anniversary of *Rerum novarum*, whose very title speaks of "new things." The pope's introduction to his encyclical points out that the tradition of the church, in keeping with the biblical image of Matthew 13:5, brings out of the treasure of its tradition what is old and what is new; but notice the relationship between the two—"'What is old'—received and passed on from the very beginning . . . enables us to interpret the 'new things' in the midst of which the life of the Church and the world unfolds" (*CA 3.3*). John Paul II sees *Centesimus annus* as continuing the approach of the earlier documents in this tradition, which paid tribute to *Rerum novarum* "and applied it to the circumstances of the day" (1.1). *Centesimus annus* looks back at *Rerum novarum* "in order to discover anew the richness of the fundamental principles which it formulated" (3.1). *Centesimus annus* "seeks to show the fruitfulness of the principles enunciated by Leo XIII which belong to the Church's doctrinal patrimony" (3.5).

All recognize the great discontinuity in Catholic social teaching between the teaching on religious freedom of the Second Vatican Council and the teaching proposed earlier by Leo XIII at the end of the nineteenth century.[8] However, John Paul II emphasizes some continuity even in this case. *Centesimus annus* recalls that Leo XIII insisted on the rights of the worker to discharge freely one's religious duties, including Sunday rest. "It would not be mistaken to see in this clear statement a springboard for the principle of the right to religious freedom, which was to become the subject of . . . the Second Vatican Council's well-known Declaration and of my own repeated teaching" (9.2). But in this case, Leo XIII is speaking of the rights of Catholics to religious freedom. This was definitely not the same as the teaching of Vatican II.

Economic Moral Teachings

Why should church and papal teaching be concerned about economic issues and problems? *Laborem exercens* begins by recalling the basic teaching of *Redemptor hominis* that "man is the primary and fundamental way of the church" (1.1). For this reason, the church is interested in all that happens to human beings in every sphere of their existence. *Sollicitudo rei socialis* takes off from Pope Paul VI's description of the church as an "expert in humanity" to justify extending "her religious mission to the various fields in which men and women expend their efforts in search of the always relative happiness which is possible in this world, in line with their dignity as persons" (41.2). The church's social teaching is concerned with whatever affects the dignity of individuals and persons, but the church does not have competence in technical problems (41.3). John Paul II, as mentioned, sees the teaching role of the church in terms of principles, criteria, and directives. The church presents no economic models, because such models can only arise within different historical situations through the efforts of those who responsibly face concrete problems (*CA* 31).

The moral teaching of John Paul II in the economic area involves three moral considerations: workers' dignity, the role and distribution of material goods, and a criticism of the existing economic systems.

Workers

The dignity of workers grounds the priority of labor over capital and the rights of workers. John Paul II recognizes a significant number of rights, especially the right to a just wage that cannot be left merely to the forces of the marketplace or the consent of the parties involved. Wages ensure the natural right of workers to procure what is necessary to live (*CA* 8). In developing the Catholic understanding of a living and family wage, John Paul II adds some new elements. *Laborem exercens* calls for a reevaluation of the mother's role and espouses family allowances or grants to mothers devoting themselves exclusively to their families (19.3–4). *Laborem exercens* also develops the concept of the indirect employer to ensure that workers receive a just wage (17). In keeping with the dignity of the worker, John Paul II repeats the earlier teaching proposing joint ownership of the means of work and the sharing of workers in management and profits (14.5). The pope is concerned, however, not only that workers "have more," but above all "be more" (20.6). Here again one sees how the teaching of John Paul II is based on the ontological truth and incomparable dignity of the human person—what the person is and what the person is called to be.

John Paul II endorses and develops the Catholic recognition of the rights of workers to organize and even to strike (*LE* 20). Unions exist to defend the vital interests of workers. In their own way, unions are a sign of the solidarity among workers. Unions, however, can be guilty of group egoism and need to be conscious of the common good. John Paul II recognizes the legitimacy of a strike as a last resort but cautions about abuses. His approach to unions threads a middle way between class struggle on the one hand and a fear of any kind of conflict on the other hand. Some contemporary Catholic commentators, myself included, have criticized Catholic social teaching for not giving enough importance to the roles of conflict and power.[9] John Paul II here recognizes the struggle and conflict that at times occur between labor and management. Conflict with other human beings is not an end in itself or a struggle against others but a means to achieve the end of social justice. Thus the pope is willing to accept some conflict, but not class struggle, as governing all of social life. All should work for the same end of social justice.

Material Goods

John Paul II follows in the Catholic tradition by recognizing both the importance and limitations of material goods. Material goods are necessary for human welfare and flourishing, but there are more important goods. The pope frequently insists on the truth of the fundamental distinction between being and having. To have objects and goods does not perfect the human subject unless it contributes to the enrichment of the subject's being or, in other words, to the human vocation. The difference between being and having grounds the quality and hierarchy of goods. Genesis tells us that the human person is an image of God with reason, consciousness, and self-direction. We can never forget that the highest dimension of human existence is the transcendental aspect of the human person, who can respond to God's gift and direct the self as an image of God. It is through this free gift of self that the human person truly finds self and achieves authentic personhood. This interior dimension of the human person as an image of God grounds the highest and most important human goods (*SRS* 27–34).

The person's capacity for transcendence makes possible the free gift of the person to God and others, which is the true fulfillment of the person. The person who refuses to transcend self and live the experience of self-giving is alienated. Both the Marxist countries and the West have suffered from alienation. Marxists have only a mistaken and materialistic notion of alienation. Alienation means the loss of the authentic meaning of life. Conversely, too often in the West materialism and consumerism can snare people in a web of false and superficial gratification. The pope has frequently pointed out the dangers of materialism and consumerism in the West (*CA* 41). *Laborem exercens* condemns an economism that treats labor as just another factor of economic production. Economism is reduced to materialism because it subordinates the spiritual and truly personal aspects of the human to the material (13.3).

The contemporary world in a paradoxical way suffers from both underdevelopment and superdevelopment. The whole thrust of *Sollicitudo rei socialis* challenges both the East and the West to recognize the plight of the developing world. According to John Paul II at that time, poverty in developing nations has become notably worse (16). A striking fact in the political causes of poverty in the developing world is the existence of the two opposing blocs of East and West (19–21). But side by side with the underdevelopment of poor countries is the superdevelopment of many in industrial countries. This superdevelopment consists in the ready availability of material goods that make people slaves of possession and immediate gratification. Such superdevelopment only leads to a radical alienation and dissatisfaction because it cannot satisfy the basic yearnings of the human person (28).

Sollicitudo rei socialis calls for an authentic development of persons and societies based on the truth of the human person, whose nature includes not only the material but also the personal, cultural, and religious dimensions. In the developing world especially, "modern underdevelopment is not only economic but also cultural, political, and simply human" (15.6). John Paul II here mentions illiteracy, the inability to share in developing one's own nation, exploitation, oppression in many forms, and discrimination (15.1).

The Catholic tradition has put a primary emphasis in its teaching on the proper distribution of material goods but has generally not developed the other side of the coin—the creation of material goods.

One can readily understand why the tradition with its emphasis on helping those in need put primary and even exclusive emphasis on the just distribution of material goods. John Paul II, to his great credit, is the first pope to emphasize the need for the creation of wealth.[10] This emphasis corresponds not only to the reality of the situation but also to John Paul II's understanding of the human person. Throughout his huge corpus, the pope frequently appeals to Genesis to explain the nature, dignity, and role of human beings. The greatness of the human person in Genesis comes from having dominion over the earth and all creation and the call by God to subdue the earth. In dominating and subduing the earth, the human person carries on the creative activity of God. The human person involved in creative work is an image of God. *Laborem exercens* develops this understanding of the creation of wealth (25). "The word of God's revelation is profoundly marked by the fundamental truth that *man*, created in the image of God, *shares by his work in the activity of the Creator* and that, within the limits of his own human capabilities, man in a sense continues to develop that activity, and perfects it as he advances further and further in the discovery of the resources and values contained in the whole of creation" (*LE* 25.2).

Sollicitudo rei socialis insists on "the right of economic initiative" that is important not only for individuals but also for the common good. This spirit of initiative is based on the creative subjectivity of the citizen (15.1–3). *Centesimus annus* develops in more detail the emphasis on initiative and entrepreneurial ability based on the subjectivity and creativity of the human person. Besides the earth, the human person's principal resource is the self. Discipline and creative human work create wealth. Modern business economy recognizes the role that initiative and entrepreneurial ability play, but the pope also goes on to point out the risks and problems connected with this business economy (32).

Distribution of Material Goods

The characteristic principle of Christian social doctrine with regard to the just distribution of material goods insists that the goods of this world are originally meant for all (*SRS* 42.5). The common destiny of material wealth comes from the creative act of God, who gave the earth to the whole human race for the sustenance of all its members without excluding or favoring anyone (*CA* 31.2). John Paul II recognizes that the common purpose of goods is the traditional teaching of the church as proposed in the Pastoral Constitution on the Church in the Modern World, and he develops this teaching in a number of different places (*CA* 30). The Pastoral Constitution on the Church in the Modern World refers to the "common purpose of created things." John Paul II tends not to use the word "created goods," but he still grounds the common or universal destiny of material goods in the gift of God's creation. But here a problem arises in his reasoning.[11] As has been pointed out, John Paul II differs from his predecessors by insisting that human creativity and initiative have contributed much to the growth of material goods and wealth. The wealth of individuals and nations today is based much more on human creativity and initiative than on the resources given by God in creation (*CA* 32). One could make the argument that what individual human creativity has brought into existence belongs to the individual who has done it.

To defend adequately the common destiny of material goods and wealth, including the vast majority of what has come into existence through human creativity and initiative, John Paul II needs to develop an argument that is not based solely on the gift of creation. Within his own thinking, John Paul II has the resources to develop a much better argument based on solidarity (*SRS* 38–40). Solidarity reminds us of our interdependence with others. We have obligations to all human beings to protect and to promote the basic dignity of all. A sufficiency of material goods is necessary to protect such human dignity. Solidarity also points out that the individual's creativity and initiative are not merely individualistic. Many others have contributed in various ways even to the creativity and entrepreneurship of the individual. Thus an emphasis on solidarity would provide a better and more complete reason for the common destiny of material wealth to serve the needs of all.

The universal destiny of material goods thus means that the primary canon of just distribution of material goods is human need. The social encyclicals of John Paul II do not develop the point in a systematic way but frequently point out the obligation to fulfill the needs of human beings. The forces of society and the state should see that the basic needs of the whole of society and of individuals are satisfied (*CA* 35.2). But there are also other needs besides material ones. Here, too, the pope claims, "It is a strict duty of justice and truth not to allow fundamental human needs to remain unsatisfied and not to allow those burdened by such needs to perish" (*CA* 34.1). Once again, as is in keeping with the genre of an encyclical, the pope does not develop all the canons of the distribution of material goods but simply insists on human need as being a basic criterion.

John Paul II invokes the "preferential option for the poor" to bolster the emphasis on satisfying basic human needs, especially in the material order. The option for the poor first came to the fore in the context of liberation theology, especially in its South American roots.[12] John Paul II opposes liberation theology for a number of reasons, including its openness to Marxist approaches (*SRS* 46.2), but he supports "authentic liberation" (*SRS* 46.5) and "true liberation" (*SRS* 47.1). He is willing to accept to some extent the preferential option for the poor. *Sollicitudo rei socialis* refers to "the *option or love of preference* for the poor" as a special form of primacy in the exercise of Christian charity to which the whole tradition of the church bears witness (42.2). Notice the attempt to distance himself from liberation theology by emphasizing love and charity and by referring to the entire tradition of the church. Elsewhere, he points out that the emphasis on the poor in Leo XIII's *Rerum novarum* testifies "to the continuity within the church of the so-called 'preferential option for the poor'" (*CA* 11.1).

John Paul II's conclusion from the "so-called preferential option for the poor" is strong. The love or preference for the poor inspires us to "embrace the immense multitudes of the hungry, the needy, the homeless, those without medical care, and above all, those without hope for a better future" (*SRS* 42.3). This preferential option is never exclusive or discriminatory toward other groups. In keeping with the truth about the human person, *Centesimus annus* recognizes that the preferential option is not limited to material goods, because it is well known, especially in the modern world, that there are many forms of poverty. The pope notes the contrast between the mass of material poverty in the developing world and the different forms of poverty in the industrial world (*CA* 57.2). But he should give more importance to the role of the poor in changing their situation.

John Paul II sees the common destiny of material goods to serve the needs of all as limiting and qualifying the right to private property. Here again, the truth about the human person recognizes both the dignity and the solidarity of human persons. All three encyclicals deal with private property in this light. The Christian tradition has never upheld the right to private property as an absolute. "*The right to private property is subordinated to the right to common use*, to the fact that goods are meant for everyone" (*LE* 14.2). In light of this approach, John Paul II repeats a teaching of the modern popes that one cannot exclude the socialization in suitable conditions of certain means of production (*LE* 14.3). The pope understands the universal destiny of goods as claiming a "social mortgage" on private property (*SRS* 42.5). The entire fourth part of *Centesimus annus* is devoted to private property and the universal destination of material goods (30–43). But here again, the pope is primarily concerned with general meaning and approaches and not with specific structures.

Communism

The truth about the human person serves as the basis for John Paul II's analysis of the opposing economic positions of capitalism and communism. John Paul II, like most commentators, recognizes different types of capitalism and communism or socialism—for example, early capitalism (*LE* 13.4), rigid capitalism (*LE* 14.4), and real socialism (*CA* 56.2). However, the pope analyzes these systems in the light of their generic thrust and does not usually get involved in various distinctions within the systems. One can readily see how the truth of the dignity and solidarity of the human person relates to these two systems. Marxism or communism tends to deny the dignity or freedom of the individual person, whereas capitalism fails to recognize the social aspects and solidarity of human persons. In general, John Paul II follows such an approach, but in a fascinating way, he also sees socialism and capitalism as having a common root in materialism (*LE* 7.2–3).

Marxism or communism goes against the truth about the human being in terms of the transcendent dignity of the human person. Dialectical and historical materialism constitutes the essential core of Marxism. In principle, this materialism radically excludes the presence and action of God, who is Spirit, in the world and also in the human person (*DV* 56.2). "Thus, the root of modern totalitarianism is to be found in the denial of the transcendent dignity of the human person who, as the visible image of the invisible God, is therefore by his very nature the subject of rights which no one may violate—no individual, group, class, nation, or State" (*CA* 44.2). Thus "the fundamental error of socialism is anthropological in nature. Socialism considers the individual person simply as an element, a molecule within the social organism" (*CA* 13.1). Socialism denies an objective criterion of the good and tends to absorb all reality within itself, denying the legitimate autonomy and sovereignty of the family and other organizations (*CA* 45). Marxism has a mistaken concept of the nature of the person and the subjectivity of society (*CA* 13.3). John Paul II logically condemns the strategy of class struggle associated with Marxism because class struggle fails to respect the dignity of persons and the common good of society. Yes, there is a need for some conflict in the struggle for justice, but the struggle is for the common good and for justice, not simply a struggle against others (*CA* 14; *LE* 11–15, 20.2). Likewise, the pope opposes the collectivist system, which eliminates private ownership of the means of production (*LE* 11.5). But *Laborem exercens* also recognizes in suitable conditions the need for the socialization of certain means of production (14.3).

The fall of the Iron Curtain and the communist countries in 1989 bore out the force of the truth of the above analysis of Marxism. The protests that led to the collapse of Marxism were almost everywhere peaceful, "using only the weapons of truth and justice" (*CA* 23.2). According to *Centesimus annus*, Leo XIII in 1891 foresaw the negative consequences of socialism that resulted in the 1989 revolution (12.1–2). The encyclical highlights two reasons for the collapse of communism in 1989. First, "The true cause of the new developments was the spiritual void brought about by atheism," which led many to search for the deeper meaning of life (24.2). Second, the decisive factor that gave rise to the changes was the violation of the rights of workers, as illustrated by the Solidarity movement in Poland (23.1).

John Paul II thus is in general continuity with Catholic social teaching in his condemnation of Marxism, but he differs significantly from Paul VI. Paul VI developed the idea first proposed by John XXIII concerning the differences between ideologies and historical movements that arose from these ideologies. Paul VI, by distinguishing between the various levels or expressions of socialism, saw room for some dialogue and even cooperation with Marxism.[13] In practice, Paul VI tried to secure the freedom and growth of the church in countries behind the Iron Curtain by working out political agreements and compromises with some of these countries.[14]

Why did John Paul II not continue in the more nuanced approach of Paul VI to Marxism? Their different social locations help to explain the differences. Paul VI, as universal pastor, was more willing to make some accommodations with communist countries to protect and promote the freedom and growth of the church behind the Iron Curtain. Karol Wojtyla, under the leadership of Stephan Cardinal Wyszynski, saw the Catholic Church as the main opposition in Poland to the communist regime. After becoming pope, his support for Solidarity gave international support to the struggle against the communist government of Poland. The Polish church, during the pontificate of Paul VI, was fearful that the pope at some time was willing to make an accommodation with the Polish government and undermine the role of the Polish church as the opposition movement. Wojtyla, in theory and in practice, saw the Catholic Church in opposition to communism and felt no need for any type of cooperation or compromise. John Paul II's strong opposition to communism played a significant role in the ultimate collapse of communism.[15]

Capitalism

As has been mentioned, John Paul II recognizes different types of capitalism and sees some positive change from the early and rigid capitalism of the late nineteenth century (*LE* 7.3). However, he remains critical of capitalism in general and also of capitalism as it exists in the West today. His opposition to capitalism is not of the same type as his opposition to Marxism. In general, he follows the approach of the older Catholic social teaching that sees Marxism as intrinsically wrong or fundamentally flawed because of its atheism, materialism, and denial of personal human dignity and human rights. Capitalism, however, is not as fundamentally flawed, and its abuses can and should be corrected.[16]

The truth about the human person with the twofold aspect of human dignity and human solidarity grounds John Paul II's criticism of capitalism. Early capitalism failed to appreciate the dignity, subjectivity, and fundamental rights of workers. "The key to reading the Encyclical [Leo XIII's *Rerum novarum*] is the dignity of the worker as such" (*CA* 6.1; see also *LE* 1–2). Such an approach coheres with John Paul II's own emphasis on the priority of labor over capital (*LE* 12). Among the rights denied to the worker in the past were the right to private property (although this is not an absolute right), the right to form unions or trade associations, and the right to a just wage (*CA* 6–9).

The solidarity aspects of John Paul II's criticism of capitalism focus primarily on the role of the state. The state has a special obligation to defend and promote the rights of the defenseless and the poor. "The State has the duty of watching over the common good and of ensuring that every sector of social life, not excluding the economic one, contributes to achieving that good" (*CA* 11.2). According to "an elementary principle of social political organization, . . . the more that individuals are defenseless within a given society, the more they require the care and concern of others, and in particular, the intervention of governmental authority" (*CA* 10.2). On the contemporary scene, John Paul II points out, "There are many human needs which find no place on the market" (*CA* 34.1). The market must be "appropriately controlled by the forces of society and by the State, so as to guarantee that the basic needs of the whole of society are satisfied" (*CA* 35.2). Business and the market exist not just to make a profit but also to satisfy basic human needs (*CA* 35.3). The following section develops at greater length Pope Wojtyla's understanding of the role of the state to protect and promote the common good on the basis of the principles of both socialization and subsidiarity.

John Paul II and the Catholic social teaching tradition recognize that capitalism and communism are two opposing approaches both in theory and in practice (*LE* 7.3). John Paul II, however, develops Catholic social teaching in a significant manner by also showing the similarities between capitalism and Marxism.

First, capitalism and Marxism share the same root problem—materialism. Karol Wojtyla made this point in his writing before becoming pope. For political reasons at that time, he could not use the term communism or socialism, but he "appears to have located in the term *utilitarianism* the root both of Soviet style materialistic communism and of the materialistic consumerist capitalism of the West."[17] Wojtyla's philosophical personalism opposes the materialism of both Marxism and capitalism. *Laborem exercens*, the first social encyclical of the Wojtyla papacy, continues the same approach by showing that capitalism and Marxism are based on what the pope calls "materialistic economism," a form of materialism that gives priority to the objective rather than the subjective aspect of work (*LE* 7.2). Early capitalism treated man "on the same level as the whole complex of the material means of production, as an instrument and not in accordance with the true dignity of his work—that is to say, where he is not treated as subject and maker" (*LE* 7.3).

Marxism too comes from materialistic economism. "The error of thinking in the categories of economism went hand in hand with the formation of a materialist philosophy, as this philosophy developed . . . to the phase of what is called dialectical materialism." Dialectical materialism does not treat man as first and foremost the subject of work but on the basis of its materialistic philosophy treats the worker as a kind of "resultant" of economic and productive realities (*LE* 13.4).

But there is also a second similarity between capitalism and communism. *Sollicitudo rei socialis* dealt with the issue of development especially as it involved the developing world before the fall of communism. The pope recognizes the complexity of the situation but concentrates on one political cause for the underdevelopment of the South—"the *existence of two opposing blocs*, commonly known as the East and the West" (*SRS* 20.3). Liberal capitalism represents the system of the West, while Marxism's collectivism is the system of the East. Each of the two blocs tries to gather around it other countries in the world (*SRS* 20.3). "Each of the two *blocs* harbors in its way a tendency toward *imperialism*, as it is usually called, or toward forms of neocolonialism: an easy temptation to which they frequently succumb as history, including recent history, teaches" (*SRS* 22.3). The developing world, which is mostly identified with the South, suffers from the tension between the two blocs. "The present division of the world is a *direct obstacle* to the real transformation of the conditions of underdevelopment in the developing and less advanced countries" (*SRS* 22.5). In this context, in a rather evenhanded way, the pope criticizes both East and West as very significant causes of the underdevelopment of poor countries.

After the fall of communism, the pope asked the obvious question: "Can it perhaps be said that, after the failure of Communism, capitalism is the victorious social system, and that capitalism should be the goal of the countries now making efforts to rebuild their economy and society"? (*CA* 42.1). John Paul II's complex assessment is in keeping with his general approach to capitalism and needs to be quoted in full:

> If by "capitalism" is meant an economic system which recognizes the fundamental and positive role of business, the market, private property, and the resulting responsibility for the means of production, as well as free human creativity in the economic sector, then the answer is certainly in the affirmative, even though it would perhaps be more appropriate to speak of a "business economy," "market economy," or simply "free economy." But if by "capitalism" is meant a system in which freedom in the economic sector is not circumscribed within a strong juridical framework which places it at the service of human freedom in its totality and sees it as a particular aspect of that freedom, the core of which is ethical and religious, then the reply is certainly negative. (*CA* 42.2)

The pope is only too aware of the continued marginalization and exploitation remaining on this planet, especially in the developing world. "Indeed, there is a risk that a radical capitalistic ideology could spread which refuses even to consider these problems" (*CA* 42.3).

One comment in *Centesimus annus* occasioned much commentary. John Paul II criticizes the "welfare state" that has come into existence in some countries to better respond to the many demands and needs of people. He opposes the welfare state, or what he also calls the "social assistance state," for giving too big a role to the state by "intervening directly and depriving society of its responsibility . . . [which leads to] a loss of human energies and an inordinate increase of public agencies, which are dominated more by bureaucratic ways of thinking than by concern for serving their clients and which are accompanied by an enormous increase in spending" (*CA* 48.5).

As one might expect, people from different perspectives have interpreted this passage differently. Proponents of neoconservatism, such as Michael Novak, see it as a recognition of the dangers of too much state involvement in economic freedom in many parts of the world. Just as Vatican II accepted the concept of religious freedom, now "in *Centesimus annus* Rome has assimilated American ideas of economic liberty."[18] In light of some of the negative comments in *Centesimus annus* mentioned above, David Hollenbach insists, "It would be a serious mistake to think that the pope has blessed the form of capitalism existing in the United States today."[19] Donal Dorr acknowledges that many Catholics were disappointed in the papal criticism of the welfare state, but he sees the criticism as a move beyond the welfare state. The state should empower people to take their own initiatives and should not create dependency among poor people.[20] At the very minimum, it is obvious that *Centesimus annus* is not blessing the American system.

This book focuses on the moral teaching of John Paul II from the perspective of Catholic moral theology. But one should always see this narrow focus in light of the broader picture. John Paul II's moral teaching is not found only in encyclicals and in documents of various sorts. As is well known, he has traveled all over the globe to proclaim his message. No other person in the world has spoken more often and to more people on economic issues. He has preached his message of authentic development in season and out of season, to rich and poor, North and South, to people of all races and creeds throughout the world. His voice has echoed across the globe in support of the poor and the oppressed. Authentic development requires that all have the basic minimum necessary to live a minimally decent human life. But he has also constantly reminded the rich that authentic and integral development is based on the spiritual nature of the human person and that materialism and a consumer mentality stand in the way of authentic development.

The Political Order

The truth about the human person, with its twin emphases on human dignity and human solidarity, grounds John Paul II's understanding of the political order. His three social encyclicals and other significant writings tend to address specific issues or particular occasions and do not attempt to present a systematic political ethic. However, there can be no doubt that his thought comes from the Catholic social tradition in general and the recent hierarchical social teaching—but with significant contributions of his own.

The Role of the State

The pope's emphasis on both human dignity and human solidarity, as in the economic realm, results in an understanding of the state that avoids the opposite extremes of individualism and collectivism. From a theological perspective, the state owes its origin to the God-given nature of the human person, who is called to live in solidarity with others. For some Christians, the state owes its origin to its need to serve as an order of preservation in the light of human sinfulness. God uses the coercive power of the state to preserve order and prevent chaos. Without the state, sinful human beings would tend to kill one another.[21] The Catholic tradition sees the origin of the state in light of the nature of the human person confirmed by revelation's understanding of our solidarity, and thus it has a more positive understanding of the role of the state.[22]

In the Catholic tradition, the purpose of the state is to protect and promote the common good.[23] Individualism recognizes only individual goods that the state protects. Collectivism recognizes only collective goods and subordinates the individual to the good of the collective. In the Catholic tradition, the common good is the good for society that ultimately redounds to the good of the individual.

Think, for example, of clean air, which is not only good for society in general but also for all the individual members of society. John Paul II recognizes the interdependence in our world and in all human relationships as a moral category. The correlative response to this interdependence is the virtue of solidarity, which "is a *firm* and *persevering determination* to commit oneself to the *common good*; that is to say to the good of all and of each individual, because we are *all* really responsible *for all*" (*SRS* 38.6). The common good "is not simply the sum total of particular interests; rather it involves an assessment and integration of those interests on the basis of a balanced hierarchy of values; ultimately it demands a correct understanding of the dignity and rights of the human person" (*CA* 47.2).

The proper role of the state avoids the individualistic notion of the state as minimalistic and the collectivist notion of the state as maximalistic. In the Catholic tradition and in Catholic social teaching as enunciated by Pope Pius XI, the principle of subsidiarity recognizes the various levels in society—the individual, families, neighborhoods, voluntary associations of all types, and local, state, and federal governments. The elements on the higher level should do everything possible so that the lower levels can do all that they can on their own, and the higher levels should take over only what the lower levels are not able to do.[24] The principle of subsidiarity exists in tension with the principle of socialization. In *Mater et magister*, John XXIII recognized this principle of socialization, according to which—in light of the multiplication of social relationships and the correlative interdependence of citizens—there is a greater need today for government intervention.[25]

John Paul II recognizes this very realistic tension in describing the proper role of the state. He points out that *Rerum novarum* condemned both state control of the means of production, which would reduce every person to a "cog" in the state machine, and also a concept of the state that completely excludes the economic sector from its interests and concerns. The state contributes to the achievement of the good of justice for workers and others in two ways. Indirectly, in accord with the principle of subsidiarity, the state creates favorable conditions for the free exercise of economic activity, which leads to opportunities for employment and wealth. Directly, in accord with the principle of solidarity, the state defends the weakest by placing limits on the autonomy of owners and capitalists and by ensuring the necessary minimum support for unemployed workers (*CA* 15).

John Paul II sees the principle of subsidiarity in light of the subjectivity of society. With his personalistic approach, he has stressed not only the subjectivity of the person but also the subjectivity of society. The subjectivity of society opposes totalitarianism and recognizes that the social nature of the human person needs the state but above all needs the family and various intermediate groups, including economic, social, political, and cultural ones (*CA* 13.2; *SRS* 15.4). The subjectivity of society calls for the creation of structures of participation and shared responsibility (*CA* 46.2). The family and intermediate associations create networks of solidarity that prevent society from becoming an anonymous and impersonal mass (*CA* 49.3). John Paul II thus strongly supports the subjectivity of society and the principle of subsidiarity, although it is somewhat curious that he does not develop in any depth the important distinction between society and the state. Implicitly, such a distinction is there. But it could have been developed more explicitly. The state with its use of coercive force is only a small and limited part of the broader public society with its social, cultural, and economic activities.[26]

Conversely, the pope recognizes that at times the state must intervene when the family and intermediate groups cannot promote and safeguard justice and the common good. The state has the responsibility to safeguard the basic human rights of all. These include the right to religious freedom, the right to life, the right of workers to organize, to a just wage, and the right of all people to participate in society (*CA* 47.7–8). The state has the responsibility to circumscribe the economic sector within a strong juridical framework and thus to safeguard the true freedom of all (*CA* 42.2). The state also has a role in planning, along with all other intermediate groups, to bring about justice in the economic sphere (*LE* 18.2). In *Laborem exercens*, John Paul II introduced a new concept into Catholic social teaching: the indirect employer. The labor contract does not involve only the employer and the employee. The indirect employer, which includes many aspects, substantially conditions the employment contract and the role of the direct employer. "The concept of indirect employer is applicable to every society and in the first place to the State. For it is the State that must conduct a just labor policy" (*LE* 17.2).

Democracy and Human Rights

The Catholic Church at the beginning of the twentieth century strongly opposed both democracy and human rights. By the end of the twentieth century, however, the Catholic Church and Catholic social teaching had come to strongly defend democracy and human rights throughout the world. George Weigel, the self-proclaimed neoconservative Catholic,[27] describes this strong Catholic support for democracy as the second twentieth-century revolution, the first having been the Russian Bolshevik Revolution of 1917. The Roman Catholic Church transformed itself from a bastion of the ancien régime to one of the foremost supporters of democracy.[28] With regard to human rights, it was only in 1963 that John XXIII in *Pacem in terries* developed the full spectrum of human rights.[29]

The historical development of these significant changes lies beyond the scope of this book.[30] Briefly, at the beginning of the twentieth century, the Catholic Church associated both democracy and human rights with the Enlightenment and individualistic political liberalism. Such an approach absolutized individual reason and freedom cut off from any relationship with God and God's law. But as the twentieth century unfolded, the Catholic Church began to see that totalitarianism and not political liberalism was the primary problem. Against the century's growing totalitarianism, Catholic teaching began to insist on the freedom, equality, dignity, and basic rights of the individual person and on the need for democracy.

Catholic teaching, however, did not simply accept individualistic philosophical liberalism. Thus, for example, in the matter of human rights, Pope John XXIII insisted on both political and civil rights, such as freedom of religion, freedom of association, and freedom of meeting, as well as social and economic rights, such as the right to food, shelter, clothing, education, medical care, and basic social services.[31] Political liberalism emphasized only political and civil rights, whereas communism and socialism emphasized only social and economic rights. In keeping with the Catholic insistence on both the dignity of the individual person and the social nature of all human beings, John XXIII insisted on the need for both types of rights. In theory and in practice, John Paul II has strongly supported democracy and human rights throughout the world. His personalism emphasizes not only the person as a subject but also the subjectivity of society, calling for structures that facilitate the participation and shared responsibility of all in society. Totalitarianism ultimately denies the subjectivity of society. The Catholic understanding of subsidiarity and the need for many intermediary groups supports such subjectivity. Democracy calls for the participation and shared responsibility of all citizens working for the common good. Democracy also guarantees to the governed the possibility of both electing and holding accountable their leaders and of replacing them peaceably whenever appropriate (*CA* 46.2, 13.2, *SRS* 15.4). In practice, John Paul II has campaigned vigorously throughout the world in support of democracy against totalitarianism not only of communist states behind the Iron Curtain but also against many other totalitarian and "national security regimes."

The worldwide quest for freedom and democracy, which came to the fore at the end of the twentieth century, finds its cause and basis in universal human rights (*CA* 47.1–3). The dignity and value of the human person constitute the basis for all human rights. The human person is the only creation on earth that God willed for itself. God has conferred God's own image and likeness on the human person, conferring on the person an incomparable dignity.

John Paul II, in *Redemptor hominis*, his first encyclical, sees human rights as a fundamental principle of human welfare in our world today (*RH* 17). Such rights have their origin in the dignity of the human person and God's gift. They are not simply conferred or granted by the state. Totalitarianism in the twentieth century restricted or denied basic human rights. All states must recognize these fundamental human rights. Human rights constitute the basis for social and international peace. War springs from the violation of human rights and brings with it greater violations of human rights. The principle of human rights is a profound concern for social justice and is the basic criterion for testing the existence of social justice in countries. *Sollicitudo rei socialis* maintains that true development requires "a lively *awareness* of the *value* of the rights of all and of each person" (33.5).

In his encyclicals, John Paul II does not draw up a detailed list of rights. But in keeping with his anthropological emphasis on both human dignity and human solidarity, he recognizes both political and civil rights as well as social and economic rights (*RH* 17; *CA* 47.1). His most explicit recognition of both types of human rights came in his "1999 World Day of Peace Message: Respect for Human Rights—The Secret of True Peace." [32]

Human rights correspond to the authentic development of the human being. The apex of human development is the exercise of the right and duty to seek God, to know God, and to live in accord with God's directions. In a certain sense, religious freedom is the source and synthesis of all human rights (*CA* 47.1). But the right to religious freedom itself follows from the broader rights of conscience properly understood. The primary foundation of every authentically free political order comes from the right of the human conscience that is bound only to the truth, both natural and revealed (*CA* 29.1).

Truth, Democracy, and Rights

John Paul II, in a very consistent way, insists on the primacy of truth in his understanding both of human rights and of democracy. The truth about the human person grounds all human rights. The basic error of totalitarianism is its denial of objective truth. Without transcendental truth, there is no sure basis for human rights. Self-interest and power will eventually take over. No one may violate human rights—no individual, group, class, nation, or state, nor the majority within any society (*VS* 99; *EV* 96.2; *CA* 17). In its discussion on democracy, *Centesimus annus* asserts that "freedom attains its full development only by accepting the truth" (46.4). The pope maintains that "obedience to the truth about God and man is the first condition of freedom" (*CA* 41.4).

Pope Wojtyla is well aware that many today see an emphasis on truth as incompatible with democracy. Today there is a tendency to claim that agnosticism and skeptical relativism ground democratic forms of political life. Those who are convinced they know the truth are unreliable supporters of democracy. Because all people cannot agree on what the truth is, in a democracy the majority decides what is true. But the pope insists that a democracy without truth and values easily turns into open or thinly disguised totalitarianism (*CA* 46.2).

What is the proper relationship between freedom and truth in democracy? The papal encyclicals and other writings do not address the issue directly in a systematic way, but the papal writings touch on this significant theoretical and practical issue.

Centesimus annus, on four different occasions, cites Leo XIII's encyclical, *Libertas praestantissimum* (fn. 7, 47, 48, 91). The pope appeals to this encyclical of Leo in pointing out the error of understanding human freedom as detached from the truth (17.1, fn. 47, 48). Earlier, the text of *Centesimus annus* explicitly cites *Libertas praestantissimum* in calling attention to "the essential bond between human freedom and truth" (4.5, fn. 7). On the basis of the concept of freedom and its relationship with truth developed by Leo XIII in the nineteenth century, that pope denied religious freedom and called for the union of church and state. Error has no rights.[33] The heavy dependence of John Paul II on Leo XIII thus raises the question about whether his notion of democracy is acceptable to many people today. Perhaps the citation of Leo XIII fits in with John Paul II's attempt to show continuity with all of his predecessors. However, it certainly raises the question about John Paul II's understanding of the relationship between freedom and truth and his understanding of democracy.

Without doubt, John Paul II claims to have knowledge of the truth about the human person and the truth about what is good for society. The question then arises: How does the church try to convince others of the truth? John Paul II has frequently mentioned the need for dialogue, even on matters of faith in terms of ecumenical dialogue. The encyclical *Centesimus annus*, for example, mentions dialogue on six occasions. The complex problems humanity faces can be resolved through dialogue and the solidarity of Christians with all people of goodwill rather than by war or violence (22.2). Unlike the Marxist insistence on violent confrontation, the protest against Marxism, which resulted in the fall of the Iron Curtain, "relied on trying every avenue of negotiation, dialogue, and witness to the truth appealing to the conscience of the adversary and seeking to awaken in him a sense of shared human dignity" (23.2). The Christian affirms in dialogue with others "all that his faith and the correct use of reason have enabled him to understand" (46.4). The human person seeks the truth and strives to live in that truth, "deepening his understanding of it through a dialogue which involves past and future generations" (49.3). *Centesimus annus* also recognizes that the one truth about humanity needs dialogue with the various other human disciplines in order to incarnate the truth in constantly changing social, economic, and political contexts (59.3). Near its close, this encyclical insists that openness to dialogue and to cooperation is required of all people of goodwill (60.4).

If dialogue is the way to arrive at truth, proponents of democracy have less to fear with John Paul II's approach. But there are still some tensions, both theoretical and practical. On a theoretical level, John Paul II strongly insists that the church has the truth and it teaches the truth. But the church is not only a teacher of truth; it is also a learner of truth, especially in the area of social teaching. Catholic social teaching has learned much from others in this very area of the appreciation of freedom and the need for democratic forms of government. But nowhere in his encyclicals on social teaching does the pope explicitly admit and recognize how much the church has learned in this area from other people of goodwill and even from those who have strongly disagreed with Catholic positions. At times, John Paul II gives the impression that dialogue is a method for others to accept his truth. His recognition of the need for dialogue would be stronger and more acceptable to proponents of democracy if he explicitly recognized how much the Catholic Church itself has learned in the matter of social teaching through dialogue with others.

But there exists a deeper problem. John Paul II fails to recognize explicitly the different roles of freedom in the moral or ethical order and in the political order. The failure of Leo XIII to make this distinction resulted in his opposition to political and civil rights and his insistence that error has no rights. John Courtney Murray has described Leo XIII as having an ethical view of the state rather than a political view. Leo had an authoritarian or at best a paternalistic notion of the state, according to which the state tells people how to live their lives.[34] Leo could not accept the teaching espoused by the Declaration on Religious Freedom of Vatican II—"For the rest, the usages of society are to be the usages of freedom in their full range. These require that the freedom of man be respected as far as possible and curtailed only when and insofar as necessary."[35] Murray pointed out the fundamental importance of this position: "Secular experts may well consider this to be the most significant sentence in the Declaration. It is a statement of the basic principle of the 'free society.'"[36] Nowhere in his encyclicals does John Paul II explicitly accept this basic principle of the free society.

Civil Law and Its Coercive Power

John Paul II's failure to accept explicitly the basic principle of the free society comes to the fore in his understanding of the role of civil law and of the coercive power of government. He has been a most vocal and visible spokesperson on the world scene, calling for civil laws against abortion and euthanasia. *Evangelium vitae* (68–77) devotes ten paragraphs to his understanding of the role of law in a democracy. His notion of democracy opposes the moral relativism that is so prevalent today. Democracy is not simply a matter of majority vote. The almost universal consensus today exalting democracy is a positive sign of the times, but the value of democracy stands or falls with the values that it embodies and promotes. Democracy is a means to an end and not an end in itself. "Its 'moral' value . . . depends on conformity to the moral law to which it, like every other form of human behavior, must be subject" (70.4). These values depend on "the acknowledgment of an objective moral law which, as the natural law written in the human heart, is the obligatory point of reference for civil law itself" (70.5).

Pope Wojtyla, however, recognizes that the purpose of civil law is more limited in scope than the moral law. The real purpose of civil law is to guarantee ordered social coexistence and true justice. Civil law must protect fundamental human rights. First and foremost among these rights is "the inviolable right to life of every innocent human being" (71.3). Laws that legitimize the direct killing of innocent human beings through abortion and euthanasia are in complete opposition to the inviolable right to life proper to every individual and thus deny the equality of everyone before the law (73.1). "The doctrine on the necessary *conformity of civil law with the moral law* is in continuity with the whole tradition of the Catholic Church. . . . This is the clear teaching of St. Thomas Aquinas" (72.1). Human law must be in conformity with right reason, natural law, and eternal law. If a civil law is opposed to natural law (which is an ordering of reason based on the eternal law), then it is not really a law but the corruption of law (72.1). In his exposition, the pope discusses and refutes the arguments that have been proposed in favor of a permissive abortion law—unenforceability, the danger of illegal and medically harmful abortions, human autonomy and freedom, and the lack of consensus in society on abortion (68–69).

John Paul II's understanding of the relationship of civil law and morality definitely follows the traditional Thomistic approach. But Vatican II, in its Declaration on Religious Freedom, proposed a different theoretical framework for the law–morality relationship. The declaration, as its title indicates, deals primarily with religious freedom, but, in keeping with the approach of Murray, the correct understanding of religious freedom involves the notion of the proper role and function of a limited constitutional state. The "religious freedom approach" begins with the principle of a free society—as much freedom as possible and as little restraint as necessary. The first limit on freedom in society is the responsibility of the individual person in the exercise of freedom. However, the state can and should intervene with the coercive power of law to protect and promote public order, which has a threefold content—justice, public peace, and public morality.[37]

The religious freedom approach differs from the Thomistic approach in two significant ways. The Thomistic approach begins with natural law, even though civil law is a somewhat more restricted reality. The religious freedom approach begins with the principle of a free society—as much freedom as possible and as little restraint as necessary. Second, the criterion for state intervention through civil law differs. In the Thomistic approach, the state intervenes for the common good. In the religious freedom approach, the state intervenes to protect and promote public order. Public order is a more restrictive concept than the common good. The limited constitutional state, unlike the totalitarian state, insists on an important distinction between public society and the state. Society embraces all those factors and institutions that affect public life in all its manifold dimensions—cultural, social, economic, intellectual. The state is the narrower reality in the broader public society that alone can use the coercive force of law. The common good is the end corresponding to the broader public society and all who act in public society. Public order is the end of the state and the criterion that justifies the use of the state's coercive power. Such an understanding of law and morality also recognizes some pragmatic aspects about law in the light of pluralistic societies. Law must be enforceable and equitable. Likewise, at times, proponents of stronger laws will be willing to settle for less if that is the best that can be attained. Murray himself strongly supported Thomistic natural law in general, but only in the context of democracy can and should one distinguish between the broader and more inclusive concept of society with the common good as its end and the narrower concept of the state with the more limited end of public order.[38]

One could readily conclude, on the basis of the religious freedom approach, that the justice requirement of public order calls for the protection of all human rights, including the right of the unborn. However, some Catholics, including myself, use the religious freedom approach to give more emphasis to the benefit of the doubt favoring freedom from law, especially where there is no societal consensus against abortion.[39]

John Paul II could still come to the same conclusion of opposing permissive abortion laws using the religious freedom approach. But his failure to use the religious freedom approach indicates that he does not accept its basic idea of giving greater importance to freedom in political society. The Declaration on Religious Freedom holds in tension the two realities of truth and freedom. Freedom in the political sphere is not the same as freedom in the moral sphere.

Freedom in the political sphere does not result from moral relativism but from respect for the dignity of the human person, who is to be free from external coercion in order to freely embrace the truth. John Paul II fails to state explicitly that freedom is an analogous concept and that freedom in the political order is not the same as freedom in the moral order. Thus, in my judgment, he fails to recognize the significance of political freedom and its role in democracies. He has not accepted the understanding of political freedom found in the Declaration on Religious Freedom.

On the basis of such an understanding of political freedom in democracies, the primary role of influence for the church in matters of social justice is in the broader public arena of culture and public opinion and not in the narrower realm of coercive law. Under certain conditions, however, I think it is appropriate for church leaders and members as such to work for specific laws and public policies, but here the criterion is public order.[40]

John Paul II obviously does not accept the religious freedom approach to the understanding of political freedom in democracies. Throughout his writings, he invariably refers to the common good as the end of the state and does not invoke the narrower concept of public order as proposed in the Declaration on Religious Freedom. For example, the section on law and morality in *Evangelium vitae* maintains that "*the purpose of civil law* . . . is that of ensuring the common good" (71.3). The common good is "the end and criterion regulating political life" (70.4; see also 71.4 and two references in 72.2). This section of *Evangelium vitae* twice cites paragraph 7 of the Declaration on Religious Freedom (fn. 91, 93), but it never mentions the need for as much freedom as possible and as little restraint as necessary. Likewise, *Evangelium vitae* does not mention the concept of public order. The encyclical does refer to the threefold content of the public order—"fundamental rights, and the promotion of peace and of public morality"—but explicitly refers to these three goods as constituting the common good (71.3).

John Paul II is correct in recognizing that in democracies there are certain truths that all must accept and that a majority vote cannot overturn. The Bill of Rights, the first ten amendments to the United States Constitution, well illustrates such truths. But he fails to recognize explicitly that truth plays an analogous role in the ethical and political sphere. By citing Leo XIII on truth and freedom, and by his failure to cite the presumption in favor of freedom in political society proposed by the Declaration on Religious Freedom, he appears in this particular matter not to accept the basic principle of a free society—as much freedom as possible and as little restraint as necessary.

One might maintain that John Paul II does not explicitly mention the religious freedom understanding of the state and the role of civil law because he is dealing only with particular issues and not writing a theoretical treatise on the role of the state. Most people agree with him that the truth of basic human rights should be present in every society. I pointed out above that he could still logically work for legislation against abortion and euthanasia on the basis of the more limited understanding of law in the religious freedom approach. As was mentioned above, he strongly supports the limited role of the state based on the principle of subsidiarity, his insistence on the subjectivity of society, and his opposition to totalitarianism. But by emphasizing the subordination of freedom to truth and by failing to acknowledge explicitly the religious freedom approach, he opens himself to the charge that he fails to appreciate the proper understanding of freedom in a democracy.[41]

One can only conclude that John Paul II purposely refused embracing the religious freedom notion of the relationship between law and morality because it weakens somewhat his understanding of the close connection between truth and freedom, morality and law.

Peace and War

John Paul II has not devoted an encyclical to the precise topic of peace and war. His three major social encyclicals, especially *Centesimus annus*, discuss peace and war somewhat in passing, but one can find here his general approach to the question. He has often talked about peace, nonviolence, and war in his travels throughout the world and has commented on some of the world situations that have occurred during his papacy.

John Paul II has protested that he is not a pacifist who rejects all use of violence in all circumstances today,[42] but he has been a forceful proponent of peace and an avid advocate for nonviolent means of fighting injustice. His primary contribution in the area of peace lies on the two levels of a theology or vision for peace and more specific ways of working for peace. He has used his worldwide platform to try to change the culture of our world and the hearts of all people to recognize the value and importance of peace. And he has made his own the cry of Pope Paul VI at the United Nations: "War—never again!" (*CA* 52.1). He constantly teaches the "truth about man" to influence the hearts of human beings and the broader human culture to reject violence and promote and secure peace. The church's primary contribution is on this level of changing hearts and culture (*CA* 50.2).

Human solidarity on a global plane furnishes the basic foundation for peace in this world. Pope Pius XII's motto was peace as the work of justice, but John Paul II proposes "*Opus solidaritatis, pax*—peace as the fruit of solidarity" (*SRS* 39.9). The meaning of human interdependence and solidarity is spelled out precisely in terms of human rights. "After all peace comes down to respect for man's inviolable rights . . . while war springs from the violation of these rights and brings with it still greater violations of them" (*RH* 17.2). The pope recognizes that at the root of war there are essentially real and serious grievances—injustices suffered, legitimate aspirations frustrated, poverty, and the exploitation of multitudes of desperate people who see no real possibility of improving their lot by peaceful means. Just as there is a collective human responsibility for avoiding war, so too there is a collective human responsibility for promoting authentic development throughout the world. Borrowing a phrase from Paul VI, John Paul II asserts that another name for peace is development (*CA* 52.1–2). "Peoples excluded from the fair distribution of the goods originally destined for all could ask themselves: why not respond with violence to those who first treat us with violence?" (*SRS* 10.2). Thus, solidarity, human rights, and authentic development constitute the true bases for lasting peace.

In keeping with his strong emphasis on the primacy of truth, John Paul II sees an intimate connection between the power of truth and nonviolence. The fall of communism in 1989 testifies to the power of truth and of nonviolence. This fall "was accomplished almost everywhere by means of peaceful protest, using only the weapons of truth and justice" (*CA* 23.2). He praises and salutes "the nonviolent commitment of people who, while always refusing to yield to the force of power, succeeded time after time in finding effective ways of bearing witness to the truth" (*CA* 23.3). The pope prays that others throughout the world will follow this example.

Most of John Paul II's efforts have focused on trying to change the culture and attitudes of people with regard to war and violence. But he also realizes that peace cannot come about without the proper international structures. "What is needed are concrete steps to create or consolidate international structures capable of intervening through appropriate arbitration in the conflicts which arise between nations" (*CA* 27.2). "The United Nations, moreover, has not yet succeeded in establishing, as alternatives to war, effective means for the resolution of international conflicts. This seems to be the most urgent problem which the international community has yet to resolve" (*CA* 21.2). One could raise to the pope a more fundamental question: Will such structures ever be possible in our world?

John Paul II works for peace in many different ways. On the broader level of working toward a culture of peace and nonviolence, he has brought together religious leaders from all over the world to come to Asissi to pray and work for peace.[43] He had been an actor, and he has a flare for the dramatic. He brought the bishops of Argentina and the United Kingdom together to celebrate the liturgy with him in the midst of their countries' war in the Falkland Islands–Malvinas.[44] In his journeys throughout the world, and especially in his world day of peace messages released every New Year's Day, he has developed, and at times made more specific, the general approach found in the social encyclicals.

John Paul II frequently points out the great evils connected with war. In his social encyclicals, especially *Centesimus annus*, he highlights the problems with war. War destroys the lives of innocent people, teaches people how to kill, and throws into upheaval even the lives of those who do the killing (52.1). It is practically impossible to limit the negative consequences of war today in light of the terrifying power of the means of destruction—to which even medium-sized and small countries have access—and the ever closer links among all the people of the globe (51.2). There exists the danger of total war, which would result in the suicide of humanity (18.3). John Paul II, like his predecessors, strongly criticizes the arms race, in both industrial and poor countries, because it diverts huge sums from the authentic development of all peoples (*SRS* 10.3). The arms race is "insane" (*CA* 18.2). The arms trade only adds to the world's problems. This is a trade without frontiers and crosses all blocks and boundaries. Ironically, "while economic aid and development plans meet with the obstacle of insuperable ideological barriers, and with tariff and trade barriers, *arms* of whatever origin circulate with almost total freedom all over the world" (*SRS* 24.1). Despite the condemnation of the arms race and the need for disarmament, John Paul II never calls for unilateral disarmament.

John Paul II insists "that true peace is never simply the result of military victory, but rather implies both the removal of the causes of war and genuine reconciliation between peoples" (*CA* 18.1). He uses the European situation after World War II to prove his point. World War II, "which should have reestablished freedom and restored the rights of nations, ended without having attained these goals" (19.1). War itself does not produce peace.

With regard to international wars, John Paul II opposed war as a solution to the Falkland Island–Malvinas dispute between the United Kingdom and Argentina in 1982 and later opposed the Gulf War in 1991. In both cases, the pope recognized that aggression and violations of international law had occurred, but war still was not justified in these cases.[45] In 2003, he opposed the United States' involvement in Iraq.[46] In his trips around the globe, he has opposed violence as a means of achieving justice within countries in Africa, in Latin America, and in Ireland.[47]

In light of his strong support for nonviolence and his very negative attitude toward war, some might conclude that John Paul II is a pacifist. In light of such claims, he protests that he is not a pacifist, as was mentioned above. Nowhere do the encyclicals explicitly develop the justification of using force to repel unjust aggression, but they also never espouse a totally pacifist position. *Centesimus annus* condemns "total war" (18.3). Elsewhere, John Paul II has clearly expressed the legitimacy and at times even the need to use violence to prevent unjust aggression. His "2000 World Day of Peace Message" states: "Clearly when a civilian population risks being overcome by the attacks of an unjust aggressor and political efforts and nonviolent defense prove to be of no avail, it is legitimate and even obligatory to take concrete measures to disarm the aggressor."[48]

John Paul II allows for and even urges humanitarian intervention by force in the case of very severe violations of human rights. Other states cannot be indifferent to the intense sufferings that might occur in another nation. Humanitarian intervention is "obligatory when the survival of populations and entire ethnic groups is seriously compromised."[49] This is a duty for nations and for the international community.

Thus, John Paul II continues to maintain a just war position, but he has considerably narrowed the legitimate use of force. The pope has strengthened the presumption against war by insisting on its terrible evils and on the fact that war or force can never bring about true peace.

In summary, John Paul II has tried to create a climate and culture of peace while insisting on the limitations and evils connected with violence and the resort to war. In the light of the present world scene, in which there are no effective international structures to peacefully resolve conflicts, the pope recognizes the justification of war as a last resort to stop unjust aggression when all other means have failed. Thus, he still follows a just war approach, but he has significantly limited and restricted the conditions that could ever justify resorting to violence. [50]

Globalization and the Global Ethic

Perhaps the best way to conclude this discussion of the social teaching of John Paul II is to use the lens of the contemporary discussion about globalization and the global ethic. Today we are conscious of the reality of globalization and the global interdependence of all of us who live together on planet Earth. Even a generation ago, we never realized how climate and weather were global. Recently in the United States, we have come to understand how much of the weather is affected by El Niño. Environmental concerns today are global. Global warming and the destruction of rain forests have effects all over the world. Today we are well aware of the role of multinational corporations in our world. The economic power of such corporations has a huge impact on human existence in all parts of the world. Truly today we are living in a global village.

William Schweiker accepts the understanding of globalization as the rapidly developing and ever-desensing network of interconnections and interdependence that characterizes modern social life. The global vision is marked by an increasing social density that affects the way we see reality and how we live in the global village. This compression of the world and our reaction to it generate the problem of proximity, which confronts us with the issue of how to live so near others, most of whom are very different from us and some of whom are even enemies. Our global awareness and our proximity to all others can result in either greater cooperation or greater conflict. This precarious situation, which could move toward cooperation or conflict, global order or global chaos, is exaggerated by the tremendous growth of human power—especially technological power, which is so difficult to control. Today one thinks especially of huge economic power but also of the need to control it for the good of all.[51]

In light of globalization, there is a crying need for a global ethic. We are faced with the alternatives of cooperation or conflict. The danger is that power will ultimately triumph and the powerless will become even more oppressed. One of the earlier responses to the challenge came from the World Parliament of Religions in 1993, with its "Declaration toward a Global Ethic." Hans Küng was the primary mover behind the declaration and has continued to write and work for the cause of the global ethic.[52]

But can there be a global ethic?[53] Problems abound. From a philosophical perspective, some claim that there cannot be a global or common ethic precisely because of the great diversity of human cultures, languages, and traditions. No one comes to the conversation with a truly universal and unprejudiced perspective. We cannot arrive at an ethic that all people can and will accept. At the very minimum, even if agreement can be found, it will only be on the level of great generality; but, as we all know, the devil is in the details. Even if we can agree on recognizing basic human rights, all also recognize the conflicts between and among these rights in the complexity of everyday life.

A Christian realist perspective acknowledges the continuing and powerful presence of sin and its effects. Powerful groups and nations will always be tempted to protect and augment their own power and to not care about the concerns and needs of others. From a political perspective, as long as national sovereignty continues to be the controlling force in the world, there will be no way to enforce a global ethic. Independent and powerful nations will continue to insist on what is in their best interests.

John Paul II's social encyclicals do not directly address the contemporary discussion about globalization and global ethics, although he spoke to the Pontifical Academy of Social Sciences in 2001 on the topic of globalization. In this short speech, he focuses primarily on the reality of economic globalization in light of the market economy. He points out the dangers of neocolonialism and the need for a truly global ethic. We need an ethic to direct the economy to truly human needs, but the priority of ethics does not mean that all forms of ethics are worthy of the name.[54]

John Paul II's social teaching shows that he is a strong advocate of a global ethic, even though he does not use the term. His perspective on social ethics has been consistently global in scope. His role in the Catholic Church gives him a global perspective beyond the boundaries of race, culture, language, and nation. He serves a universal church. In addition, he addresses his social encyclicals to all people of goodwill. His teaching shows a special concern for persons in need and in the developing world. Thus, his vision and perspective have been consistently global.

The content of his ethics is also global. His anthropology insists on the dignity of all individuals and upholds the equality of all, despite the many diversities among human persons. Human dignity comes from the fact that God has made each human person in God's own image and likeness. But the human person exists in solidarity with other human beings and is not just an isolated monad. Solidarity affects the person in many different relationships but also includes the broadest relationship of solidarity with all other people on the globe. The pope's insistence on human rights presents a very important part of a global ethic. These rights, both political and civil, as well as social and economic, belong to all human beings. In the economic sphere, the destiny of the goods of creation to serve the needs of all also supports universal human rights.

John Paul II calls for both a change of attitudes and a change of structures. Both aspects are necessary for a global ethic. Solidarity as a virtue can and should appeal to all people on the basis of their common human experience and nature. All are called to practice justice and respect the rights of fellow human beings. John Paul II thus proposes a global common good that has a universal dimension to it based on solidarity and human rights.

But there will never be a truly global ethic in the political realm unless there is also a change of structures. The pope has acknowledged the need for the necessary structures in the political and social order that will ensure a global ethic. He has consistently recognized the importance of the United Nations and called for its strengthening. I think, however, that the pope is too optimistic in his hope that there might be an effective, unified, international political structure. The reality of the world's tremendous diversity together with human sinfulness bring me to the conclusion that there can be no all-encompassing, effective, and truly just international political structure. The existing nations, especially the powerful ones, will never be willing to give up their sovereignty to join in an effective international political structure that respects the rights and diversity of all. However, all can and should agree with the pope on the need to make international structures more effective.

To bring about a truly global ethic, we also need various international structures of an intermediary kind to work for a global ethic. John Paul II's social ethics, with its recognition of the need for intermediate groups and organizations, is certainly open to the need for institutions and groups working for peace, justice, human rights, and the environment in the whole world.

John Paul II's political and economic ethics also recognize an important limitation. Such ethics at best can only be quite general.

Thus, in the area of economics, the pope does not claim to propose any economic structure but only principles or criteria by which all existing structures can be evaluated. By definition, any global ethic will have to exist only on the level of the more general. There will thus always be room for diversity and even great disagreement on specifics. A global ethic on the level of the general will never ensure that specific conflicts can ever be fairly adjudicated.

In light of the lens of the important need today for a global ethic, the many strengths of John Paul II's approach to social teaching come through. But, in this light, one also sees some of the weaknesses. First, the top-down method, moving from the universal to the particular, has some inherent weaknesses, as does any approach. Moving from the universal to the particular one tends to claim more universality than exists and a greater certitude than the complexity and diversity of our global existence warrants today. The particular and the diverse may be somewhat overlooked from such a perspective. Also, no approach, including the pope's, is truly universal. We all bring with us the limitations of our own experience and knowledge, together with our shortcomings. Papal reason and experience, like all others, are embedded and therefore somewhat limited. In light of Catholic ecclesiology, the role of the bishop of Rome does have a universal perspective—but, at the same time, a call to be in dialogue with all the local churches. John Paul II could learn much more from what has occurred on the local level and thereby show greater appreciation for the particularity and diversity found there.

Second, John Paul II's social teaching tends to some extent to be too optimistic and fails at times to recognize the depth and stubbornness of the problems existing in our world, as is illustrated above by his failure to recognize explicitly the significant obstacles in the way of world government. A number of factors influence the somewhat optimistic tone of the pope's approach. As one trying to teach and inspire others, the papal language does not want to discourage such participation by bringing up the many problems in the way of recognizing both human dignity and human solidarity in our world. From a theological perspective, the Catholic tradition in general has not recognized enough the power and negative effect of sin in our world. To his credit, the pope has recognized sinful social structures and has not neglected the effects of human sinfulness. His emphasis at times on the struggle of the culture of life and the culture of death, which I have criticized as being too extreme, also recognizes in its own way the reality of sin. But one gets the impression that human beings working together can overcome the existing sinful structures. A more explicit emphasis on the eschaton as future would also make him more conscious of the limited possibilities in the present. But here too, he is obviously aware of how a one-sided emphasis on eschatology in the past influenced many Christians merely to accept the existing negative realities and not try to change them.

Third, the pope does not give enough importance to the role of power in social and political relationships. The role of teacher by definition tends to downplay the importance of power, whereas the activist perspective recognizes much more readily the role of power. His top-down approach, going from the general to the particular, fails to recognize the positive role that the poor and marginalized can play in changing their situation through a constructive use of power and organization. In addition, Catholic social teaching has traditionally not given enough importance to the role of power in bringing about social change. But despite these shortcomings, John Paul II makes a very important contribution in his social teachings to all who are striving to achieve greater justice and peace in our world today.

Notes

1. John Paul II and most commentators refer to Pope Leo XIII's encyclical, *Rerum novarum* (1891), as beginning the tradition of Catholic social teaching. There is no official canon of the documents belonging to Catholic social teaching, but there is general agreement on the papal and conciliar documents belonging to it. For an English collection of the documents of Catholic social teaching, see David J. O'Brien and Thomas A. Shannon, eds., *Catholic Social Thought: The Documentary Heritage* (Maryknoll, N.Y.: Orbis, 1992). For the fact that papal social teaching arose much earlier than Leo XIII, see Michael J. Schuck, *That They May Be One: The Social Teaching of the Papal Encyclicals 1740–1989* (Washington, D.C.: Georgetown University Press, 1991).

2. Pope Leo XIII, *Rerum novarum*, n. 38, in *Catholic Social Thought*, ed. O'Brien and Shannon, 33.

3. International Synod of Bishops, *Justitia in mundo* (Justice in the world), in *Catholic Social Thought*, ed. O'Brien and Shannon, 289. There are no paragraph numbers in this document.

4. For my analysis of this development at Vatican II, see Charles E. Curran, *Catholic Social Teaching 1891–Present: A Historical, Theological, and Ethical Analysis* (Washington, D.C.: Georgetown University Press, 2002), 23–37.

5. Pope Pius XI, *Quadragesimo anno*, nn. 141–48, in *Catholic Social Thought*, ed. O'Brien and Shannon, 75–77.

6. See, for example, R. Bruce Douglass and David Hollenbach, eds., *Catholicism and Liberalism: Challenges to American Public Philosophy* (Cambridge: Cambridge University Press, 1994).

7. John Coleman, ed., *One Hundred Years of Catholic Social Thought: Celebration and Challenge* (Maryknoll, N.Y.: Orbis, 1991); Donal Dorr, *Option for the Poor: A Hundred Years of Catholic Social Teaching*, rev. ed. (Maryknoll, N.Y.: Orbis, 1992).

8. John Courtney Murray, "Vers une intelligence du développement de la doctrine de l'Église sur la liberté religieuse," in *Vatican II: La liberté religieuse, declaration "Dignitatis humanae personae,"* ed. J. Hamer and Y. Congar (Paris: Éditions du Cerf, 1967), 111–47.

9. Curran, *Catholic Social Teaching*, 85–91.

10. In the United States, Michael Novak has criticized older Catholic social teaching for its failure to develop the importance of creating wealth but has praised John Paul II for doing so. See Michael Novak, *The Catholic Ethic and the Spirit of Capitalism* (New York: Free Press, 1993). For Novak's failure to recognize fully economic rights and his difference with John Paul II on this issue, see Todd David Whitmore, "John Paul II, Michael Novak, and the Differences between Them," *Annual of the Society of Christian Ethics* 21 (2001): 215–32.

11. Daniel R. Finn, "Creativity as a Problem for Moral Theology: John Locke's 99 Per Cent Challenge to the Catholic Doctrine of Property," *Horizons* 27 (2000): 44–62.

12. For the best one-volume compendium of liberation theology, see Ignacio Ellacuría and Jon Sobrino, eds., *Mysterium Liberationis: Fundamental Concepts of Liberation Theology* (Maryknoll, N.Y.: Orbis, 1993). For the understanding of the option for the poor in the thought of the father of liberation theology, see Gustavo Gutiérrez, "Option for the Poor," in *Mysterium Liberationis*, ed. Ellacuría and Sobrino, 235–50.

13. Pope Paul VI, *Octogesima adveniens*, nn. 30–34, in *Catholic Social Thought*, ed. O'Brien and Shannon, 275–77.

14. Jonathan Luxmoore and Jolanta Babiuch, *The Vatican and the Red Flag: The Struggle for the Soul of Eastern Europe* (London: Geoffrey Chapman, 1999); Pedro

Ramet, ed., *Catholicism and Politics in Communist Societies* (Durham, N.C.: Duke University Press, 1990).

15. Many recent biographies of John Paul II discuss his role in the fall of communism in Eastern Europe. See, for example, Jonathan Kwitny, *Man of the Century: The Life and Times of John Paul II* (New York: Henry Holt, 1997); Tad Szulc, *Pope John Paul II: The Biography* (New York: Scribner, 1995); George Weigel, *Witness to Hope: The Biography of John Paul II* (New York: Cliff Street Books, 1999).

16. Pope Pius XI, *Quadragesimo anno*, nn. 101–26, in *Catholic Social Thought*, ed. O'Brien and Shannon, 64–70.

17. George H. Williams, "Karol Wojtyla and Marxism," in *Catholicism and Politics in Communist Societies*, ed. Ramet, 361; see also Williams, *The Mind of John Paul II: Origins of his Thought and Action* (New York: Seabury, 1981).

18. Michael Novak, "Tested by Our Own Ideals," in *John Paul II and Moral Theology: Readings in Moral Theology No. 10*, ed. Charles E. Curran and Richard A. McCormick (New York: Paulist Press, 1998), 323.

19. David Hollenbach, "The Pope and Capitalism," *America* (June 1, 1991): 591.

20. Dorr, *Option for the Poor*, 345–47.

21. Helmut Thielicke, *Theological Ethics*, vol. 1, *Foundations* (Philadelphia: Fortress Press, 1966), 141–46, 272–73, 277–78.

22. For the classical neoscholastic work on the state in Catholic social thought, see Heinrich A. Rommen, *The State in Catholic Thought: A Treatise in Political Philosophy* (Saint Louis: B. Herder, 1947). For an influential mid-twentieth-century approach to the state, see Jacques Maritain, *Man and the State* (Chicago: University of Chicago Press, 1951).

23. David Hollenbach has written extensively on the common good and the Catholic tradition. For his latest work, see David Hollenbach, *The Common Good and Christian Ethics* (Cambridge: Cambridge University Press, 2002); see also Brian Stiltner, *Religion and the Common Good: Catholic Contributions to Building Community in a Liberal Society* (Lanham, Md.: Rowman & Littlefield, 1999).

24. Pope Pius XI, *Quadragesimo anno*, nn. 79–80, in *Catholic Social Thought*, ed. O'Brien and Shannon, 60.

25. Pope John XXIII, *Mater et magistra*, nn. 53–58, in *Catholic Social Thought*, ed. O'Brien and Shannon, 92–93.

26. The distinction between society and state was very important for John Courtney Murray's approach to religious freedom. See Murray, *The Problem of Religious Freedom* (Westminster, Md.: Newman Press, 1965).

27. George Weigel, "The Neo-Conservative Difference: A Proposal for the Renewal of Church and Society," *Pro Ecclesia* 4, no. 2 (spring 1995): 190–211.

28. George Weigel, "Catholicism and Democracy: The 'Other Twentieth Century Revolution,'" in *Morality and Religion in Liberal Democratic Societies*, ed. Gordon L. Anderson and Morton A. Kaplan (New York: Paragon, 1992), 223–50.

29. Pope John XXIII, *Pacem in terris*, nn. 11–27, in *Catholic Social Thought*, ed. O'Brien and Shannon, 132–35.

30. Curran, *Catholic Social Teaching*, 152–56, 215–22.

31. Pope John XXIII, *Pacem in terris*, nn. 11–27, in *Catholic Social Thought*, ed. O'Brien and Shannon, 132–35.

32. Pope John Paul II, "1999 World Day of Peace Message: Respect for Human Rights—The Secret of True Peace," *Origins* 28 (1998): 490. For an attempt to downplay the idea of economic rights in John Paul II, see Michael Novak, "The Future of Economic Rights," in *Private Virtue and Public Policy: Catholic Thought and Economic Life*, ed. James Finn (New Brunswick, N.J.: Transaction, 1990), 76–80. For a response to Novak, see Whitmore, "John Paul II, Michael Novak, and the Differences between Them," 215–32.

33. For an exhaustive study of Leo XIII's understanding of the state, see the following five articles published by John Courtney Murray: "The Church and Totalitarian Democracy," *Theological Studies* 13 (1952): 525–63; "Leo XIII on Church and State: The General Structure of the Controversy," *Theological Studies* 14 (1953): 1–30; "Leo XIII: Separation of Church and State," *Theological Studies* 14 (1953): 145–214; "Leo XIII: Two Concepts of Government," *Theological Studies* 14 (1953): 551–67; and "Leo XIII: Two Concepts of Government II: Government and the Order of Culture," *Theological Studies* 15 (1954): 1–33. A sixth article, "Leo XIII and Pius XII: Government and the Order of Religion," existed in galley proofs but higher authority did not allow it to be published in *Theological Studies*. It was published much later in John Courtney Murray, *Religious Liberty: Catholic Struggles with Pluralism*, ed. J. Leon Hooper (Louisville: Westminster / John Knox, 1993), 49–125. For a summary of Murray's analysis of Leo XIII and the role of the state, see Murray, *Problem of Religious Freedom*, 52–64.

34. Murray, *Problem of Religious Freedom*, 55–58.

35. Declaration on Religious Freedom, n. 7, in Walter J. Abbott, ed., *Documents of Vatican II* (New York: Guild, 1966), 687.

36. Declaration on Religious Freedom, n. 21. The footnotes in Abbott in regular print are not official footnotes of the document but were written by John Courtney Murray.

37. Declaration on Religious Freedom, n. 7.

38. Charles E. Curran, *Directions in Catholic Social Ethics* (Notre Dame, Ind.: University of Notre Dame Press, 1985), 27–45.

39. Charles E. Curran, *Transition and Tradition in Moral Theology* (Notre Dame, Ind.: University of Notre Dame Press, 1979), 230–50.

40. Charles E. Curran, *The Church and Morality: An Ecumenical and Catholic Approach* (Minneapolis: Fortress Press, 1993), 65–91.

41. For a similar interpretation of John Paul II's understanding of the role of freedom and truth in a democracy, see Hermínio Rico, *John Paul II and the Legacy of Dignitatis Humanae* (Washington, D.C.: Georgetown University Press, 2002).

42. Pope John Paul II, "We Are Not Pacifists," *Origins* 20 (1991): 625.

43. Giuseppe Chiaretti, "Lo spirito di Assisi," *Studi Ecumenici* 16 (January–March 1998): 31–43.

44. Joseph Joblin, "Le Saint-Siege face à la guerre: Continuité et renouvellement de son action pour la paix à l'époque contemporaine," *Gregorianum* 80 (1999): 333–52.

45. Joblin, "Le Saint-Siege face à la guerre."

46. John L. Allen, "Rome, U.S.: Differing Worldviews," *National Catholic Reporter*, January 16, 2004, 3–4; Brian V. Johnstone, "Pope John Paul II and the War in Iraq," *Studia Moralia* 41 (2003): 309–30.

47. J. Bryan Hehir, "Catholic Teaching on War and Peace: The Decade 1979–1989," in *Moral Theology: Challenges for the Future: Essays in Honor of Richard A. McCormick, S.J.*, ed. Charles E. Curran (New York: Paulist, 1990), 359–64.

48. John Paul II, "2000 World Day of Peace Message: Peace on Earth to Those Whom God Loves," *Origins* 29 (1999): 452.

49. Pope John Paul II, "The World's Hunger and Humanity's Conscience," *Origins* 22 (1992): 475; see also Pope John Paul II, "Address to Diplomats: Principles Underlying a Stance toward Unjust Aggressors," *Origins* 22 (1992): 583–87.

50. For a similar approach but developed in greater depth, see Joblin, "Le Saint-Siege face à la guerre," 299–352.

51. William Schweiker, "A Preface to Ethics: Global Dynamics and the Integrity of Life," *Journal of Religious Ethics* 32, no. 1 (spring 2004): 17–22; see also Schweiker, *Theological Ethics and Global Dynamics: In the Time of Many Worlds* (Oxford: Blackwell, 2004).

52. Hans Küng and Karl-Josef Kuschel, eds., *A Global Ethic: The Declaration of the Parliament of the World's Religions* (New York: Continuum, 1993); Hans Küng, ed., *Yes to a Global Ethic* (New York: Continuum, 1996); Hans Küng, *A Global Ethic for Global Politics and Economics* (New York: Oxford University Press, 1998).

53. For different approaches to a global ethic from a Catholic perspective, see Lisa Sowle Cahill, "Toward Global Ethics," *Theological Studies* 63 (2002): 330; Hollenbach, *Common Good and Christian Ethics*, 212–44; Jean Porter, "The Search for a Global Ethic," *Theological Studies* 62 (2001): 105–21; and Charles E. Curran, "The Global Ethic," *The Ecumenist* 37, no. 2 (spring 2000): 7–10.

54. Pope John Paul II, "The Ethical Dimension of Globalization," *Origins* 31 (2001): 44–45.

AFTERWORD

My appraisal of John Paul II's moral teaching is much more positive about his social teaching than about its other aspects. One might argue that the difference comes from the fact that I am in general agreement with the particular positions taken in his social teaching and opposed to some of the positions he takes on sexual matters. But especially in light of moral theology as a moral theory and a second-order discourse, there are significant differences between his teaching on social issues and on sexual and personal issues. Some of what I have called the negative aspects of his method are found in dealing with some personal and sexual issues and do not appear in the social area.

John Paul II's theological presupposition insists that the church "teaches the truth about man." He clearly claims the same role for the church and the hierarchical magisterium in social issues, but there are important differences here.

Discussing the teaching role of the church and the hierarchical magisterium, I pointed out that the church and the hierarchical magisterium need to learn the truth before they teach it. Although John Paul II nowhere explicitly recognizes the need for the church to learn in the area of social teaching, the fact of such learning is evident.

Pope Paul VI in his 1971 apostolic letter *Octogesima adveniens* refers to significant new understandings. "While scientific and technological progress continues to overturn man's surroundings, his patterns of knowledge, work, consumption, and relationships, two aspirations persistently make themselves felt in these new contexts, and they grow stronger to the extent that he becomes better informed and better educated: the aspiration to equality and the aspiration to participation, two forms of man's dignity and freedom."[1] Paul VI thus recognizes the fundamental importance today of human freedom, equality, and participation.

But Leo XIII, less than a century earlier, firmly denied all three. In his papal writings, Leo strongly condemns the modern liberties—such as freedom of religion, freedom of speech, and freedom of the press—especially in his 1888 encyclical *Libertas praestantissimum*.[2] Leo also stresses the existence and need for inequalities. Inequality is a fact of nature. Differences exist with regard to human thought, intelligence, health, beauty, and courage. These natural inequalities involve social inequalities that are essential for the good functioning of society. Society for Leo is analogous to a human body with very different and unequal parts that all work together for the good of the whole.[3] Leo does recognize a basic equality of human beings with regard to origin, value, and end, and with corresponding rights and duties; but the differences in abilities, powers of mind and body, and manners and character call for inequalities in the social life and institutions.[4]

The nineteenth-century Pope Leo XIII also has a hierarchical, authoritarian, and paternalistic notion of political society with no room for the active participation of citizens.[5] He actually refers to the people as the ignorant or untutored multitude that need to be led by their rulers.[6] However, in *Rerum novarum*, he calls for the participation of workers in struggling for justice by joining unions.[7] The dramatic change in beginning to appreciate the fundamental importance of human freedom, equality, and participation came to the fore in Vatican II's recognition of religious freedom—despite Leo XIII's denial of it.

What explains these dramatic changes? In my judgment, the enemy—or, if you prefer more conciliatory language, the dialogue partner of the church—changed. Leo XIII opposed Enlightenment liberalism with its emphasis on the freedom of the individual person cut off from any relationship with God and even with others. But the twentieth century witnessed the rise of totalitarianism, both of the right and of the left. Especially in opposition to communism, Catholic social teaching tended to stress the freedom, equality, and participation of the person. In this connection, only in the middle of the twentieth century did Pope Pius XII gingerly indicate some hint of endorsement for democracy as the best form of government.[8] Without doubt, the church learned much from what was happening in the world in the twentieth century, while at the same time it correctly challenged some of the negative aspects of the times.

John Paul II, in his major writings, does not explicitly recognize these very significant changes and developments. But he certainly makes no claims about a plan of God for political society existing from the beginning of the world, as he does for marriage and sexuality. In social areas, the church has learned much from the world, and even John Paul II's teaching in social areas uses this new knowledge without explicitly recognizing where it came from. The one place he reverts to the older Leonine position concerns the complete subordination of political freedom to truth.

Another negative aspect of John Paul II's approach comes from the claim to have the certitude of truth too quickly and too readily. As has been pointed out above, the very nature of moral truth dealing with contingent practical realities means that one cannot have the same certitude in practical truth as exists in speculative truth. Pope John Paul II's teaching on social issues tends to be general and not too particular. As a result of staying on the level of the general, his social teaching does not claim to have certitude on very specific concrete issues, as is the case in papal sexual teaching. The problem of claiming too much certitude on particular issues is not that great a problem in papal social teaching.

As mentioned above, John Paul II moves away from the more historically conscious and inductive methodology employed by Paul VI in his social teachings. Some of the negative aspects of that have already been noted. John Paul II's approach to social issues definitely tends to be classicist and move from the top down. However, even here there are differences with the method used in the teaching on sexuality and marriage. In social matters, John Paul II does not claim to find the plan of God for these issues found in the creation narrative of Genesis, as he does with regard to sexuality and marriage.

With regard to the ethical model, John Paul II definitely employs a legal model in his writings on personal and sexual issues. Aspects of a legal model also appear in his social teaching, but the relationality–responsibility model is more prominent. Recall the emphasis on interdependence and solidarity, especially in *Sollicitudo rei socialis*. This encyclical sees authentic and integral development in relational terms. People without faith cannot accept their relationship with God, but they can and should recognize the relational nature of the human person (38.3).

A strong criticism of John Paul II's use of natural law was the problem of physicalism—the identification of the human moral act with the physical structure of the act. The problem of physicalism comes to the fore in papal sexual teaching. But physicalism is not a problem in the social areas. In none of the social areas does John Paul II identify the moral aspect with the physical structure of the act. Precisely because of the complexity of social reality and relationships, there is no tendency to absolutize the physical structure of the act.

My more positive appraisal of John Paul II's social teaching comes not only from the fact that this teaching avoids some of the methodological problems found in his sexual teaching but also because the positive aspects of his moral theological method are evident in the social teaching. He correctly recognizes that anthropology constitutes the most significant factor in moral theology. My more positive appreciation of his social teaching comes especially from the anthropological basis for this teaching.

John Paul II insists on the dignity of the human person and the solidarity of the person with many different relationships and ultimately a relationship including all other human beings. Many people insist on human dignity, but John Paul II bases that dignity on the loving gift of God in creation and redemption. Such an approach underscores the true equal dignity of all human beings. Too often in contemporary society, human dignity seems to be based on what one does, merits, or accomplishes. We usually treat influential and rich people differently from the way we treat poor people. The equal dignity of all demands a special concern for those who can so easily be written off or forgotten—the needy, the poor, the institutionalized, and the helpless.

But the fundamental God-given dignity of the individual human person exists together with the solidarity of the human person with all other human beings. The Catholic tradition has historically insisted on this aspect of solidarity, which is often based on the Thomistic understanding that the human being is by nature social and even political.[9] John Paul II has developed this understanding by introducing the concept of solidarity, which he sees as a Christian virtue that can and should be recognized by all human beings. Such an approach flies in the face of the individualism that is so often prevalent in our world today, especially in the United States. Individualism absolutizes the self and reduces all other things and persons to means to help the individual achieve one's own goals.

The two aspects of anthropology—the equal dignity of all and our interdependence governed by the virtue of solidarity—form the basis for criticizing the two extreme political and economic positions of collectivism and individualistic liberalism while insisting on the need for both political and civil rights as well as economic and social rights.

The social teaching also shows forth the influence of John Paul II's eschatology, both in general and in its effects on anthropology. The pope rightly insists on an eschatology that sees the goodness of creation, the fallenness of sin, the existence of redemption through Christ Jesus, and the final coming of the reign of God at the end of time. Such an eschatology recognizes the possibility of bringing about some change in the hearts of people as well as in the structures of society. The pope acknowledges that the fullness of the reign of God will never be present in this world, but at times he still seems too optimistic.

In the area of social teaching, John Paul II is neither an idealist nor a sectarian. Sectarians see Christians as called to separate themselves from a sinful world and to bear witness to the Gospel within their own enclave. John Paul II constantly calls Catholics and all Christians to work together with all people of goodwill for greater justice and peace in our world, but the struggle will never be easy nor will it develop always in an ongoing progressive manner.

Such an eschatology undergirds John Paul II's position on peace and war. We must all work for peace—especially by overcoming the problems of injustice through authentic and integral development and true solidarity, by bearing witness to peace in all aspects of personal and social life, and by establishing more effective international institutions. In this imperfect world, where the lamb and the lion have not lain down together, the pope does not rule out the possibly legitimate use of force against unjust aggressors, but he strongly cautions that human beings and nations are tempted to resort to force much too readily and quickly. War by itself cannot bring peace.

Thus, my generally positive appraisal of John Paul II's social teaching comes not only from the particular positions taken in his social teaching but also from the more positive appraisal of the moral theology lying behind such teachings.

In conclusion, my primary objection to John Paul II's approach, involving both ecclesiology and moral theology, is his failure to emphasize and at times even to recognize the Catholic approach as a living tradition. In my judgment, the glory of the Catholic self-understanding is its insistence on a living tradition.[10]

Historically, Catholic theology has insisted on both scripture and tradition. Thus, the Catholic approach has never been tempted by scriptural fundamentalism. Over the years, there have been some problems with the understanding of the relationship between scripture and tradition, but the emphasis on tradition is most significant. Tradition means that the church constantly strives to understand, appropriate, live, and bear witness to the word and work of Jesus in light of ongoing historical and cultural circumstances. The history of the church bears witness to this understanding of a living tradition even in its understanding of fundamental realities such as God, Jesus Christ, and the sacraments. In moral theology, the recognition of the important roles of human reason, experience, and changing historical and cultural circumstances testifies to the need for a living tradition.

Because much of John Paul II's authoritative moral teaching opposes possible developments and changes in Catholic positions, he not only does not emphasize the living tradition, but, for all practical purposes, he fails to recognize its role in the area of morality.[11] In addition, he emphasizes other aspects that tend to downplay and even seem to oppose the understanding of a living tradition. Three aspects of his moral teaching take on this character of downplaying the role of a living tradition. First, in claiming too much certitude for noninfallible moral teachings, he in principle insists on an artificial barrier to change or any kind of development in moral teaching beyond the verbal. Second, by downplaying any role for historical consciousness and experience in arriving at moral truth, and especially a proper role for the *sensus fidelium*, he eliminates important sources that contribute to a living tradition. Third, by failing to point out that the magisterium needs to learn before it can teach, he gives the impression of an unchanging deposit of truth over which the magisterium presides.

The Catholic Church is not going to change radically and should not change radically the core aspects of faith, even though there can be some significant development. But my problem is not with core aspects of faith, the call to conversion, the significant Christian virtues, or general moral considerations such as the need to respect persons. On specific moral issues that are greatly affected by changing historical and cultural circumstances, the magisterium must recognize that it cannot claim absolute certitude and that its teachings have changed in the past. By insisting on the certitude of truth for complex and specific moral issues, John Paul II has downplayed and even implicitly denied what has been the glory of the Catholic tradition: It is a living tradition.

Notes

1. Pope Paul VI, *Octogesima adveniens*, n. 22, in *Catholic Social Thought: The Documentary Heritage*, ed. David J. O'Brien and Thomas A. Shannon (Maryknoll, N.Y.: Orbis, 1992), 273.

2. Pope Leo XIII, *Libertas praestantissimum*, nn. 19–37, in *The Church Speaks to the Modern World: The Social Teachings of Leo XIII*, ed. Etienne Gilson (Garden City, N.Y.: Doubleday Image, 1954), 70–79.

3. Pope Leo XIII, *Quod apostolici muneris*, nn. 5–6, in *Church Speaks to the Modern World*, ed. Gilson, 192–93.

4. Pope Leo XIII, *Humanum genus*, n. 26, in *Church Speaks to the Modern World*, ed. Gilson, 130–33.

5. John Courtney Murray, *The Problem of Religious Freedom* (Westminster, Md.: Newman Press, 1965), 55–56.

6. Pope Leo XIII, *Libertas praestantissimum*, n. 23, in *Church Speaks to the Modern World*, ed. Gilson, 73.

7. Pope Leo XIII, *Rerum novarum*, nn. 36–38, in *Catholic Social Thought*, ed. O'Brien and Shannon, 32–34.

8. Paul E. Sigmund, "Politics and Liberal Democracy," in *Catholicism and Liberalism: Challenges to American Public Philosophy*, ed. R. Bruce Douglass and David Hollenbach (Cambridge: Cambridge University Press, 1994), 225–27. For an analysis of the change in Catholic social teaching culminating in the acceptance of social democracy, see Roger Aubert, *Catholic Social Teaching*, ed. David A. Boileau (Milwaukee: Marquette University Press, 2003).

9. Thomas Aquinas, *Summa theologiae*, 4 vols. (Rome: Marietti, 1952): *Ia*, q. 96, a. 4; *Ia IIae*, q. 61, a. 5; *Ia IIae*, q. 72, a. 4; *Ia IIae*, q. 95, a. 4; *IIa IIae*, q. 109, a. 3, ad 1; *IIa IIae*, q. 114, a. 2, ad 1; *IIa IIae*, q. 129, a. 6, ad 1; *IIIa*, q. 65, a. 1.

10. My good friend and colleague, the late Richard A. McCormick, frequently cited Jaroslav Pelikan's comment that tradition is the living faith of the dead and not the dead faith of the living. See Richard A. McCormick, *The Critical Calling: Reflections on Moral Dilemmas since Vatican II* (Washington, D.C.: Georgetown University Press, 1989), 121, 130, 216. For the original statement, see Jaroslav Pelikan, *The Vindication of Tradition* (New Haven, Conn.: Yale University Press, 1984), 66. For my further development of the understanding of the Catholic approach as a living tradition, see Charles E. Curran, *The Living Tradition of Catholic Moral Theology* (Notre Dame, Ind.: University of Notre Dame Press, 1992).

11. On occasion, the documents we have studied do mention the term "living tradition" (e.g., *VS* 27.1, 37.3, 109.2; *EV* 54.2; *FR* 93.1; *FC* 29.2; *CL* 14.2). The concept is never developed and sometimes is linked with the role of the magisterium.

INDEX

Abbott, Walter J., 6n2, 158n27, 246nn35, 36, 37
abortion, direct. *See Evangelium vitae*
Aertnys, I., 156n1
Allen, John L., 247n46
Allsopp, Michael E., 89n9, 158n33
Alphonsus, Saint, 128–29, 147
Anderson, Gordon L., 245n28
Aquinas, Thomas: on human acts, 128; and *imago dei* doctrine, 190; on natural law, 32, 103, 120, 132; and speculative truth, 34, 132; and teleology, 103, 105; and Thomism, 22, 43nn5, 10, 108, 111, 112, 114, 123nn12, 13, 16, 18, 147, 157n15, 201n28, 231, 255n9
Aubert, Roger, 255n8
Augustine, Saint, 22, 96, 101, 126, 147
authoritative papal documents, 2, 253: and apostolic exhortations and letters, 4; audience talks, 5

Babiuch, Jolanta, 244n14
Baum, Gregory, 90nn26, 29
Beal, John P., 157nn12, 18
Biggar, Nigel, 123n17
Bilgrien, Marie Vianney, 123n7
Black, Rufus, 123n17
Boilean, David A., 255n8
Bouscaren, T. Lincoln, 159n38
Boyle, Philip, 124n19
Brady, Bernard V., 200n9
Brown, Raymond E., 89n5, 90n21
Buttiglione, Rocco, 7n5, 122n2

Cahill, Lisa Sowle, 119, 124nn23, 25, 26, 201n32, 247n53
Caldecott, Léonie, 90n15

canon law: definitive teaching on, 27, 131–32
capital punishment. *See Evangelium vitae*
Catechism of Catholic Church: morality of lying, 142–43, 147
Catholic Church: and ecumenism, 35–36; learner and teacher, 41–43; metaphors for, 38–39; nature of, 37; and reign of God, 35, 40; and sinful church, 38; teaching about person, 35; and Vatican II, 36
Catholic moral theology: as academic discipline, 1, 21; authoritative teachings, 1, 27, 56; and complex reality, 33, 119–20; and critical historical method, 47; and empirical data, 18; and humanity as way, 27; and living tradition, 253; and manuals, 142; and metaphysics, 18–19; and method, 6, 18, 45–90, 103; and natural law, 23, 30, 31, 42, 62, 66, 67, 88, 103, 109–22; and philosophical ethics, 1, 4, 18; and principles, 27, 105, 108; and reason, 4, 9–10, 15, 17, 18, 112; as second-order discourse, 1, 102, 248; and subjectivism, 10
Catholic social teachings: and common good, 20, 25, 61, 68, 222; and democracy, 225–30; and divinizing role of church, 205; and globalization, 238–43; and Enlightenment, 225, 249; and legal model, 105, 106; and Marxism, 218, 249; and natural law, 21, 205; and principles, criteria, directives, 27, 105, 108, 207; and social doctrine, 27, 62–64, 205; and state, 222–34; and subsidiarity, 218, 223; and theological and scriptural foundations, 205; and truth, 20, 30, 31,

INDEX

259